PRAISE FOR *CA*

MW00643882

"*Careeranista* is one of the most comprehensive career guides I have read, period. In addition to being jam-packed with practical advice and personal accounts, it addresses the psychological aspects of the career search and on-the-jobs issues as well. As a professional who provides both clinical and career counseling, this is an integral but often overlooked topic in the career books I have reviewed. I would not hesitate in recommending this guide to my career clients."

—HEIDI VAN DER WALDE,
Licensed Clinical Professional Counselor
and founder of Professional Advancement

"In today's competitive market, the successful individual will be one with believability, a good work ethic, knowledge, and a copy of Pitts-Kyser's *Careeranista: The Woman's Guide to Success After College.* The content is priceless and will be a winner for all readers that turn the pages from start to finish."

—JOANN HAYSBERT, PhD, Executive Vice President,
Hampton University

"It is imperative for recent graduates to read *Careeranista.* The book provided me with the encouragement I needed, as well as practical steps to success."

—ASHLEY BENSON, 2013 graduate,
University of North Texas

"*Careeranista* is applicable to women at any stage of life, but an excellent guide for women just entering the professional world. And finally, someone is able to accurately capture the unique underpinnings of how gender plays a role in professional success. The advice from other professionals will also be helpful to women as they navigate barriers in the job market."

—LAUREN LOEFFLER, Director of Career Services,
University of West Florida

"An invaluable resource for those in need of direction, whether they are fine-tuning their personal lives, seeking a new career path, or trying to confirm that they are already on the right one."

—BETTYE BLACK, Director of Library Services,
Langston University

"Chaz Pitts-Kyser has done it again! Her new book, *Careeranista*, delivers timely, practical strategies that would benefit any young woman seeking to successfully advance in today's job market. Whether you are just entering the job market, or seeking a promotion, Chaz's book provides a clear and comprehensive road map to success."

—KIM R. WELLS, Director, Executive Education,
Howard University School of Business

"Pitts-Kyser has written another ground-breaking guide to successfully living life after college. This is a masterpiece as no one ever provides instructions for getting on to the business of being an adult . . . detailing how to become a Careeranista—setting goals, searching for a job, interviewing, and maintaining your life whether you get the job or not. Pitts-Kyser also uses motivating quotes and human resource tips to encourage those entering their careers to do better and be better. A must-have gift for anyone stepping out into the world."

—MONIQUE MILES BRUNER, Associate Dean,
Social Sciences, Rose State College

"In reading *Careeranista*, women will feel as if they have their own personal career coach, encouraging them to conquer their fears, set and achieve their goals, and overcome any obstacle in their path. I highly recommend!

—ALONZO JONES, Associate Dean of Students,
Arizona State University

"Chaz covers nearly every issue a young professional may face, providing insight and information that you just can't get inside a college classroom."

—CLYDE MONTGOMERY, PhD, Vice President
of Academic Affairs, Langston University

Utietiaug,
Best wishes
at Howard
+ beyond!
Ch
Nov 14

CAREERANISTA

THE WOMAN'S GUIDE
TO SUCCESS AFTER COLLEGE

CHAZ PITTS-KYSER

Seshet Press

Careeranista: The Woman's Guide to Success After College

Copyright © 2014 Chaz Pitts-Kyser

Published by Seshet Press

All rights reserved. No part of this publication may be reproduced, stored in a retrieval system, or transmitted in any form by any means—electronic, mechanical, photocopying, recording, or otherwise—without written permission from the publisher.

To make requests for excerpts, send an email to cpkyser@careeranista.com

ISBN: 978-0-9788188-2-1
LCCN: 2013920946

Cover design by Jeff Greenwood
Interior design by Katherine Lloyd, The DESK
Author photo by Buchi Akpati of BA Photo and Faces

Printed in the United States of America

First Edition

Dedication

To my sister, Cameron Allen-Kyser,
a wonderful sibling and fabulous friend.

◈

"If opportunity doesn't knock, build a door."
—Milton Berle

Table of Contents

Introduction

Let the World Make Room

You are the designer of your destiny;
you are the author of your story.
—Lisa Nichols, motivational speaker

Just 30 minutes of watching the news is enough to make the average graduating senior want to crawl beneath the covers. The headlines always seem to come back to the sluggish economy, high rate of unemployment, fierce competition for well-paying jobs, Americans' mounting personal debt, and ultimately, just how unlucky young professionals are for having to build a career amid such misfortune.

The bad news? It really is a tough time for recent graduates. The good news? It doesn't have to be a tough time for *you.* You know that countless women are out there making a name for themselves despite the obstacles in their path—and there is no reason why you can't do the same. You are a Careeranista: A smart, sophisticated, success-driven young woman committed to carving out a career she loves. And this book will show you how.

Careeranista: The Woman's Guide to Success After College is the book I wish I had been given the day I graduated from college in May 2000—if not my freshman year. Like so many bright-eyed but a tad bit naïve graduates, I had all the book smarts needed to start a rewarding career, but not necessarily the professional smarts. Sure, all the English, journalism, and sociology classes I was required to take were more than beneficial, but one year into my first professional position, I began wishing courses like handling conflicts with co-workers, working your way up within a company, and paying off debt had also been listed in the university's class catalog. Years later, experiences of job loss and the frustrations of job searching also made me stumble, and I wished I had been given key pieces of professional advice *before* I actually needed it.

Well, they say necessity is the mother of invention, so I longed to develop a book that would put future graduates on a clear path to career success. In 2007, I published *Embracing the Real World: The Black Woman's Guide to Life After College,* a niche book that proved a benefit to thousands of black women entering the workforce. Because of the guide's success, I was urged to pen one for women of all ethnicities—as we face common challenges and share common goals.

The book that you hold in your hands is a blueprint you can use to get where you want to go faster and easier. It is filled with all the great advice that career-related books should have, based on my experiences, those of other college graduates, the insights of more than 50 career experts, and tons of research. You'll get schooled on everything from applying and interviewing for jobs, negotiating your salary, succeeding in a new position, networking effectively, budgeting, and coping with job loss. But what sets this book apart from others on the market is that it's specifically written for young professional women and covers topics that most career-related books ignore. Handling sex discrimination in the workplace, achieving some semblance of work-life balance, working in corporate America, and overcoming the fear of failure are just a few of the chapters you'll discover in *Careeranista: The Woman's Guide to Success After College.*

When you turn the last page of this book, you will be better prepared to face the challenges ahead, and just as crucial, to take advantage of the myriad opportunities available to you. You will feel more excited about your future as a young professional from the encouragement you will receive along the way. Despite the economy and any other thing out of your control, you will know that there truly is enough room in the world for you to construct the life you want. And, as a newly minted Careeranista, you will have the knowledge and power to start claiming your space.

Careeranista (noun): A smart, sophisticated, success-driven young woman committed to carving out a career she loves.

part one

BECOMING A CAREERANISTA

Mapping Out
Your Future

The future isn't a place that we are going to go;
it's a place that we get to create.
—Nancy Duarte, communication expert

A s a beginning freshman, you may have worked with a counselor on what is commonly called a degree plan. This plan stated the degree you were trying to achieve, outlined the classes needed to receive that degree, and then gave you a timeline indicating how long it would take before you could don a cap and gown.

Now, you may have followed your plan to the letter. Or perhaps, if you were like me, you had to adjust it a couple of times. If you were very indecisive you might have changed your plan frequently and ended up adding a few more semesters to your college experience. But what matters is that you graduated. You would still be in a classroom, however, if you had not created that degree plan mapping your way in and out of college.

With the start of a new phase of your life, a new plan is needed. This plan will map out what will hopefully be an exciting and rewarding career, thus we'll call it your Career Map.

Besides mapping out your future, your Career Map will also help keep you focused. Sometimes we forget exactly what our goals are and the reasons we chose these goals. Having something written down can reassure us that we're heading in the right direction and remind us why we're working so hard.

Now You Tell Me?

Create a definite plan for carrying out your desire, and begin at once, whether you are ready or not, to put this plan into action.
—Napoleon Hill, author of *Think & Grow Rich*

The Career Map you develop should answer four basic questions:

1. What are my career goals?
2. Why have I set these goals?
3. How will I achieve these goals?
4. When should I reasonably be able to achieve these goals?

What are my career goals?

This part of your map will state the goals you want to reach both now and further on in your career. This can be as simple as stating what titles you want to hold, such as an assistant account executive and eventually an advertising director, or a junior accountant and eventually an owner of a medium-sized accounting firm.

If you have two very different career goals, like you want to be a high school principal and a clothing designer, then you will need to make a Career Map for both goals. It's okay if you're unsure about exactly which positions you hope to hold, but it's good to at least know what field you want to work in. For example, instead of writing that you want to be an occupational therapist, you could put that you want to work in healthcare. However, the more specific you are, the more helpful your Career Map will be.

Why have I set these goals?

This part of your map will explain why you've set your stated career goals. The explanation should be straightforward. For example: I am

4

going to be an assistant account executive and then work my way to an executive position in advertising because (1) I am a creative person with business sense and have other key skills that will help me succeed in advertising; (2) I love the idea of coming up with game-changing commercials and other forms of advertising for big and small companies; (3) I enjoyed my advertising internships and have been told by former professors and respected professionals in the field that this is the right career for me; (4) I get bored easily and would be able to work on a variety of projects and with a variety of people and clients throughout my career; and (5) advertising executives tend to be paid very well.

Now You Tell Me?

A vision is a magnet. Seeing, believing, being, and articulating your vision with confidence is an effective tool for influencing others and for gathering the right people around your vision.

—Rebecca Shambaugh, author of *It's Not a Glass Ceiling, It's a Sticky Floor*

How will I achieve these goals?

This part of the map explains what you have to accomplish to achieve your goal(s) step by step. You will need to research your desired profession to fill this section out. If you wanted to eventually be an advertising executive, for example, then talking to professionals at all levels within advertising would be essential.

Once you've done your research, you should be able to write out a general path you have to follow. For example, you might write: In order to be an advertising executive, I need to:

1. Secure an entry-level position within an advertising agency, such as assistant account executive. Consistently work hard, learn all that I can, and build and leverage my network. Continue to do this throughout my career.
2. Get promoted to account executive or move to a different agency to secure this position. Earn my MBA while in this position to increase my marketability.

3. Secure an account manager position.
4. Land an account supervisor position.
5. Secure an executive position, such as advertising director or vice president.

When should I reasonably be able to achieve these goals?

The biggest question is almost always "when?" Answering the "when" question will help keep you on track once you decide what you're focused on becoming. The word "reasonably" is inserted into that question so you'll set a realistic timeline. Setting deadlines in your timeline that are impossible to meet will lead to discouragement. On the other hand, setting deadlines that are too easy to meet will keep you from working hard and going as far as you can in your career.

The timeline you make will be based on what you wrote down in "How will I achieve these goals?" For each step you wrote down, you should give a maximum amount of time allotted to get past that step and on to the next one. Research will definitely be needed to determine how long each step may take, and in doing so, you can get guidance from looking at the career paths of the people whose shoes you hope to fill. Some steps will be taken simultaneously and should be written as such. The following is a sample timeline:

CAREER TIMELINE

- Work as an assistant account executive (0–3 years)
- Work as an account executive and obtain an MBA (3–6 years)
- Work as an account manager (6–8 years)
- Work as an account supervisor (8–12 years)
- Work as an advertising executive (12+ years)

Estimated time to working as an executive director: 12 years

SAMPLE CAREER MAP

What are my career goals?

- To work as an assistant account executive and then work my way to an executive position in advertising.

Why have I set these goals?

- I am a creative person with business sense and have other key skills that will help me succeed in advertising.
- I love the idea of coming up with game-changing commercials and other forms of advertising for big and small companies.
- I enjoyed my advertising internships and have been told by former professors and respected professionals in the field that this is the right career for me.
- I get bored easily and would be able to work on a variety of projects and with a variety of people and clients throughout my career.
- Advertising executives tend to be paid very well.

How will I achieve these goals?

- Secure an entry-level position within an advertising agency, such as assistant account executive. Consistently work hard, learn all that I can, and build and leverage my network. Continue to do this throughout my career.
- Get promoted to account executive or move to a different agency to secure this position. Earn an MBA to increase my marketability.
- Secure an account manager position.
- Land an account supervisor position.
- Secure an executive position, such as advertising director or vice president.

When should I reasonably be able to achieve my goals?

- Work as an assistant account executive (0–3 years)
- Work as an account executive (3–6 years)
- Work as an account manager (6–8 years)
- Work as an account supervisor (8–12 years)
- Work as an executive director or in similar position (12+ years)

End Goal: Advertising Executive
Estimated Time: 12 Years

GOING OFF COURSE

It is important to keep in mind that life hardly ever goes according to plan. Given this, your Career Map will undoubtedly have to be adjusted in some way—and probably several times—because of unforeseeable circumstances throughout your life. It may take you much longer to snag the job you believe will propel your career forward. You may not get into graduate school or may find yourself going much later than anticipated. Or you may discover that you want to work in an entirely different field—again. And that's okay. As any trusty GPS can show you, there are multiple ways to get to a destination—that destination being a career that fully utilizes your talents, not necessarily a specific job or employment within a specific company. So you shouldn't be so set on one path that you keep trudging along it even as you're obviously being rerouted. Flexibility on your part will be one of the keys to your success. You must be open to possibilities and opportunities presented to you; they may ultimately get you to where you want to go faster or to an even better place.

In the case of not landing your dream job, realize that there are similar positions out there that will allow you to leverage the exact same skills as your self-described dream job and connect with the right people. For example, I was once mentoring a young woman, Kristen, who, despite earning an accounting degree and having several internships under her belt, found that after almost a year she hadn't landed a junior accounting position at a large accounting firm like she expected. Urging her not to wallow in self-pity, I reminded her that practically every large organization has its own accounting/business department. While it might not be Ernst & Young, she would be able to use her degree while subsequently getting more real-world experience that might make her more appealing to a top accounting firm. I also pointed out that she could look into working for a successful private accountant in need of an assistant—a position in which she would likely learn more about the many aspects of the business. Kristen liked this option most and altered her Career Map to reflect her desire to work for such a person as part of her end goal of being employed at a major accounting firm.

She soon found herself working for a two-person accounting firm that dealt with mainly upper-class clients, many of whom weren't too good with their finances despite having lots of money. A year later, Kristen changed her Career Map again from landing a job and working her way up in a top accounting firm to being both a CPA and financial planner in private practice. She is now well on her way toward this goal. Like Kristen, whenever and however you are rerouted, you should be creating a new Career Map. Each new map should have clear goals leading to bigger clear goals.

WAIT! BUT I DON'T KNOW WHAT I WANT TO DO

What do you want to be when you grow up? I distinctly remember being asked this question multiple times throughout my childhood, and as with most kids, the answer always rolled off my tongue easily and with confidence. Of course, it changed as I got older, going from gymnast, astronaut, and then dance choreographer, to an FBI agent and finally a women's magazine editor by the time I was headed to college. Looking back, the answer must have always come so easily because it wasn't one that I really had to take seriously at the time. But fast-forward to the day I sat half-listening to my college commencement speaker, and this question consumed me. Trouble was, like many of my peers who looked ready-for-the-world decked out in their gown and decorated caps, I wasn't all too sure I now knew the answer. And it wasn't because I had wasted my college education. More than anything, college had shown me that there were countless career paths I could take given my talents and interests—despite my majors in journalism and sociology. The question I should have been asking myself, and which I pose to you if you find yourself unsure about the field you want to enter, is what do you want to be *right now?*

Don't think 20 years down the line, or even five years. Think about six months to one year from now. What can you see yourself doing? What would you like to be doing? The answer should be based on what interests you *right now*—not the degree you earned. This is because many entry-levels jobs are open to people with any degree, and sometimes employers care more about whether a person is passionate about something than whether or not they have experience in something. What's more, in looking at the career paths of many people—including some of the most successful ones—you may notice something that at first seems peculiar: they have switched fields multiple times, or eventually chosen paths that had absolutely nothing to do with their majors.

So don't despair. You don't have to have everything all figured out. However, you do have to figure out *something*, and the best way is to start applying for jobs you are qualified for that appeal to you in some way—no matter the reason. Or, if you can afford not to work full time for a while (perhaps by living with your parents), start looking for an internship that will allow you to learn more about a field that interests you. The bottom line is that sometimes you can only know what you really want to do by finding yourself actually doing it.

The next two chapters focus on getting the position you desire so you can begin gaining the experience needed to move forward in your career.

2

Job Searching in a Tough Job Market

Perseverance is a great element of success;
if you only knock long enough
and loud enough at the gate,
you are sure to wake up somebody.
—Henry Wadsworth Longfellow, poet

It would be terrific if every degree came along with a job we loved, but then we wouldn't be living in what has appropriately been dubbed "the real world." In the real world, a great job is a prized possession, and what's more, it's something that the average college graduate must work increasingly hard to get. According to the National Center for Education Statistics, more than 1.6 million bachelor's degrees are conferred every year in America. Roughly all newly minted college grads look for some type of employment, which means you face some pretty tough competition.

I lost a managing editor position one year after graduation and thought I would have a nervous breakdown as I frantically searched for a new job. My ego shrunk to the size of a penny when weeks went by and not one person I sent a resume to called me back. "Don't they know how smart I am?" I thought. "I have two degrees and they seem worthless!" I complained to my friends. "Doesn't my experience count for anything?" I whined to my sister's cat, which I envied for not having to get a job, much less its own food. Because I had worked for the same company since my freshman year, and thus was offered a great full-time position before I graduated, I had skipped the job-hunting phase that so many of my friends had complained about. Now, I seemed to have landed on the "start over" square of some horribly unfair board game.

But eventually I did secure a job, albeit at Radio Shack near the high school I graduated from. I felt so humiliated that I hid in the office when anyone I knew walked in. Seriously. But my car note didn't care where I worked, so I had to sell those batteries and cell phones. However, I kept sending out resumes while working at "the shack," as one of my girlfriends teasingly called it. Two months later, I was offered a job more in my field, journalism/publishing, which I kept until I left for New York to work on my master's degree in publishing. What's odd is that I almost didn't want to take the new job because I had finally gotten over my stuck-up self and had become a pretty good saleswoman.

Years later, when I had even more experience, better connections, *and* my master's degree, I couldn't believe the amount of time it took me to land a job—full time, part time, any time. My friends, who by now had achieved varying levels of career success, also were dumbstruck when they applied for positions and were not immediately snatched up by employers awestruck by their awesomeness.

As you are searching for the position that will jumpstart your career, keep in mind that the job search process can be a long and tedious one for both the recent graduate and seasoned professional. In fact, because of the current higher-than-average unemployment rate, unemployed older professionals often apply for entry-level positions— the same ones new graduates need to begin their careers. And the job market you're entering has also not been helped by the growing number of companies now outsourcing professional positions overseas or that have had to downsize to stay in business.

Since these and many other factors are beyond your control, it may take you months upon months to land the type of job you're searching for. Until you find a job appropriate for your career, consider your job search as your temporary full-time job—one that doesn't pay anything but has good benefits.

The job search tactics you use can mean the difference between a slightly mind-numbing job search experience and a painful one. Instead of playing hit or miss, you should take smart, time-efficient, calculated steps to secure a position. Once you've decided on the career you want, your goal should be to locate those companies or organizations that offer jobs relative to your career aspirations. Make a point of thinking outside the box as you job search. Magazines, websites, TV stations, book publishing houses, and PR firms aren't the only companies looking for people with English and communication degrees. There are plenty of places nurses work besides hospitals. And accounting firms aren't the only entities hiring accountants.

It's also important to apply to companies of varying sizes. Many people apply only to well-known, large-sized companies because they think the pay will be more and it will look better on a resume, but this isn't necessarily true. You might actually earn more and put your career on the fast track through "thinking small." As a plus, smaller companies tend to be easier to get into because less people are applying for positions within them and it's easier to gain the interest of the actual owner. And, as I have found, working for companies that have relatively few employees gives you an opportunity to learn and do more, which is what really helps build your career. The point: The faster you are able to recognize not-so-blatant opportunities and expand your idea of where you should work, the closer you will be to getting hired in a position you will enjoy.

JOB SEARCH STRATEGIES

Although many people rely on the more formal methods of job searching, such as applying to positions listed on websites, the fastest way to secure a position is by using both formal and informal strategies. Informal strategies, such as job searching through networking (online and off) and contacting employers directly, will take more time on your behalf but are definitely worth the effort. It's estimated that more than 80 percent of all jobs are secured through using informal job search strategies.

Informal Job Search Strategies

Cold calling: If you learn about a company that might have a position of interest to you, but you don't know if they're hiring, be proactive and find out. When you speak to a manager, briefly tell him or her about your background, the type of position you are seeking, and the career you want to pursue. But how do you get their contact info? The Internet has made this simpler than ever. The name, phone number, and email address to human resources (HR) staff and the people you would ultimately work for are often listed on a company's website.

Email and direct mail campaigns: This is a "wait and see" strategy. After identifying companies that offer (but may not be hiring for) positions in your field, you email or mail the hiring manager a customized cover letter and resume and hope you get a response. You will need to be quick about following up on all the emails and mail you send out to make the most of this approach.

Informational interviews: An informational interview is a meeting that you initiate with a potential employer to ask for career advice and learn more about a particular field. Unlike a regular interview, *you* ask the majority of the questions. Requesting an informational interview is a great way to network, get yourself on a company's radar should they be hiring for a position that fits you in the future, and learn about opportunities with other businesses.

During an informational interview held over lunch with a senior book publishing professional, I was actually invited to apply for a position I didn't even know she was hiring for. My "informational interview" turned out to have doubled as a real interview, and I was soon offered the job. If you ask intelligent questions, confidently discuss your goals, and come dressed to impress, someone may decide that they need you on their staff, too.

Your personal network: Tell all your friends, relatives, former professors, and mentors about the type of jobs you are seeking. To inform them all at once and take real advantage of social media, put up a tactful but direct post on Facebook, LinkedIn, Twitter, and whatever other social networking tool you use. *Example:* I have a business degree, strong work ethic, and excellent analytical and communication skills needed to start my career in [fill in the blank]. All I need now is a position I can prove myself in. If you know of a position I might be right for, please let me know! Or, even simpler: I want to work at [fill in the blank]. Can you help?

Your end goal is to have as many people as possible on the lookout for your first or next job. If there are certain people in your life who seem to know any and everybody, make sure they have a copy of your resume.

Professional organizations: Joining an organization related to your career is a great way to network with people who can give you leads on job openings within your field or hire you themselves. Many organizations provide members with lists on who is hiring or have companies recruiting people specifically from their organization. Find, join, and become actively involved in a professional organization in your city as soon as possible.

Alumni associations: Check with your alma mater to see if they offer placement services for their graduates. If the alumni association provides a list of alumni and the fields they now work in, take the initiative to call or email those working in your field for job leads.

Volunteerism: Volunteering is an excellent way to network with people working in different fields.

HRinsider Tip: It's one thing to identify employment opportunities, and another to turn them into career prospects for yourself. The most effective job seekers follow each lead until the end and keep lines of communication open, making sure to send thank-you notes, reply in a timely fashion, and make follow-up calls when necessary and appropriate.
—Sudy Bharadwaj, CEO of Jackalope Jobs, Jackalopejobs.com

The people you meet may open you up to job opportunities you never considered. As an added bonus, you can use your skills to help an organization or business and include this work on your resume.

Formal Job Search Strategies

Internet ads: There are tons of sites on the Internet with job listings, and this is where you will likely find the positions that are advertised. However, you should choose just a select handful to browse so you have time to spend job searching through informal methods. You can search sites like Indeed.com, CareerBuilder.com, Craigslist.com, and Idealist.com, which have listings for nearly every field in every city, or field-specific sites like ones for counselors. If you find a great listing that doesn't show the date it was posted, or the posting is more than a month old, call the company to see if they are still hiring for the position and if they have any other positions open that fit your interests.

HRinsider Tip: Post your resume on job search websites such as Indeed.com and Careerbuilder.com and then update it once a week or so by adding a blank space, deleting the blank space, and then saving it. This way, when your resume is looked at by a potential employer, it will appear to be a few days old, instead of a few months old. Also, instead of checking job boards every day, set up search agents for each website and then save them. This way, new jobs that meet your specifications will be sent directly to your inbox.

—Dale Abrams,
CEO of Temporaries Now

Newspaper ads: Millions of people still look in newspapers across the United States for job listings every week, but thanks to the Internet, it's almost pointless because employers have found advertising online to be cheaper and faster. Also, keep in mind that most newspapers have websites now. Their websites will allow you to check for job listings every day so you don't have to constantly buy papers.

Employment/staffing agencies: Generally, employment agencies (also referred to as temp agencies) get paid by companies to find new temporary or permanent staff, so they can be extremely helpful in securing a position that interests you. Often the agency pays you instead of the actual company you are working for. Some employment agencies are industry-specific, only dealing with techies or creatives, for example. Look for an agency that specializes in placing people within your field—particularly in entry- to mid-level positions—before you go with one that works on a broader scale. You can also register with temp agencies to just help you find a job that will pay the bills while you look for something better. Run from agencies that ask you to pay them for anything.

Job fairs: Job fairs offer a convenient way for you to market yourself and learn more about companies in your field. Always dress like you are going to an interview and bring plenty of resumes and business cards.

JOB HUNTING NO-NO'S

An unprofessional online presence: Reading about the wild night you just had (that you barely remember because you were soooooooo freaking drunk) may be very amusing to fellow Facebookers, but not so much to a potential employer digging around to learn more about you. And chances are that they are digging. A CareerBuilder.com survey of 2,184 hiring managers and HR professionals found that nearly two in five companies use social networking sites to research job candidates. Of those checking the net to scope people out, 43 percent said they have found information that has caused them *not* to hire a candidate. So, if your profiles on social media sites aren't set to ultra private and feature unprofessional (mean, controversial, sexual, anything but positive) posts, you could lose a job you didn't even know you were seriously being considered for. Ditto for sexually suggestive photos.

Beyond checking you out on social media platforms, potential employers may simply Google you. Through search engines, would-be employers can find posts, photos, and video left on various websites from long, long ago. If the content is questionable, they aren't going to call you anyway and ask if you have matured since then. Bottom line: If your overall online presence paints you as anything less than a sophisticated and charming young woman, clean it up immediately.

Now You Tell Me?

A Jobvite survey of more than 1,600 recruiting and HR professionals found that recruiters use LinkedIn 93 percent of the time to search, contact, and keep tabs on candidates in the hiring process.

An unprofessional email address: How seriously do you think you'll be taken by an employer if you email your resume from prettybrown eyes22@hotmail.com? Not very seriously at all. If you haven't done so, create a professional-sounding email address using Gmail (because some employers consider Hotmail and Yahoo to be youngster) and use your name or part of your name as the email address. Keep it simple by avoiding the use of hyphens, periods, and multiple numbers. Your email address should be both easy to remember and type. Also, don't use your birth year, graduation year, or anything else that indicates your age.

Cold: Jessiethegenius21@yahoo.com
Warm: JessicaDeniseParker_21@gmail.com
Warmer: JDParker2@gmail.com

An unprofessional voice message: Talking sexy on your voice mail, making a joke, using a ringback tone, and even having a long-winded inspirational message are potential employer turn offs. Even your friends don't want to hear all that. While you're job searching—and even once you've snagged a position—you'll need to have a professional voice message. Think upbeat (so you don't sound monotone or like you don't play well with others) and short (so people don't forget what they want to say by the time your message is over).

Sending emails using your company email address: This indicates to employers that you don't see a problem with using work time for personal business, and this is never a good sign.

LEVERAGING YOUR DIGITAL SELF

Harness the power of social media to help, not hinder, your job search.

Facebook

Help: Post cool, but non-eyebrow-raising photos of you and your friends. Update your status with information that inspires or educates others, not informs them of what you ate for lunch or how rude your waiter was. If you want to be free to post info as you wish, only allow your information to be viewed by friends.

Hinder: Allow anyone to access your page so they can see photos of you dancing on top of a table at the last girls' night out and read all of your poorly punctuated, negative posts. Let other people post inappropriate/distasteful content, which sends the message that you think inappropriate content is funny too.

LinkedIn

Help: Have a professional headshot and a profile that is as thorough as your resume. Be able to show off recommendations by former bosses and colleagues.

Hinder: Neglect to post a picture and let your profile remain only halfway filled out, and thus, entirely uninteresting.

Twitter

Help: Have a fun but professional photo, and use tweets to share knowledge about your industry and links to interesting articles. Interact with professionals through providing insightful and positive comments about their tweets.

Hinder: Have a somewhat lewd photo or one in which you are not looking your best, and use your tweets to comment on the latest celebrity gossip, disparage other people, or provide links to bizarre and disturbing videos.

YouTube

Help: Create and post short educational or inspirational videos for other people that show off your confidence, eloquence, and knowledge in an area.

Hinder: Let friends record and post videos of you doing or saying inappropriate things. Create your own videos in which you talk at length about religion, politics, or whatever controversial issue is in the news.

Pinterest

Help: Show an interest in companies you would like to work for and people you would love to meet through commenting on and liking their pins. Share pins associated with one of your interests; interesting, positive pins in general; and if applicable, pins of your work.

Hinder: Share pins that are sure to be commented on, but only because of their shock value.

Google Plus

Help: Create a professional profile that includes a great head shot and information on your background and career goals. Link your profile to the new blog you created and the pages to the other social networking sites you use so people can learn more about you and your interests. Make sure people are in their appropriate circles, such as family, friends, and associates.

Hinder: Share totally inappropriate content that contradicts the professional image you are trying to portray, and use a cute but unprofessional photo taken a few years back that makes you seem too young and immature to potential employers.

Applying
for Positions

It's a long old road,
but I know I'm gonna find the end.
—Bessie Smith, blues singer

Sometimes it seems the most you can do is wish your resume and cover letter well after you send them off. However, there is something else you can do: Take extra steps to get your materials into the hands of the right person. The right person is someone who has the authority to say, "You're hired!"

I finally figured this out after writing what seemed to be gazillions of brilliant and perfectly punctuated cover letters and resumes (I hoped!) to would-be employers. Despite double-checking the "where to send your resume line" on job posts, I was always a little afraid that I had used all that brain energy for nothing and my application materials were in a black hole somewhere. I had heard the very true statistic that employers get hundreds of applicants for every one position, and I worried that my email may have been the sole one to go into a junk folder, or my work samples were lost by the postal service. Although I am prone to imagining worst-case scenarios, when it comes to applications getting to the right person—and actually being read—it really doesn't hurt to be extra careful and proactive.

Now You Tell Me?

When applying for a job, don't name your resume file "resume." If your name's good enough for you, it's good enough for your resume. Name it "M. Allen resume.doc" for example. The same goes for your cover letter. —David Gaspin, HR director

---

Sending your materials to the right person is easy when the job advertisement directs you to send it to a specific person. However, this simple task becomes trickier when you are asked to send your valuables to human resources. Most large organizations and companies now have HR departments, which serve as gatekeepers between applicants and employers. The people who work in HR often decide if your resume merits the consideration of the person hiring for the position. You take the gamble of your resume ever being seriously looked at when you send it to these well-meaning, but potentially career-blocking people. To overcome this barrier, you can find out who your resume really needs to go to and send it to them *and* the HR department.

Finding out who the real decision maker is may take a little time and snooping, but it's worth it. The easiest approach is browsing the company's website and searching for the email address to the person you would most likely be working for, or the person who manages the department you would work in. If the information is not on the website, call the company, ask who's who, and then try reaching out to the person through LinkedIn or another professional social media website.

Once you know whom your materials should be directed to, you're one step closer to getting them into their hands. Keep in mind that just because you sent your resume and cover letter off, it doesn't mean that they were received and reviewed. Again, an employer can get hundreds of applications every week—for your position and others—and you don't want yours to be the one that gets lost in the shuffle.

The following are simple rules to follow when sending your application materials via email, through a company's website, by mail, and in person.

By email: Unless a company gives specific directions for applying via email, paste your cover letter directly into the body of the email (beginning with the salutation, Dear X), and attach both the cover letter and resume in .pdf format, not in Microsoft Word (.doc or .docx). Sending a document as a .pdf is wise because a company may not have your font, which could cause a Word document to look formatted poorly.

If you're directed to email your resume to a specific person, call him or her to verify that it was received a few hours after you send it. Although you do risk the chance of being annoying, you also put your name in the person's mind. However, if the job advertisement specifically says "No phone calls, please!" then follow up with another email one to two weeks later. In the email, provide your name, the position you applied for and when, and write that you just wanted to follow up. Also briefly reiterate your interest in the position. The key here is letting your potential boss know you really want the job.

FOLLOWING UP BY EMAIL

Email subject line: Follow up on Program Coordinator position

Dear Ms. Janice Pines,

My name is Paige Prince, and I emailed my resume and cover letter to you last Wednesday to apply for the program coordinator position within GreenPoint Solutions. As I expressed, I am very interested in speaking with you about this opportunity, and given my experience and passion for developing and launching grassroots sustainable initiatives, I am confident I would be an asset to your organization. Please let me know if you received my application materials. I look forward to your reply.

Sincerely,
Paige Prince

Through a website: As with email, upload your resume and cover letter as .pdf files unless directed otherwise. Normally, you will receive an email from a company indicating that your materials were received. If you don't, call the HR office and ask someone to check to make sure all your materials came through.

By mail: When applying by mail—which is increasingly rare now—print your resume and cover letter on matching white or light-cream resume paper. Send your materials in an envelope that matches your resume and cover letter, or in a paper-sized envelope so your materials will still be neat when received. Call the employer two to three days after they should have received your materials to make sure they got them.

By fax: When sending your resume and cover letter via fax, make doubly sure the cover sheet is directed to the right person. Wait an hour after you send it to call and verify that it was received and that your materials are in the process of being given to the person who should review it. It won't hurt to call the next day to make sure it got into the right person's hands.

HRinsider Tip: While there is nothing wrong with applying for a job that is a bit vague on the prerequisites, putting your name in for something that is outside of your expertise can come off as wasting the company's time, especially in this competitive job market. If it's pretty clear that you aren't the ideal candidate (and you don't know the hiring manager or have a great inside referral), your time may be better spent applying for a position more suitable for your qualifications.

—Linsey Knerl, writer for Financialhighway.com

In person: Applying in person gives you the chance to present yourself to a potential employer and to take a look at your potential workplace. Although this option just isn't available for most large companies (because it can be hard to even get into a building and your name may need to be on a list), the in-person route could be worth a try for small businesses.

Call the company and ask when the owner or manager will be in on the day you plan to visit. It is a good idea to dress business casual or in an actual suit. Ask for the proper person once you get there, and if he or she is not there then ask for another manager or assistant manager in the department. Your goal is to introduce yourself to someone who has some decision-making authority. If you have to turn your materials into someone in HR, inquire about their hiring process and how long it usually takes for materials to be reviewed. Always be extra nice to everyone you meet while visiting the company.

OMG! MISTAKES

No matter how you apply, do not give someone a reason *not* to read your application materials because of foolish mistakes. Ones to watch out for:

Spelling someone's name wrong: Double check to make sure names are spelled correctly and the same in all places. If you must ask someone else for a person's name, ask for the correct spelling—don't assume. "Sherry" can also be spelled Sheri, Sherri, and Sherrie.

Assuming someone's gender: Like "Chaz," my name, or "Kim," a male friend's name, plenty of people have names that you would bet are a man's or woman's—and be wrong. This is also true for gender-neutral names like Cameron. Don't gamble on your application materials—find out.

Using the wrong company name: This is easy to do after sending many cover letters, but there's still no excuse. Double check to ensure you've included the correct company name and the correct name of the hiring manager and not one from a different job to which you applied.

Emailing materials to the wrong person: Again, too easy to do when emailing people back-to-back. Make the email address the last thing you enter before emailing your materials, and then make sure you have the right person.

Not actually attaching your materials: This is why I love Gmail. A nice warning pops up when you mention attachment in an email but have failed to attach anything.

CREATING COMPELLING RESUMES & COVER LETTERS

Chances are you're not 100 percent confident that the resume and cover letter you worked on for days clearly articulate how utterly amazing you are. No worries! There are fantastic print and online resources to help you whip these two key documents into shape, as well as bona fide resume writing professionals. Key resources:

PRINT

Resume 101: A Student and Recent-Grad Guide to Crafting Resumes and Cover Letters that Land Jobs (Ten Speed Press, 2012): This guide is jam-packed with tips on how to bypass the recent grad conundrum of no or limited experience by highlighting the transferable skills and strengths gained from your life experiences (e.g., school projects, travel, hobbies, part-time work, internships).

The Damn Good Resume Guide (Ten Speed Press, 2012): This bestselling resume guide packs a lot of punch in 88 pages, with a summary and breakdown of 10 essential steps to resume writing and tip sheets on cover letters. FAQs and resume samples in various fields are also provided.

Knock 'Em Dead Resumes: How to Write a Killer Resume that Gets You Job Offers (Adams Media Company, 2012): With more than 35 years of career management experience, author Martin Yate is the perfect companion for your job search journey. Yate's advice and clear examples of how to deconstruct your target job and present yourself as the solution to employers' problems will move you one step closer to career fulfillment.

Resumes for Dummies (Wiley Publishing Inc., 2011): Like the other *Dummies* books, *Resumes for Dummies* is both visually appealing and easy to follow. Regardless of your employment situation or specific challenges, this book will give you the tools to cast yourself in the most positive light and impress future employers.

ONLINE

On Monster.com (http://career-advice.monster.com/resumes-cover-letters/careers.aspx): A virtual career library containing tips on creating stand-out resumes and cover letters, handy checklists, and templates for job-seekers in diverse fields and at different career stages.

On Quintcareers.com (http://www.quintcareers.com/resres.html): A one-stop career guidance site that demystifies the process of creating powerful resumes and cover letters for job search newbies.

On Susanireland.com (http://susanireland.com/resume/examples/): Offers both new and experienced job seekers 100+ sample resumes and 50+ cover letters categorized by format, career type, work history problems solved, target audience, and more.

On Careerealism.com (http://www.careerealism.com/category/jobsearch /resume/): Career experts from across North America provide their best tips for creating bullet-proof job search documents and thriving in an ever-changing job market.

On Ubc.ca (http://www.students.ubc.ca/careers/students/get-career -guidance/job-search-skills/resumes/): Created by the University of British Columbia, this site is an excellent resource for any student or recent graduate, providing short videos on resume basics and featuring sample resumes for entry-level job candidates in a range of fields.

—compiled by Christelle Agboka

PROFESSIONAL HELP

As a resume writer, I have rarely seen a resume or cover letter that didn't need some type of work, and many were so poorly written, organized, or formatted that they were destined for the employer's recycling bin. Resume and cover letter writing is a type of craft; considering this, you may find it beneficial to hire a professional resume/cover letter writer if you think your resume isn't up to par, have been told so, or are not getting interviews. Find a professional through the National Resume Writer's Association (www.thenrwa.com) or the Professional Association of Resume Writers & Career Coaches (www.parw.com). Consider the fee an investment in your career.

Acing the Interview

Nothing about my life is lucky. Nothing. A lot of grace, a lot
of blessings, a lot of divine order, but I don't believe in luck.
For me, luck is preparation meeting the moment of opportunity.
—Oprah Winfrey

Getting that long-awaited phone call for an interview can be a big confidence booster. It means the cover letter and resume you hoped would impress your potential employer did, and your phone calls and emails weren't in vain. So be optimistic. You're now closer to getting a call saying you're hired. But just how do you make that happen? You prepare for the interview 10 times more than you would prepare for a date with the man of your dreams. How well you're prepared for the interview will dictate how well you'll do once it's begun.

The following four tasks must be accomplished before you walk in to greet any employer.

Task 1: Research the Company

Prior to an interview, you should research the company to help you better answer and ask questions. You can gather information from many sources, including the company's website, their marketing materials, and employees you may know. If you Google a company, you may also find reviews and other information posted by current and former employees. When researching a company, look for this type of information:

→ The company's products and/or services

→ The company's mission

→ How long the company has been in business and who started it

→ How successful the company is compared to others within the industry

→ Trends and issues affecting the company

→ How many employees the company has

→ If the company has offices in other cities, states, or countries

→ The company's recruitment process

→ The company's future plans

→ The company's stock performance (if it's a public company)

If you take time to gather this information, you'll be better able to confidently discuss what compelled you to apply for the position and any aspects of the company the employer brings up.

Now You Tell Me?

If you don't have immediate access to your resume, cover letter, and job announcement when a potential employer calls, letting the call go to voicemail will give you a few minutes to get them together without having to make an excuse to call back. It also gives you the opportunity to be focused on the discussion instead of distracted by what's going on around you.

—Pamela McBride, creator of the Work-Life Diva blog, Pamelamcbride.net/blog

---

Task 2: Practice Interviewing

Perhaps one of the most unnerving parts of the interview process is when the employer takes out a long sheet full of interview questions and smiles. Right then you know it's time for you to either sink or swim. In order for you to swim—float even—you need to understand the purpose of the question-and-answer phase of the interview. The questions posed by employers, no matter how mundane or unusual, simply give them a chance to gauge the following:

→ Your personality

→ If you can help meet the company's wants, needs, and goals

→ Your wants, needs, and goals

→ If you will fit into the company's culture

Just as your cover letter should be tailored to an employer, so should the answers to the questions posed. The more you've researched the company and its needs, the better you'll be able to answer the questions to an employer's liking.

For example, if you know the job requires you to work a lot in teams, then of course you "work well collaborating with other colleagues to complete assignments." The employer doesn't need to know you prefer working alone! If the position requires you to learn new software programs, then you certainly "are sure learning new programs will not pose a problem for you." The employer doesn't need to know you'll have to re-read the software manual a dozen times at home! Employers know that people are rarely perfectly suited for a position. However, you don't want an employer to eliminate you as a candidate because of preferences or small weaknesses you blabbed you have. Now, if the employer asks you if you speak Spanish and you say yes when you don't know what "agua" means, then you'll be in trouble.

Answering the interview questions can be like walking on a tight rope. You want to appear confident but not cocky, knowledgeable but not a know-it-all, energetic but not wired, and poised but not "posed" for the interview. And just as important, you don't want to say anything incorrect or silly. This is why practicing for each interview is so important.

The following are sample interview questions and tips for how to answer them. Have an older professional ask you the questions during a mock interview.

Sample Interview Questions

1. Can you tell me a little about yourself?

Focus on what led you to the career you're entering, and then briefly talk about your career-related goals. You can also talk about anything interesting/unusual about yourself that is positive, like you've traveled to several countries, speak more than one language, are a trained dancer, or volunteer in community service programs. Do not give the interviewer your whole life story, say anything negative about yourself, discuss your political or religious views, or divulge private details of your life.

2. Why are you seeking a position with this company?

Discuss certain aspects of the company that you admire, such as its reputation or mission, and how working for the company will help you reach your career goals.

3. What makes you qualified to apply for this position?

Discuss how your educational background, work history, and the skills you've acquired have prepared you for the exact position you are applying for.

4. Why do you want this position?

Explain why the position is a perfect fit for you, given your educational background, work history, or interests. Talk about specific aspects of the job that you'll enjoy and what you like about the company.

5. Why should I hire you?

Again, discuss how your educational background, work history, and the skills you've acquired have prepared you for the exact position you are applying for. However, also highlight your positive character traits, like your creativity or perceptiveness, and how having someone in the position with these traits will benefit the company. You should also talk about anything else that you think may set you apart from other candidates.

6. If hired, how long will you stay with the company?

Stress to the employer that you can really see yourself growing with the company, and that you see the company as a great place to start and build your career. Employers know you don't know the answer to this question; they just want to make sure you aren't using the position as an "in-between" job until you find something better.

7. What are your career ambitions?

Discuss your ultimate career objectives and how the position you are applying for, and the company itself, will help you meet those objectives. Do not discuss career goals that have nothing to do with the field you're in (e.g., you are applying for a financial counselor position, but you say your career goal is to become a wedding planner).

8. Why did you choose this career field?

Discuss what first drew you to the field you're in, and what aspects about the field made you passionate enough to want to build a career in it.

9. What is your ideal type of company?

The ideal type of company you describe should closely resemble the company you're trying to join. After describing this "imaginary" place, you can talk about what you like most about the company you're hoping to be a part of.

HRinsider Tip: Avoid TMI (too much information). When an interview is going well, personal topics such as kids or hobbies may come up. While that's a good sign and it's nice to discuss these things, be careful to respect the boundaries because you're still on a "first date." Realize that you've only been with this person for an hour and avoid getting too personal by discussing religion, politics, and the like.

—Adriana Llames, author of *Career Sudoku: 9 Ways to Win the Job Search Game*

10. What kind of people do you enjoy/ dislike working with?

First, stress that you are able and enjoy working with all types of people. Next, describe the type of people you enjoy working with most (like flexible or very resourceful people). Then pick a type of person that no one wants to work with (such as someone who is negative or isn't respectful of other people's time).

11. What things are most important to you on a job?

Discuss what you need most in a position to enjoy it (as long as the position offers these benefits), such as the ability to interact with lots of people, room to grow, autonomy, or supportive co-workers and managers.

12. Do you prefer working alone or with a team?

Stress that you are able to work well in a team or alone and talk about what you like about both. Then consider the position. If it requires you to work most often in teams, then that's what you prefer, and vice versa.

13. What qualities do you look for in a manager?

Discuss the positive attributes that you most admire in people and why you look for these attributes in a manager (such as someone who provides constructive feedback). If you have worked for a manager who you really liked, you can briefly talk about him or her.

14. What is your greatest strength/weakness?

Tell the employer you don't like trick questions. Just kidding! Discuss your strengths first, such as your unflappable nature or ability to explain hard-to-understand concepts simply. Next, resist the urge to say "perfectionism" or some other trait that really is not a weakness. The employer not only won't believe you, he or she probably heard the same canned response from the candidate interviewed right before you. Instead, pick a minor weakness that you really do have but would not be considered a character flaw, such as a slight fear of public speaking. After you've stated your teeny-weeny weakness, tell the employer how you are working to improve in this area.

15. Do you have any additional skills that make you a good candidate for the position?

Discuss any talents or skills you may have that aren't a requirement for the position, and explain how they can add to your effectiveness on the job.

16. What did you like most/least about your former boss?

Discuss the qualities you liked most in your boss first and what you learned from him or her. If you had a particularly good working relationship with your former boss, then you can talk briefly about how well you worked together. When asked what you liked least about him or her, pick something relatively minor, like your boss's forgetfulness. Do not badmouth your former boss or co-workers.

17. In what ways did you contribute to your last company?

Discuss specific ways you helped the company, such as increasing profits, implementing a new service, or finding a great solution to a problem that was hurting the company. You can also talk about how you performed well in your position day to day, and how doing your job well positively impacted your co-workers, managers, and the company as a whole.

18. What problems did you encounter at your former company, and how did you deal with them?

Discuss problems you had that didn't involve confrontations with your boss or co-workers, such as having an inflexible schedule or not being given enough direction on hard assignments. Then explain how you dealt professionally and maturely with whatever problem you mentioned.

19. How would your co-workers describe you?

Pick your best qualities that your co-workers generally liked, like your good sense of humor or friendliness. If possible, pick qualities that would have made you well-respected, such as being a hard worker or straightforward and honest.

20. Are you comfortable working with a diverse group of people?

The answer is always yes. Talk about why you enjoy working with people from different backgrounds (you're exposed to different cultures or beliefs, which can help you grow as a person). You can then briefly share any positive experience you have had that allowed you to work with a diverse group of people.

After the practice interview session, ask the person helping you the following questions:

1. How confident did you come across?
2. How was your demeanor while answering questions?

3. Did you answer the questions intelligently and concisely?
4. Did you fully answer all of the questions?
5. Which questions did you seem to have difficulty with?
6. In what areas do you need to improve?

SHARE YOUR ACCOMPLISHMENTS WITH *CAR*FIDENCE

Make a list of your accomplishments and the problems you have helped solve, so you will be better able to remember them during the interview. When sharing your stories or examples, use the CAR structure:

*C*ircumstance: This was the situation or problem.

*A*ction: Here is what I did to improve it and why.

*R*esult: Because of my (ingenuity, quick thinking, diplomacy, etc.), here's how it turned out.

Task 3: Brainstorm Questions for the Employer

Asking questions about the company and your position further communicates your interest. All questions you feel are appropriate and relevant are game, except questions about money. Waiting to discuss your salary until you're offered the job puts you in a better position to negotiate your salary. Write your questions in a nice notepad, which you will also be using to take a few notes. Here are a few examples:

1. What qualities does a person need to have to be successful in this position?
2. How has the job been performed in the past, and what improvements would you like to see happen?
3. What is the company's culture like?
4. What is your management philosophy?
5. What level of supervision will be given to me?
6. Does this position offer room for growth?

7. How does the employee review and evaluation process work?

8. What is a typical day like for an employee with my job title?

9. What do you like most about working for the company?

10. What is the next step in the hiring process?

It's important to note that you're not just asking these types of questions because it makes you look like a smart candidate. It may be that this job you've been doing rain dances for really isn't right for you, but you won't know that unless you act like the interview goes both ways.

For example, I once accepted an assistant editor position with a book publishing company without getting a full account of exactly what the "assistant" in the title implied. I assumed, given how the publisher and I talked mostly about the more important aspects of the job—helping to build the company's list of books, editing, and production—that I would simply be "helping out" the publisher as needed. But we all know what happens when one assumes; it turned out I was to double as an executive assistant. Being that I have chicken-scratch handwriting and can't remember to forward my own voicemail, much less someone else's, I wasn't too happy in that position.

I also neglected to ask about this company's typical work hours in fear I would appear unwilling to work hard. Yet soon, as I found myself clocking 12-hour days, and—I am not kidding—spending the night in the office, I silently cursed myself for not interviewing the employer as well as she had interviewed me.

Task 4: Get Your Wardrobe Together

Take the idea of dressing to impress very seriously because it isn't just your credentials that will be judged during the interview. Your appearance should be as sharp as you are. Your attire, hair, makeup, and accessories must reflect a professional woman who means business. Now, the problem is that different people have different ideas about what is appropriate business attire. Some women will walk into an interview looking like they should be going to a club and think their outfit is cute. Others will stroll in dressed business casual because they don't feel like the job they're applying for warrants wearing a nice suit. However, during the interview, only one person's opinion about fashion counts—the interviewer's opinion. Because you can never be sure about what someone else thinks is tasteful, you're better off playing it safe by sticking to what has traditionally been considered "proper" attire for an interview.

This can sometimes be a problem for women with a flair for fashion and accessories. Keep in mind that you'll have plenty of time to show off your fashion sense after you've gotten the job. While you're trying to get one, you'll have to play by a conservative set of rules for attire.

RULES FOR ATTIRE

Do . . .

→ Wear a suit to the interview, choosing between one with a skirt, dress, or pants. If you opt for a skirt or dress, pay close attention to how short it is. You don't want to be ashamed to cross your legs during the interview.

→ Stick with solid-colored or pinstriped suits. Most people opt for a navy blue, black, or brown suit.

→ Choose a suit made from a synthetic-blend material, cotton-polyester, or wool, so that it won't wrinkle easily. The suit should be tailored to fit you.

→ Wear a blouse that matches well with your suit, opting for a long-sleeved one (unless it's summertime) that will allow the cuff to show around a quarter or half-inch beyond the jacket sleeve.

→ Wear shoes with a closed toe, even if it's summertime. The heel should be no more than 1 1/2 inches high. The shoes should complement your suit.

→ Wear pantyhose closest to your skin tone or black if you're wearing a black suit.

Definitely Do Not . . .

- → Try to get away with wearing a business-casual outfit. You're dressing for the interview, not the job.
- → Wear a loud-colored suit or one with designs or animal prints.
- → Choose a suit made from materials that wrinkle easily or that looks cheap just from the look of it.
- → Come to the interview wearing a skirt, pants, or dress that is too tight or too big for you. You should feel and look comfortable in your clothes.
- → Wear no blouse or undershirt at all. What's more, your cleavage should be completely covered up whether you have big boobs or itty bitties.
- → Wear heels you can't walk in or ones that look worn out.
- → Wear hose with fancy designs or with a little run in them. In fact, you should bring an extra pair with you when wearing a dress or skirt.

Those rules for attire aren't too hard to follow and neither are these other rules governing fragrance, jewelry, makeup, accessories, and hairstyles.

Fragrance: Pay special attention to how you smell. Sniff yourself if you're unsure! If the perfume you wear is strong with just one spray, then opt for a nice-smelling body spray for the day, or consider wearing no perfume at all. Also make sure you don't smell like any kind of food (a burger you ate before the interview) or animal (a cat you may have at home). Ditto for cigarettes and alcohol.

Jewelry: Less is better. Don't try to "bling bling" for the interview; besides looking gaudy, big earrings, long necklaces, and clunky bracelets tend to make noise. Also lose any tongue, nose, chin, or eyebrow rings unless you're interviewing for positions where you'll look out of place without them (which aren't many places). Lastly, err on the safe side and also leave religious jewelry at home.

Makeup: Again, less is better. You want to look natural, not made up. Save the heavy blush, fake eyelashes, and seductive eye shadow for a night out with the girls to celebrate your new gig.

Accessories: A small purse that matches your suit is fine for the interview, but it's better to just bring a professional tote that holds extra copies of your resume and work samples. A scarf around your neck that matches the suit is okay, but it should have a simple design.

Hairstyles: How you wear your hair to the interview is entirely up to you. However, there are some general rules for hairstyles that you should follow. These include coming in with neat hair no matter what the style; having the simplest style possible, such as a ballerina bun if you have long hair; leaving out unnecessary hair accessories; and making sure you have absolutely no dandruff to be embarrassed about. Also, unless you're interviewing for a job in entertainment, it's wise to keep your hair color natural, or at least not dye your hair using an unnatural-looking color. Hint: no colors in the American flag.

Twenty Pointers to a Better Interview

When you're prepared, you're more confident.
When you have a strategy, you're more comfortable.
—Fred Couples, professional golfer

You only get one chance to convince an employer to hire you. Avoid playing the woulda, coulda, shoulda game by following these 20 interviewing rules.

1. *Arrive Ahead of Time:* Get good directions and plan to arrive at the place you're being interviewed at least 30 minutes early so you won't be 30 minutes late. You never know if there will be a lot of traffic or how hard it will be to find a parking space.

2. *Give Your Appearance a Double Check:* Go to the restroom in a nearby café or one in the lobby of the company's building so you can straighten yourself up before greeting the interviewer.

3. *Be Cordial to Everyone You Meet:* The person interviewing you might end up being the same person you let the elevator door shut on during your way up to their office. Briefly greet and be nice to everyone at the company because you never know just who has a say in your hiring.

4. *Make a Good First Impression:* Consider it showtime when employers first spot you; from that very moment they are sizing you up. Given this, it's best to stay off the cell phone while waiting to be called in for the interview. To keep yourself busy, read the company's literature or go over the questions you have for the employer.

5. *Be Respectful of the Employer:* Don't forget to whom you're talking. Greet the people interviewing you with their last name until they tell you otherwise. Leave the slang at home and turn the cell phone off or on silent—not on vibrate.

6. *Watch Your Body Language:* Your demeanor should exude confidence and enthusiasm, which can be shown in various ways, including a firm handshake, eye-to-eye contact, good posture, and a sincere smile. Definite don'ts include biting your lip or nails, slouching in your chair, excessive note-taking, watching the clock, fiddling your hands or feet, and looking at everything else in the room but the interviewer while talking.

7. *Have Extra Copies of Your Resume:* You may be required to interview with more than one person. Being able to hand them a crisp resume demonstrates your professionalism and thoughtfulness.

8. *Think Before You Speak*: Always make sure you understand a question before you go about answering it. People can tell when you're running off at the mouth while trying to remember what you were asked. Ask for clarification if you don't completely understand a question.

9. *Answer Questions Completely:* Try not to give simple yes or no answers. One of your goals is to show how well you communicate with others.

10. *Stress the Skills You Can Offer the Company:* Know the exact skills an employer is looking for and stress that you have these skills and enjoy using them. Also, talk about any other skills you have that are not required for your position, but that you feel will make you more attractive to an employer, such as bilingualism or public speaking.

> ———————— **Now You Tell Me?** ————————
>
> The three most deadly mistakes an applicant can make during an interview are dressing inappropriately, not being prepared, and being late, according to a poll of HR professionals conducted by the Center for Professional Excellence at York College of Pennsylvania.

11. *Stress Your Ability to Learn New Skills Fast:* If there's a skill you lack that an employer asks about, stress your ability to quickly learn that skill, possibly giving examples of how you've learned fast in other situations.

12. *Stress Your Positive Personality:* Communicate with the interviewer how easy you are to work with, how you can see the silver lining in any cloud, and how you're so very flexible, etc. The employer is looking for someone who current employees will get along with.

13. *Talk with Pride About Your Accomplishments:* Most employers believe that past performance is the best indicator of future performance. Make them realize how valuable you are by talking about accomplishments you're proud of, be they through old positions, internships, volunteer work, or hobbies.

14. *Be Prepared for Tough Questions:* While most interview questions are to be expected, some interviewers may surprise you with a curve ball. An employer knows when they've asked a hard question and probably just wants to see how you'll react. Impress them. When asked a question that makes you say "hmmmm," stay calm, take a few moments to think of a good response, and try your best to answer the question as if it didn't faze you.

15. *Tell Them Why You Want the Job:* Don't let the interview come to an end without telling the person interviewing you why you want the job and what it is that you like so much about the position. This further demonstrates your enthusiasm and that you aren't just applying for the paycheck.

16. *Have Any Work Samples Ready to Show:* Be ready to whip out work samples you've brought for the employer to review. You shouldn't have

to search for anything, and if you do, it makes you look unprepared. Don't let the interview end without showing the employer your work samples, even if he or she didn't ask to see them.

17. *Show Your Enterprising Nature:* Demonstrate to the employer that you can handle any job and how resourceful you are by relating stories of how you've handled sticky or tough situations very well.

18. *Don't Undermine Yourself:* Never talk negatively about yourself or talk about what you can't or won't do, no matter how insignificant you think what you're saying is.

19. *Don't Badmouth Anyone:* Never badmouth a past employer or your former co-workers—regardless of how comfortable you feel while talking to someone interviewing you.

IT'S *WHAT* YOU SAY AND *HOW* YOU SAY IT

Communicate with clarity and confidence during the interview and in everyday situations by following these three rules:

1. *Power up your voice:* A strong, powerful voice will exude self-confidence even when you may not be feeling that way. What's more, people often think that individuals with softer voices are less qualified for certain positions.

2. *Slow down:* People should not have to ask you to repeat yourself. Use strategic pausing to slow down your rate of speech, add impact to your spoken message, and improve your overall speech quality. Own your words and deliver them with the importance they deserve.

3. *Watch your filler words.* Using too many fillers like "um," "uh," and "well" can create the impression that you are unsure of yourself, or not knowledgeable about the topic on which you are speaking.

—*Jayne Latz, president of Corporate Speech Solutions of New York City, Corporatespeechsolutions.com*

20. *Leave a Great Lasting Impression:* No matter how good or bad you think the interview went, the show isn't over until you're out of the employer's sight. Be as cordial and enthusiastic at the end of the interview as you were at the beginning. Communicate with the employer that you are genuinely interested in the position and that you'd very much like to work for the company. Make sure you shake the hand of everyone with whom you've interviewed. Take time to tell them how much you appreciate being interviewed, to find out when you should hear from them, and to wish them a great day.

One of the most challenging/interesting interview experiences I had as a young professional was with a national newsletter publishing company. The company needed a temporary research editor while one of its employees was on maternity leave. After interviewing and taking a hard editing/layout test for an employment agency, I had to go through three more individual interviews with those inside the publishing company. The interviews were set back-to-back.

The first interview was with the managing editor. She instantly came across as friendly but strictly about business. She asked me a succession of questions about my qualifications and work history, but also made me feel comfortable by talking about what she liked about the company and what I might like about the position. She then asked me to take a typesetting exercise on a computer. I thought the interview went well and she told me I did great on the exercise.

The next interview was with a senior research editor with whom I would be closely working. I thought the purpose of this interview was to see if I would fit in her group. The lady who interviewed me was very sweet and seemed sincerely interested in who I was as a person. She wanted to know what I was passionate about, what my ultimate career goal was, and how I would use the job to get there. I talked to her for what seemed like a long time, and walked away from that interview feeling that it went extremely well.

By the time I got to the third interview, which was with the human resources manager, I felt very confident. That confidence lasted about two seconds. The person I was introduced to made me feel panicky for some reason. To this day I still don't know what it was. She was dressed regally in a long, flowing dress and had this piercing gaze. I felt like if I said or did anything wrong she would call my mother and tell her she raised me wrong. She turned out to be very down-to-earth, however, and we ended up talking quite frankly about her expectations of me, what I could offer the company, and my background.

My confidence was almost back up to sea level until she asked me what my favorite word was. "My favorite word?" I asked her, thinking I had heard her wrong. She nodded yes, and said that as an editor, I should have a favorite word.

The question should have been an easy one, as I have words that I like for one reason or another. However, as soon as I began to think of one, all the words I had ever known seemed to fly out of my brain. "I'll have to give that question some more thought," I said meekly after three minutes had passed. She frowned, gave me another look of supreme disappointment, and then shook my hand, told me I would be notified about the company's decision "soon," and sent me home. I left feeling like a complete loser.

On the train ride home, one of my favorite words finally came to me—fierce. I emailed her the word when I got home with a note about how sorry I was that it took me so long to think of it. I guess she liked the word and everyone else who interviewed me thought I was a good fit because I was offered the job two days later.

Following Up After the Interview

Sending a thank-you note to your interviewer is a good practice. It shows courtesy, respect, and that you really want the job. Although you can and should send a formal note of thanks via email, doing so by mail as well will likely score you more bonus points because people rarely do that these days. Within a day after the interview, mail a typed letter on resume paper in a matching envelope. Thank the employer for the opportunity to interview for the position, and reiterate your interest in working for the company.

If the people who interviewed you have not contacted you when they said they would, then give them a call. Let them know that you're calling to check on the status of their hiring process and that you're still very interested in the position.

SAMPLE THANK-YOU LETTER

Dear Ms. Karen Monroe,

It was a pleasure meeting you and your colleagues yesterday during my interview for the business analyst position within Perry International.

The interview strengthened my interest in the position and in working for such a dynamic, internationally recognized consultancy. I am confident that my qualifications and experience, particularly my familiarity with your current systems, fit well with the job requirements and I'm certain I could make a positive contribution to the company from day one. In addition, my strong analytical skills would benefit the new direction the company is taking.

I look forward to hearing from you regarding my candidacy for the position. Should you need further information from me, please don't hesitate to call me at 657-462-3245.

Again, thank you for the interview and for your interest.

Sincerely,

Signature

Typed name

6

Learning from Rejection

The way I see it, if you want the rainbow,
you gotta put up with the rain.
—Dolly Parton, singer

Y ou didn't get the job?" Don't you hate when people ask that question right after you told them you didn't get it!? It's okay to pout a little, but it's not okay to get depressed and let your discouragement keep you from being optimistic about the next interview.

I actually cried the first time I didn't get a position I thought I was destined to have. After the third time, I sulked around the house. *Did I come off as too confident,* I wondered. *Did I not smile enough? Did I not get hired because I was a woman, and a black woman at that?* I asked myself a dozen pointless questions like those in between checking my dwindling savings account. Well, the questions themselves weren't pointless, but my dwelling on them and bringing myself down in the process was. I stopped muttering about how life "just isn't fair" after my mother kindly let me know that I wasn't the only person praying for a job.

Understand that when you're competing with people for a position—or anything in life for that matter—someone isn't going to get it. Unfortunately, sometimes that someone may be you. You may not have been chosen for the job for any number of reasons. It might just be that you were great, but someone was better qualified than you. You can't help that. Maybe something about you reminded the interviewer of a person he or she doesn't like—and yes, this really happens.

The bottom line is that you shouldn't view a rejection as an insult or barrier to your achievement. You don't know what the universe has in store for you. Just focus on how you can do better next time. The following are various reasons employers give for not offering someone a position:

1. Poor personal appearance
2. Overly aggressive
3. Inability to communicate information clearly
4. Lack of interest and enthusiasm
5. Lack of planning for career; no purpose or goals
6. Nervousness, lack of confidence and poise
7. Overemphasis on money
8. Unwilling to start at the bottom
9. Lack of tact and courtesy
10. Lack of maturity
11. Negative attitude about past employers
12. No genuine interest in company or job
13. No eye contact with the interviewer
14. Application form is incomplete or sloppy
15. No sense of humor
16. Late for interview
17. Failure to express appreciation for interviewer's time
18. Failure to ask questions about the job
19. Gives vague responses to questions

—From "Reason's People Don't Get Hired," published in
Creative Job Search by the Minnesota Department of Economic Security,
copyright holder; used with permission.

If you really want to know why you didn't get the position, ask the person who interviewed you. Be very tactful and explain that you're inquiring so that you can be more successful on your next interview.

While many employers may be reluctant to respond, seeking feedback can't hurt you.

After taking a day to debate whether or not I should ask a woman who had interviewed me why I didn't get the job, I finally picked up the phone and called her (email is best, however, so you don't put the person on the spot). I had applied for an entry-level position as an editorial assistant for the children's books division at a major publishing house. I was qualified for the position (in hindsight, overly qualified), had what I considered one of my best interview experiences, and the woman who interviewed me actually told me how impressed she was with me before I left the interview. So naturally, I was dumfounded and upset.

Now You Tell Me?

You might not get hired because your working style would clash with the people you'd be working with. Remember, it's not just a question of whether you have the skills to do the job, it's also a question of fit for this particular position, with this particular boss, in this particular culture, in this particular company.

—Alison Green, creator of "Ask a Manager" career blog, Askamanager.org

---

The lady told me the only reason why she didn't choose me was because she thought I really wouldn't like the job. She said while I was interested in working on books, I had more of an interest in working on non-fiction or adult fiction, not children's literature, and she believed that people should work on what they really love. She then said she would notify me when an opening came up in a different division, and would personally recommend me, which she eventually did.

I thanked her for her feedback, and after I got off the phone, I realized she was right. I wanted to work at the company (which is why I applied), but I was not sincerely interested in working on children's books. In fact, when I initially applied for the position, I immediately thought about how if I got that job I would try to transfer to a different department in half a year. Someone who loved children's books deserved that job, and I hope the person she hired loved the position. The job you need and deserve is closer than you think. Wait for it.

Diary of a Careeranista

CRYSTAL HILLIARD ON
GETTING ON THE FAST TRACK TO SUCCESS

*G*rowing up a tomboy in East Lansing, Michigan, my dreams of television stardom seemed odd to many. Although my legs were covered in scars from falling in my roller blades and my long, curly hair was typically in a tangled ponytail atop my head, I still dreamed of climbing my way to stardom. When I was 17, I took my first real step toward accomplishing this goal when I enrolled into the Missouri School of Journalism.

During my junior year, I landed my first gig at an NBC affiliate in Columbia, Missouri. I began paying my dues while learning how to roll the teleprompter and edit video. It wasn't glamorous, but I knew I had to start at the bottom to become the best reporter that I could be. I realized this lesson early on: The more jobs you can do, the more likely you are to be employed. I soon mastered the art of shooting and editing video, interviewing, writing tight and compelling stories, producing, posting to the web, and anchoring. I wanted to leave the station with as many skills as possible. I also created a blog to showcase all of my stories.

Though I knew I had a pretty strong skill set, I was still shocked when the news director from an ABC affiliate in Jackson, Mississippi, came calling three weeks after I graduated. I thought it would take months to find a job. I learned that one of my professors had forwarded my blog to an executive with the company that owned the station. It was passed through some hands and within 24 hours I had a phone interview for my first job. Three weeks later, at age 21, I moved to Jackson, Mississippi, to start my professional career as a producer/reporter.

Now, while many people may assume I was just lucky, I didn't land that position by pure chance alone. While in college and upon graduating, I concentrated on marketing myself to employers—as well as making myself more marketable—because I knew just having a college degree wouldn't cut it. How can you do the same while in college and throughout your career?

Market Yourself Creatively

The news director saw the blog where I had posted all of my best work. Through my blog, he received a clear, professional picture of who I was as a budding professional and was easily hooked. I found a simple and unique way to market myself and so can you. The technology available to young professionals nowadays is remarkable. There are so many free websites that can help you market yourself, no matter what industry you're in. Maybe you can't walk resumes into everyone's office, but you can buy a URL for less than $50 and build a website! They're easy to make, and when you're done, the only work is sending out the link.

However, a website isn't the only way to snag people's attention. Think beyond the traditional resume and cover letter (though you should send those, too), and find a way to showcase your talent and achievements. For example, you could create a short video of former professors and employers discussing how much they value you and run their compliments in between clips of you hard at work.

Still, marketing yourself creatively is just one step you need to take. What else does it take to make it to the top?

Separate Yourself from the Pack

If you're like me, when you walk into a social setting wearing the same dress or outfit as another girl, you're mortified. Regardless of who looks better in it, you probably picked it out because you thought you'd stand out and look great. Well, the same thing goes for landing that first job and the ones to follow. You don't want to look and sound like everyone else! You have to come up with interesting, innovative ways to be different. For example, when reporting a story, I often try to put some personality into my standups and live shots. Many reporters seem stiff or nerdy because that's how the industry is designed, but that's just not me! I refuse to conform 100 percent to a cookie-cutter image of someone else and this has made other employers take notice.

What makes you unique? How are you different? Figure out why you're not like your competitors and use that as a selling point when you're looking for a position or promotion. But how do you find the job opportunities?

Network and Adopt Mentors

No matter where you are in your career, I guarantee someone has already been there, done that. For every mistake you made last week or the ones you'll make next year, there are countless people who have made them, too. Reach out to them. Use conferences, workshops, happy hours, and random run-ins with professionals as an opportunity to network with people in the field you want to be in. If you're looking for a job, they're the ones who will know about openings before they get posted on the web. The reality is that when a job is posted on the Internet, in many industries it's already gone. Sometimes the company only posts it because it has to. So who's getting the jobs before they go up on the net? Most likely it's the person who heard about the opening from someone who worked there and got his or her resume walked into the big boss's office by a current employee. Remember, you're only as big as your network. If you start reaching out to people in your industry who are well connected, all of their contacts will become yours. You may not know the CEO of your dream company, but if you network within your field, eventually you'll meet someone who has some type of connection to the CEO.

Beyond helping you secure a position, your newfound contacts may also become the ones you'll be able to turn to when you feel like nothing is working out. I've spent countless hours on the phone with mentors asking for job leads, getting advice, and sometimes just crying about my day. But what do you do when you find yourself *always* on the phone crying about your day? What do you do when you feel like your middle name is Failure?

Decide to "Fail Up"

Sometimes you'll fall off the ladder you were carefully climbing to move up in your industry. You may make a mistake that causes you to lose your job. Maybe your boss will put you on probation for something that wasn't your fault. Perhaps you will finally land that new job only to realize you're utterly miserable. Regardless of what bad thing happens, don't give up, "fail up," as media personality Tavis Smiley advises in his book.

When you feel as if you're at a dead end in life, you have to remember there's a bigger picture that's often hard to see. Most people are scared to fail, so when they do, they think the world is over. But I've learned to see failure as a stepping stone, not a huge, insurmountable stumbling block. Failing at something—or being at your lowest point—should serve as motivation to work harder than you knew you could to get to where you need to be. So don't wallow in self-pity when you fail; grind harder for your success.

After I lost my first job, I did a lot of soul searching. Although I didn't know exactly why I got fired, I was determined to list my mistakes and figure out how not to make them again. However, while this stage was important in my recovery, I couldn't stay in it for long. For the first three weeks of unemployment, my determination wouldn't allow me to sleep for more than five hours at a time. I would jump out of bed throughout the night to add people to my "contact for job opportunities" list. I also started coming up with creative ideas for my future.

I was soon even more motivated than before, and I've since made up my mind that whether I lose a job or have one, I have to keep myself moving toward bigger and better things. People are often amazed at my drive and motivation, but I don't think it's something to boast about. I'm hungry because I don't want to be hungry. I refuse to be another broke college graduate, or even worse (to me), a college grad living in her mother's basement working in a restaurant. Don't get me wrong, there's absolutely nothing wrong with going home after school. However, that's not something I ever want to do. I left home to chase my dreams; I'm pretty sure I won't find them at my mom's house.

I encourage you, no matter who you are or where you went to school, to chase your dreams. As long as you market yourself creatively, separate yourself from the pack, network, and keep hope alive, you will eventually catch them. One thing is for sure, they're certainly not chasing you!

Crystal Hilliard is a media maven with experience in television news, talk radio, and entertainment reporting. She has worked in Missouri, Mississippi, Illinois, and Michigan since earning a bachelor's degree in broadcast journalism from the Missouri School of Journalism in 2008. She also has a master's degree in communication from Grand Valley State University. Crystal aspires to host an international show and act in major motion pictures. Learn more about her at Crystalhilliard.com.

Evaluating
Job Offers

Failure to recognize opportunities is the most dangerous
and common mistake one can make.
—Mae Jemison, astronaut

Of course you want to make the right choice. You didn't come this far to get stuck with a low-paying job or one that doesn't challenge you. You want a salary your mom's eyes will widen over, a benefits package your friends wish they had, perks to die for, a boss who has your back, and co-workers who want to see you succeed. Okay, it would be fantastic to have all of those things, but more than anything you want to know that the chair you're sitting in at work is the chair you're meant to be in.

Well, unless you're given a pretty good sign, you'll need faith, intuition, and research on the company whose offer you're evaluating in order to make a wise decision. Even though times may be rough and working anywhere but a coffee shop may seem fine to you, you still should analyze any and all job offers. Not all jobs are worth taking. Making the right decision becomes even more important when you're considering moving away to take a position or accepting a professional position that really doesn't fall in line with your career goals.

Consider the following when evaluating a company and its job offer:

EVALUATING JOB OFFERS

1. The Industry
   - History of growth
   - Predictable future need for goods and services
   - Degrees of dependence on business trends

2. The Organization
   - Prestige and reputation
   - Growth potential
   - Size
   - Financial stability
   - Quality of management team

3. The Job
   - Training programs
   - Day-to-day activities
   - Amount of stress/pressure
   - Requirements to relocate, travel
   - Requirements to work long hours/weekends
   - Responsibility/autonomy
   - Opportunity for advancement or individual achievement
   - Salary
   - Benefits package
   - Involvement with supervisor, peer associates
   - Physical work environment
   - Social significance of work
   - Pace of work
   - Opportunity for continuing education/training

4. General Lifestyle
   - Your comfort with the organization's goals/philosophy
   - Geographic location of company
   - Recreational and cultural facilities near the company
   - Proximity of educational institutions for further study

—From the Job Search Handbook of the University of North Carolina at Chapel Hill; used with the permission of the University of North Carolina at Chapel Hill, copyright holder.

Other important factors to consider

1. *Your boss's personality and management style.* Research has found that more than anything else, your relationship with your boss will dictate how happy you are at work. Glean what you can through observance and specifically asking about their management style and the key qualities they are looking for in an employee.

2. *The existence of a work-life policy or family-friendly practices.* Many companies have family-friendly policies or systems in place that promote work-life balance, such as flexible work hours, the option to telecommute on certain days, and paid maternity leave. Other companies can make having a life outside of work seemingly impossible. While you should be expected to work hard, it's really not healthy to feel as if you are tied to your desk 24/7. Through speaking with current employees (always ask what an average work day is like); asking questions about what's expected of someone in your position (including the normal hours you would be working); and reviewing the company's HR materials, you can get a better idea of what your work life will really be like.

3. *The female-to-male ratio and the primary positions women hold (entry level, middle management, management).* If everyone interviewing you is male, or it's apparent that women hold very few mid- to senior-level positions, this may not bode well for you. Look for signs that a company values and makes a practice of supporting the career progression of women.

4. *The overall ethnic diversity of management and staff.* No matter your ethnicity, working within a company that has a demonstrable commitment to diversity is important. This doesn't mean every race/culture on the planet needs to be represented, just that everyone doesn't look like *you.* Interacting and building relationships with professionals of varied cultural backgrounds will help enhance your career in the long term and better prepare you for the global workforce.

5. *What is deemed professional and unprofessional as far as styles of dress, hairstyles, and jewelry.* Will you go into work every day feeling like

you just don't fit in? Looking professional is expected in any environment, but if you feel like you have to change too many things about yourself to look "professional enough" at a certain company, you might not be comfortable working there.

It's good to get other people's opinions on the job offers you receive, but the final choice will be yours. People determine how good a job offer is according to their own values and goals, and you must do the same. What is worth more to you? Money? Work-life balance? Autonomy? Do you want the chance to rise in the ranks, or do you really just want something that will keep you busy and provide a steady paycheck? There's no wrong or right answer; just think about the kind of person you are and the type of environment you will be comfortable in. A person who truly hates working in teams will probably despise a job that requires them to constantly assist on team projects. Someone who has no sense of time doesn't need to be in a deadline-driven environment. An ambitious person has no place in a company that hardly ever promotes from within. Also, consider your gut feeling about the company. You know, that little voice that says there's something funny going on with this company or that you and your potential boss probably won't get along.

I used to ignore my gut feelings about people or a company I might be working for because I was so happy to be offered a job. Would-be supervisors would give me all the hints I needed that they would make my workday miserable, or the company was poorly run, but I would always think, "Well, I really need a job." In one instance, everyone from the company's recruiter to its secretary warned me that the boss I

HRinsider Tip: If the position is new, being changed, or very complex, you may need to ensure that you have clarified items in detail with your future manager. Ask yourself, "Am I comfortable with the content of the job I am being hired to perform, and do I feel that I will do well with my manager and the team?

—Chris Bardwell, career & organization development consultant was about to work for was one horn away from being a devil. I took the job anyway. Two months and 30 headaches later, I was looking for another job. Now, if I get any inkling that a position I take will leave me praying for quitting time every day—because of my duties, boss, or co-workers—I won't take it.

After your interview, reflect on your initial thoughts about the company. What positive aspects of the company stood out? What did you find odd? Did you feel like you wouldn't fit in right after you met the person who may become your boss? Did the employees look or act like the last people you'd want to work with, or did they make you want to start working with them off-the-clock? You should take all these issues into consideration when you're evaluating a job offer.

8

Understanding Company Benefits

Everything that can be counted does not necessarily count;
everything that counts cannot necessarily be counted.
—Albert Einstein

When you tell someone you've been offered a position, you're bound to be asked two very important questions: what's the salary and what are the benefits? Yet, while many people seem to get super-sharp hearing when an employer talks about the paycheck they'll bring home, too many go deaf—or just don't listen carefully enough—when they start discussing the benefits. This is usually because they're so busy calculating what they can buy with the money they're offered.

Employee benefits—sometimes called "fringe benefits"—are items of compensation that are given to an employee in addition to a salary. Whether an employer offers a benefits package and the extent of their offering is often a major determining factor in whether someone will accept a job—as it should be. Most established companies will offer their employees some type of benefits package; start-ups or those with only a handful of employees may not offer benefits because they can't afford to. Usually, only full-time employees are eligible for benefits. When applying for jobs and choosing the best offer, pay attention to the benefits package an employer provides, and think carefully about choosing a job solely based on salary.

MOST COMMON BENEFITS

Health insurance: Health insurance is by far the most important benefit an employer can offer. When companies offer health insurance, they either pay your entire monthly premium themselves or pay a portion of your premium. Either way can save you a tremendous amount of money. According to recent research from the Kaiser Family Foundation, the average cost of employer-based health insurance for a single person was $5,429 per year, of which the employee paid only $921. Also, a report from eHealthInsurance found that the average monthly premium paid for individual coverage was $183—which may be a lot to pay on your own each month.

Health insurance plans cover many services, including hospital, medical, dental, vision, and mental health services. Also, many employers are able to offer disability, life, and long-term care insurance.

Now You Tell Me?

Research from the National Women's Law Center found that in states that have not banned gender rating, 92 percent of best-selling plans charge women more than men.

Retirement savings: Retirement savings benefits are funds set aside to provide people with an income when they end their careers. Given that at age 65, the average American doesn't have enough money saved to live on comfortably, this is a very valuable benefit. The type of plan companies offers differ, but they generally fall into two types: defined benefit (often referred to as a pension) and defined contribution. Under a defined benefit plan funded by the employer, you are promised a specific monthly benefit upon retirement. The amount is most often calculated through a formula that includes factors such as your salary, age, and the number of years you worked at the company. You tend to have to work a certain number of years to be eligible for this type of benefit. Through a defined contribution plan offered by an employer, such as a 401(k), you contribute money toward your individual account in the plan. Many companies match a certain percentage of your contribution, often after a certain number of years. Upon your retirement, you receive the balance in the account—withdrawing money before retirement incurs fees.

Paid annual/vacation leave: Paid annual/vacation leave is the number of days per year that you may take off for any reason. The number is usually determined by the length of time you have worked for the company. For example, you may be eligible for 10 days annual leave your first year and 15 after your fourth year. Many companies that offer annual/vacation leave require a person to complete the first 90 days of employment (referred to as the Introductory Period) before they can receive this benefit. Some allow you to begin accruing paid leave on your first day.

Paid sick leave: Sick leave days are used when you are unable to work for health reasons. The days normally accrue on a weekly or monthly basis. The number of days given varies by employer.

Paid family sick leave: This type of sick leave allows you to take time off from work for health-related reasons—including to take care of your own health problems, care for a newborn or adopted child, and care for a family member who is unwell. The number of leave days offered and how they are accrued depend on the employer.

Maternity leave: This allows women, and sometimes men, to take a leave of absence for and after the birth of a child. It also tends to cover caring for a child after adoption. The amount of time given varies per employer, and a woman or man may or may not receive her/his monthly salary as part of this employee benefit.

Now You Tell Me?

If you work part time, you can negotiate increasing your hours to the company's minimum work hour requirement to qualify as a full-time employee. Once you achieve full-time status, you should be eligible for the company's health benefit plans. —Mary Nestor-Harper, SPHR, president of MJNH Consulting

---

OTHER BENEFITS

Telecommuting: Employees are able to work from home a certain number of days or even full time. Once pretty rare, giving employees the ability to telecommute has become increasingly common—and makes a lot of business sense—given how easy it is now to communicate and get things accomplished via email, phone, and video conferencing. Not only does working from home allow people to better juggle the demands of their home lives and save precious time from being stuck in traffic, it can also lead to more productivity, since there are less interruptions from co-workers and the like.

Stock options: Employees are given stock in the company they work for or are offered them at a discounted price. Sometimes companies match the number of shares of stock an employee buys.

Educational: The employer may pay a portion or all of the costs for work-related coursework and degree programs.

Professional development: The employer may pay the cost of work-related workshops, seminars, conferences, and any training that will provide you with more knowledge in your field.

Child care: The employer pays some or all of the cost of child care or offers onsite child care facilities.

Employee discounts: The employer provides discounts or waives fees on the products or services the company offers. For example, many people who work for airlines are able to fly practically for free, and retail employees can usually expect a discount off the company's merchandise.

Which job would you choose in the following scenario?

You are looking for an entry-level caseworker position with a reputable organization in Austin, Texas, that pays at least $27,000 per year. You would prefer that they have a diverse staff, make a point of promoting from within, and offer you your own office because you don't like the idea of sharing your space with someone else. Wishful thinking, we know, but still!

Company A fits most of your criteria but only offers you a starting salary of $26,000. This, however, includes fully paid health and life insurance, paid sick leave, a two-week paid vacation, and the company will also pay for half the cost for you to earn a master's degree in a program geared toward people in your field.

Company B offers you a starting salary of $30,000, but tells you they will be unable to offer you any benefits. They do, however, offer a two-week unpaid vacation.

Which company sounds good to you? When looking just at the salary, it is easy to say that one should choose Company B. Yet, after looking at Company B's lack of benefits, you might change your mind. The difference in salary could be considered a little wide, but the benefits Company A offers overcompensate for the lower salary.

Company A will pay the full cost of health insurance. If you had to pay $100 a month for your own health insurance that would cost you $1,200 a year. They also offer life insurance, which you probably don't think you need. But still, if you paid for it at only $25 a month that would cost you $300 per year. After working there a year, Company A gives you a two-week paid vacation. Company B offers a two-week unpaid vacation, which means you would lose out on roughly $1,083 before taxes. Finally, Company A offers to pay half of your graduate expenses. If the cost was just $15,000 a year, Company A would save you $7,500.

So, although the salary Company A offers is $4,000 less than Company B's, it will provide you with more than $10,083 in benefits.

Under some circumstances, however, it would make more sense to choose Company B, which might include:

- If you only planned on working there a year or two.
- If you were covered under someone else's health insurance plan.

- If you did not plan on attending graduate school or wanted a master's degree in another field.

As you can see, benefits are a major part of the compensation package an employer offers you. Always keep in mind your needs and goals to help you make the best decision.

9

Choosing
Between Jobs

*It's not hard to make decisions when you
know what your values are.*
—Roy Disney, Disney executive

If you get the chance to choose between jobs, consider yourself lucky—many people wait and wait for just one job offer. Sometimes it will be easy to decide which job to take. But choosing the right job can become much harder when you must make a choice between equally desirable positions. A simple way to pick the job that will best meet your needs is by using a rating sheet. With a rating sheet you'll write down the work features that are most important to you at a company, and then rate each one according to those features on a scale of one to five (1 = poor / 5 = excellent).

Using this job rating method allows you to see the big picture, as you're able to take everything into consideration. You shouldn't choose a job solely because of its salary, perks, or any other single feature. Everything the job offers and doesn't offer should be taken into consideration. How long will you stay with a high-paying company if it's in a city that makes you weary? What good is a three-week paid vacation if you don't make enough money to go out of the city? Think on these things as you make your decision. The company that scores the highest is probably your best bet.

SAMPLE RATING SHEET
FOR THREE JOB OFFERS

Work Feature	Company A	Company B	Company C
Salary	4	4	3
Flexible work hours	2	5	3
Great location	5	3	3
Maternity benefits	1	4	2
Minimal supervision	1	3	5
Opportunity to travel	1	1	1
Workplace environment	4	4	3
Good male-to-female ratio	2	4	2
Advancement opportunities	3	3	3
Good 401(k) plan	5	5	5
Vacation time	5	5	5
Tuition reimbursement	1	5	5
TOTAL	34	46	40

Now You Tell Me?

Looking at the highest bidder to start is short-sighted and shallow, yet an often enticing mistake. Ten years from now, you won't remember how much you made, but you will remember if this was the right company or position to launch the rest of your career. —Andy Masters, author & speaker

---

ACCEPTING A JOB OFFER

When you're sure that you've made the best choice given your options, enthusiastically accept the job offer you've chosen. You may accept the offer over the phone, but you should also follow it up in writing. Thank them for the offer and confirm the terms of the offer (starting date, salary, benefits). Concisely summarize what impressed you most about the position/company, and close by saying that you look forward to joining the company.

Most companies will provide with you an official job offer letter after you've accepted a position. If they don't, you should request one. At a minimum, the official job offer letter should state your salary, benefits, start date, and any special things you may have negotiated.

REJECTING A JOB OFFER

Once you've decided which job you want to take, you should graciously reject every offer you received, either by phone or in writing. One day you may want to work for the company and you'll be more likely to receive another job offer if you left a good impression.

10

Negotiating Your Salary

In business, you don't get what you deserve,
you get what you negotiate.
—Chester Karras, negotiation expert

Negotiating the salary for a particular position is an unfamiliar practice for a majority of recent college grads. Many are accustomed to just being told what the pay is for a position they've applied for and gratefully accepting it. This is largely because the positions we took in college and high school weren't professional, so we didn't expect to receive much; we were just happy to have a job. But beyond being an unfamiliar practice, negotiating your salary can also be a bit panic-inducing, especially for women. Unlike men, we tend to be socialized not to be pushy or aggressive, and although neither trait is needed when seeking appropriate compensation, we often fear that's how we'll be perceived if we ask for more than what's being offered. That, and very ungrateful. Because of this, as numerous studies have found, we are far more likely than men to accept the first dollar amount we are offered for a position.

But, as the saying goes, "Closed mouths don't get fed." Or fed enough, in the case of salary negotiations. And the ironic thing is, employers actually expect to discuss and come to an agreement about the compensation they've offered a new hire—even for entry-level positions. For them, it's just business. So, when it comes to the type of "real money" you are hoping to make now, it's a mistake to leave your salary up to chance. After all, this is the income you will be using not just to pay bills, but to save and enjoy life, too.

Now You Tell Me?

Less than half of employees report feeling they are receiving adequate monetary compensation, according to a workplace survey conducted by the American Psychological Association.

If your goal is to get the highest possible salary for a position, then you will have to know how to negotiate for it. But before you can confidently negotiate your salary, you should know what you should expect to be paid for your talent. The salary you should expect to receive is determined by a variety of factors, including:

- Your occupation
- The demand within your field
- Your experience and qualifications
- Your related education in the field
- The city and state you reside in
- The particular employer

Before the interview, you should do your research to find out what people in your field, with your education and experience are getting paid. Then you need to go further and determine how much the average person within your field, with your education and experience, gets paid in the city you live in. The Bureau of Labor Statistics (www.bls.gov) is the best place to start your research. Their website offers in-depth information on every job imaginable, including general job descriptions, the qualifications needed for certain roles, and average pay. Salary.com is also a great resource.

After considering what your research reveals, you then have to look at the salary being offered for the position you're applying for. Employers often give salary ranges for advertised positions, such as $35,000–$40,000, or $40,000–$55,000. The salary range for the position can help you determine a figure before you're asked. The important thing to remember is that your salary is not carved in stone. Your earnings can and should be discussed. However, some positions are more negotiable than others.

You have more room to negotiate when:

→ People with your occupation are in demand, and there are few skilled people

→ You have a high level of experience

→ You have special skills or talents

→ You have an advanced degree

You have less room to negotiate when:

→ The position is entry-level

→ You have little experience

→ You don't have the degree normally required for the position

→ There's little demand for people in your field or an over-abundance of skilled people

→ The employer simply doesn't have the budget to provide the salary you want

→ The employer determines salaries by a strict pay scale

It's also important to keep an open mind when trying to determine your asking price. As discussed in the chapter "Understanding Company Benefits," the perks a company can provide should be considered in addition to the salary. Fringe benefits, like having the ability to telecommute or earn another degree at a company's expense, can be far more beneficial in the long run that an extra $3,000. And while an employer may not be able to offer you a higher salary, it's possible that they'll have more flexibility when it comes to fringe benefits. This is particularly true with smaller companies or when the actual owner of the company is hiring you. But as with anything, you won't know what's possible unless you ask.

LET'S TALK MONEY!

Most negotiation experts advise you to let the employer initiate questions about your salary expectations. When the employer does start asking salary-related questions, take time to ask some as well. Two very important questions are: "What is the salary range for this position?" and "What would be the salary range for someone with my qualifications?" You can ask these questions even if you've already found out the answer from another source. The employer's answers can help you determine the amount of money he or she is considering offering you. Armed with this information, you can keep from underpricing yourself and missing out on more money or overpricing yourself and not being offered the job. It's actually wiser to not ask for or agree to a specific figure until after you've been offered the position. An employer is more likely to give you your desired salary (or come as close as possible to it) if they've already chosen you to fill the position.

When asked about your salary requirements in an initial interview, you can give a salary range that you're willing to work with. You can say something like, "I'd expect to make somewhere between $45,000 to $55,000, but I'm sure we could come to an agreement at that time." And what do you say if the employer asks what you made on your last job and it wasn't anything to brag about? After answering the question directly and honestly, share

HRinsider Tip: Don't make the mistake of only comparing the salary offer to what you presently earn. You might be underpaid now and not realize it, which means you could still end up underpaid even after accepting a new position.
—Paul McDonald, senior executive director of Robert Half International

the background information relative to the salary you made in the past. Then speak on your desire to now advance and take on more responsibilities, which will warrant a salary that's comparable to the role.

It's time to really talk money when you've been offered the position and the salary question is presented by the employer. But never just throw out any old number! The salary you ask for should depend on the information the employer gave you, what your research has revealed to be appropriate compensation, and your own realistic salary expectations.

During the salary negotiation, you should practice the following rules:

- Ask for more than what you're really shooting for, but not so much more that the salary is completely outside of the range
- Act like you deserve the salary, not like you need it. There should be no mention of the cost of living, your bills, or any other financial obligation during the discussion
- Be confident
- Stress how much you are suited for the role and how your skills will add value to the company's bottom line

The last rule is particularly important. At the end of the day, an employer really wants to hire someone who will fit into the company's culture, help the company to grow, and improve the company's profit margin (in other words, make more money, not drain it). The key to getting the salary you desire is being able to convince the employer that you're worth every penny. The best way to accomplish this is to stress how your skills and experience will support the company's mission, vision, and growth. If you're lucky, your asking price will be acceptable and you won't have to play the money game. If the figure isn't what the employer had in mind then you will have to do your best to change his or her opinion. This is where your research will come in handy. When you're trying to negotiate a higher figure than what you've been offered, you can use the following reasons to support being given the salary you're aiming for:

1. Other companies are paying more: If similar companies are paying more money to people with the same position, then kindly enlighten the employer (and yes, they know it already). "My research has shown that the average salary for a junior systems engineer in Kansas City is $58,000. I understand that this is just an average, but considering this, I think $58,000 is more appropriate than $53,000." However, before you take this option, make sure the company's benefits don't make the total compensation you're offered actually more attractive than other companies.

2. You have special talents/skills: If you have more to offer than just what the position calls for, remind the employer of this. "I understand that $40,000 is more than the average entry-level accountant at your company is paid. However, as you told me earlier, you currently don't have any Spanish speaking accountants. I would be able to work with clients you've been having to turn away, thus producing more revenue for the company."

3. Your qualifications merit you more money: Don't get stuck with entry-level pay when you have experience. Politely remind the employer of your qualifications. "Actually, $40,000 seems a bit low for someone with my professional experience and education. I have worked as a graphic designer for three years and have a master's degree in graphic design. Based on this, I feel that I should receive a minimum of $50,000."

4. Your occupation is in demand: If you work in a field that has a lot of job openings but few skilled people to fill them, then remind the employer of this. "Well, I am basing a starting salary of $65,000 partly on the fact that nurses are in very high demand. There's a shortage of nurses in this area and many hospitals and clinics are actually offering $70,000 per year plus sign-on bonuses."

5. The position should obviously pay more: If they're offering you a salary that seems ridiculous considering your duties, explain this to them in the nicest way possible. "The public relations specialist position seems like it should pay more than $40,000 given the wide range of duties it comes with. If I understand correctly, I would also be serving as the back-up administrative assistant to the director and handle all the company's social media campaigns. Given this, I feel that a salary of $45,000 would be more fair and appropriate given the wide range of duties I would have."

6. *You have other job offers:* Tactfully let the employer know that you've been offered another job that pays the amount you're asking for or more. "I really want to be a part of this team and $42,000 sounds reasonable, however, I've been offered $46,000 at another company. Is it possible for you to also offer $46,000?" However, be careful not to create a "bidding war" by going back and forth with an employer by saying things like "Company X really wants me and now offered $47,000. Can you match that, too?" Employers do not like the bidding war game. From their perspective, if you engage in this tactic you are more interested in the money and not the job and the opportunities that the company can afford you.

SALARY NEGOTIATION TECHNIQUES

The negotiation for your salary usually begins after the employer has done one of the following:

1) Offers you a specific figure

2) Gives you his or her salary range

3) Avoids discussing the salary range for the position and asks you what your expectations are

Here are tips on handling all three situations:

1. *When given a specific figure:* If the employer gives you a specific figure, it's likely for one of three reasons: They've already considered your qualifications and the amount given is what they feel you deserve; they pay according to a scale/system; or this is the amount they've budgeted for the position. If you're offered much more than you hoped for, your best bet would be to tell the employer that the amount is fair and in line with what you were expecting. If the figure is less than the amount you were shooting for, then it's time to negotiate.

For example, Amanda is being interviewed for an entry-level social worker position with a non-profit agency that she knows doesn't pay very well. She's determined that if offered the job she'll only take it if it pays at least $30,000 plus benefits. Still, she'd like more. Here's how she handled the salary negotiation.

Employer: "Well, Amanda, the position pays $30,000 plus benefits."

Amanda: "Oh? (nice pause here) . . . I expected that this position would pay at least $34,000, given the duties you described and the degree required. In fact, my research has shown that the starting salary for the majority of entry-level social workers hired by non-profit agencies in Portland is closer to $37,000."

Employer: "I know. However, as you are aware, we are a relatively small agency and are on a really tight budget. Would $32,000 suffice?"

Amanda: "Actually, Ms. Harper, I really was expecting at least $34,000 as a social worker. And again, I really want to work here. I respect this organization for what it has done to serve the community, and know I could come in and make an immediate impact."

Employer: "Hmmmm. Okay. I think I can stretch the budget a little bit to get you in here. You'll be happy starting out with $34,000?"

Amanda: "Yes."

2. *When given a salary range:* If the employer gives you a salary range you should always ask for something at the high end of the range or at least more than you are expecting. This way, if the employer feels the figure is too high and offers you a lower salary, chances are that it'll still be more than you were expecting. Here's how Mia worked with the salary range given to her after being offered a job as an admissions counselor at a large university. She knows the salary range is $32,000–$38,000. She's hoping to start off at the high end of that range even although she'd be happy just to get the job and $30,000 a year.

Employer: "I'm very impressed with what you've accomplished thus far, Mia. I'm sure you'll be a wonderful addition to our admissions staff and learn a lot working here. As you know, the salary range for the admissions counselor position is $32,000 to $42,000, and the salary is commensurate with experience. What are your salary expectations?"

Mia: "I'm certain I'll enjoy working here, too! Thank you so much for offering me the position. Regarding my salary, I'd like to start off at at least $37,000."

Employer: "I see. Actually, someone with your experience would probably start off at around $33,000, which I can certainly offer. Individuals who have served three or more years as actual admissions counselors for a university would generally be the only ones offered more than this. And of course, you have to take into consideration that we offer an excellent benefits package."

Mia: "That's true, the university's benefits package is very good, and I know that admissions counselors come up for a pay raise every two years. But would it be possible for me to start off at $36,000? Although I've never worked as an admissions counselor, I did work for two years as the senior resident assistant at the university I attended. As I explained earlier, a large part of that role was advising students regarding their majors and class schedules."

Employer: "Aren't you a savvy negotiator? You know what? I do think you'll relate to the students very well and fit right in. I can do that."

3. When not given a salary range: This is always a tricky situation because the salary you ask for could be much less than what an employer is really prepared to offer. When faced with this dilemma, all you have to base your decision on is the research you've done and the amount you're shooting for. If it's lower than what they would've offered you'll never know, but if it's too high you're sure to hear about it. When they feel it's a little up there, all you can do is try to justify your figure with your research and speak on all that you're bringing to the table.

Let's look at how Tatyana handled herself when faced with this problem. She's at the salary negotiation stage of her interview for a math teaching position at a charter school. She's found that second-year charter school teachers make about $28,000, far less than second-year math teachers at public schools. Still, she'd like to start off at $33,000 or more.

Employer: "It looks like you're our candidate of choice, Tatyana. The only thing left to discuss is your salary. What are your salary expectations?"

Tatyana: "Well, I know that teachers' salaries can vary widely. Do you know the salary range for the position?"

Employer: "We don't really have salary ranges. The salary is just commensurate with experience."

Tatyana: "I understand. What do you feel would be appropriate for someone with my qualifications?"

Employer: "I'm not sure. I'm pretty open. Just tell me what you're aiming for and I'll see what we can do."

Tatyana: "Well, other charter school teachers I've talked to say that the average salary for a teacher with two years of experience should be a minimum of $34,000."

Employer: "Really? Unfortunately, because we're grant funded, most of our teachers don't make

HRinsider Tip: When you're up for a raise, or think you deserve one, be prepared to explain, in a straightforward and factual manner, why you believe your work effort should be rewarded with more money. Ask yourself what your "value add" is to your company, and look for ways to quantify your performance. Be rational, be reasonable, and be unemotional.

—Lisa Quast, founder of Career Woman, Inc.

over $31,000, and I really can't afford to pay you that much. I was thinking more along the lines of $30,000."

Tatyana: "I understand, but please keep in mind I would also be volunteering my time to coach the girls' volleyball team, and at many schools this is a paid position or a teacher is given supplemental pay."

Employer: "That's true, and we really do need you as a coach. However, I have to keep our budget in mind."

Tatyana: "Yes, I am very sensitive to that. And of course, I didn't become a teacher for the money, but $34,000 doesn't seem too far out there, especially considering I will be teaching math."

Employer: "Hmm. Well, math teachers do tend to be paid more and I do know you'll be working a lot of hours coaching. I can agree to 34,000."

Tatyana: "Great. Thank you so much."

Amanda, Mia, and Tatyana all managed to secure a salary of at least $4,000 more than what they were shooting for or offered by following the salary negotiation rules. They asked for more than what they were really shooting for; they acted like they deserved the salary (not like they needed it); they were confident; and they made it a point to stress how much they wanted the position and how they will use their talents to support the mission and vision of the organization.

TAKE IT OR LEAVE IT?

Of course, you have to be prepared for salary negotiations that don't work out in your favor. An employer may not budge at all when you ask for more money. You will basically be asked to take it or leave it. Only you can decide if the money is right. Don't take an employer's unwillingness to pay you what you feel you deserve personally. They're operating from a totally different perspective than you, and they may feel you deserve the salary you desire but really can't fit it into their budget. Don't flat out refuse a job when you're asked to take it or leave it. Ask the employer if you can take a day to think about their offer, and then go home and consider your options. This may be a great opportunity to negotiate on other fringe benefits such as the option to telecommute a certain number of days per week after you have proven yourself during the probationary period. However, if you really need a job, you can always take it and keep interviewing for other positions. You can also work a part-time job to bring in some extra money.

Just remember that the salary you start out with will determine the salary you will have throughout your career with the company, despite raises and promotions. If you start out feeling poorly compensated, it's likely that you will never feel like you're earning what you deserve. Also, a future employer may base the salary they offer you on what you received at your former job. If you worked for peanuts at the company you left, they may expect for you to work for peanuts for them, too.

ANSWERING SALARY QUESTIONS BEFORE THE INTERVIEW

Some employers will ask you to state the salary you desire for a position on your application or with the resume and cover letter you submit. This is often done to screen out candidates who don't fall within the salary range they've set. This poses two problems: You may overprice yourself and not get an interview, or underprice yourself and be locked into the salary you stated if offered the job. Because of this, it's best to write that your salary is "negotiable" or "open" unless employers won't accept your application or resume without your salary requirement.

When you must write something, put the minimum amount that you will work for, and state that you would like to receive a starting salary of *at least* whatever you've decided is the lowest amount (Example: "I'd like to receive a starting salary of at least $60,000."). Writing "at least" keeps you from locking yourself into a specific figure if hired, and positions you to ask for more.

Diary of a Careeranista

SANDRA SOTO ON GETTING PREPARED FOR THE NEXT OPPORTUNITY

So now you have the job you've always wanted. You have convinced your new employer that you have the skills, background, and knowledge to get the job done and support the growth of the organization. You deserve all the kudos your family and friends are giving you, but please resist the urge to get comfortable, or worse, complacent. Just because you landed the job doesn't mean that your job is over. When you start your new position, in addition to doing everything necessary to please and even over-deliver for your employer, you should also prepare yourself for the next big opportunity.

This is advice I wish I had been given when I graduated from college and was offered my first professional position in human resources. I was a hard-working, dedicated employee and I managed to get through the 90-day introductory period with ease and then performed the job proficiently throughout my two-year tenure. However, when I was ready to get my next job, I stumbled a bit because I didn't know anything about the World Wide Web (and yes, there was a time when "www" didn't mean a thing to most people).

But in my company, everyone who was really trying to get ahead did know what the web was. Meanwhile, I was still holding on to my electronic typewriter, Smith Corora, thinking I was one step ahead of my peers, when in fact I was behind. I was also using Quattro Pro and Word Perfect, which were becoming obsolete because of the introduction of the Microsoft Office programs Excel and Word. So, when I interviewed for my next opportunity, I got a rude awakening and quickly realized that I was lacking the technical skills to compete with other candidates.

Of course, I recovered from that mistake, although I didn't like playing catch up. To avoid this and other self-inflicted career pitfalls, you should focus immediately on making yourself a better young professional and preparing for your next big opportunity. Do this, and you will have the keys to doors that would have been locked otherwise.

Preparing for the Next Opportunity

Build strong company relationships: Relationship building is the key ingredient to successfully catapulting your career to the next level. Thus, it's extremely important to make quick connects with people within your company. Take advantage of your first 90 days of employment—often considered the "introductory period"—to become well acquainted with your new colleagues and management. As you do so, align yourself with positive, talented individuals within the organization who are willing to mentor and train you.

Network with a purpose: You should also make a practice of actively networking with professionals outside of work. There has only been one job I've secured that didn't come through networking—as is true for most people. Luckily, networking is as easy as it is important. In this era of social media, you can take advantage of popular social outlets such as LinkedIn and Facebook. Confidently and politely reach out to seasoned professionals who you know have the knowledge and contacts you need. Don't wait for someone to take an interest in you. Also, join professional groups to meet and stay connected to individuals with similar skills and career interests.

Never stop increasing your skill set: To know which skills you'll need, conduct research on what companies in your industry are looking for from a skills perspective, as well as the specific skills required for the next two to three positions you hope to secure. Sometimes the best "quick research" is to check out job postings on career boards like Monster.com and Careerbuilder.com. Review the postings and requirements needed for the job. Then, make some honest assessments of your weaknesses. Do you have the skills to function in a higher-level role? If you don't, then find ways to enhance them by going back to school, attending seminars and workshops, or taking advantage of on-the-job training.

Perhaps a more fun way to conduct this type of research is to shadow someone at your job who is in your role of interest. Take note of the skills they demonstrate and how they utilize those skills in the workplace. Lastly, you can also ask your boss or other leaders in the company what key things they have done to be successful, and what they think you need to learn, improve, or focus on so you can one day be in their shoes—or bigger ones. You would be surprised at how helpful senior managers can be. Most people love to talk about themselves and offer advice. Let them talk, and you listen closely.

Stay abreast of issues affecting your industry: You need to know where your industry is headed and the important changes taking place within it. To know what factors are shaping your industry—including economic and political ones—read magazines, journals, and blog sites created for those who desire to be in the know. In addition to helping you be one step ahead of your competition, you will have so much more to say during interviews and conversations with those in a position to hire or help you.

Assess and reassess yourself: Getting prepared means doing some self-assessments on where you are now and where you want to be. It's just like when you completed high school and went off to college. You assessed your interests/passions and determined the major you wanted to study. You may have changed your major several times before you held firm on a major. This reassessment process will continue throughout your career as you will likely make several career moves before you retire.

Lastly, keep in mind that your next career move—and all the rest—will be based on internal and external factors. Internal factors include skills, job knowledge, passion, and interests. External factors include the economy, industry trends, politics, and inflation. Focus on those areas you can control (internal). Invest in and support those areas that will get you to the next level. Be aware of those areas you can't control (external) and be flexible in making adjustments as needed when faced with these external issues. You will be able to best do this by assessing and reassessing your skills and job knowledge along the way.

Sandra M. Soto is a human resources professional with an extensive background in staff and management consulting. During the past 20 years, Sandra has worked in the private sector supporting and consulting businesses through exercising her expertise in talent acquisition, employee engagement, and professional development. Sandra holds a Professional Human Resources Certification and is an active member of the Society for Human Resource Management, the Civilian Human Resources Agency, and the Professional Association of Resume Writers and Career Coaches. She earned a bachelor's degree in business administration from Bowie State University and a master's degree in teaching from the College of Notre Dame of Maryland.

Networking Effectively

Each person represents a world in us,
a world possibly not born until they arrive.
—Anais Nin, author

S hyness is not one of my attributes. I've learned to ask for what I want—as nicely as possible—from those who have the power to give it to me. I've found that if you're sincere in your desires and approach people correctly, most people are more than willing to help you.

Yet some people cringe when they hear the word "networking," especially those just starting out in their careers. The idea of "meeting and greeting" strangers intimidates them, and seeking out people who can possibly help them advance professionally brings out the fear of rejection. But the old adage, "It's not what you know, but who you know," could not be truer for young women. Our social circles tend to contain mainly other young women, and this isn't very beneficial given the gender makeup of American businesses and those who hire for them. Also, we tend to focus on meeting people of our same ethnicity, age, and socio-economic background. This excludes entirely too many people. You should be networking with any and everyone.

This is something I was told and took to heart after I decided to uproot myself from Texas to pursue a career in book publishing in New

York. One of the first things I did was seek out people in the field who could give me advice and job leads. I was taken out to breakfast by the founder of a very influential media website, Mediabistro.com, after I expressed my love of her website and future goal of entrepreneurship. Because I was taking publishing classes, I had access to many publishing executives who came to speak to my class. I hardly ever missed a chance to talk with them after class and to get their email addresses so I could tell them about my interests. I also went to seminars, conferences, and even book signings that I knew publishing professionals might attend. My networking led to freelance work, actual jobs, and new friends.

Just as networking proactively worked in my favor, so can it for you. Networking is what the most successful and savviest business professionals say got them to where they are today. They built mutually beneficial relationships that served as a support system and boosted their careers. Building a network of people that will help you grow and thrive is a task you will be both consciously and unconsciously doing for the rest of your life. You have to always be on the lookout for people in both high and low places who can be added to your network—not just your Facebook friends list. There are individuals out there who can help you land your dream job, turn you on to professions you never thought twice about, give you an idea to bring in truckloads of dough, or simply change your life just by being supportive—and you haven't even met them yet. And you won't if you don't make networking an ongoing task. There are various ways you can build your network:

HRinsider Tip: You have to start feeling comfortable reaching across generational, gender, and racial boundaries to start developing relationships with people that may not look like you or share anything in common on race or ethnicity.

—Wilka Toppins,
former Fortune 100 VP & founder
of Ask The Corporate Latina

- Through colleagues and business associates
- Through memberships in professional and social organizations

- Through your relatives, friends, and their peers
- Through religious involvement
- Through social functions and community events
- Through volunteering
- Through conferences and programs for people in your profession
- Through leveraging social media using websites like LinkedIn

Most of the networking you will do will take place informally—with people you will meet without even trying. Because of this, it's important not to make assumptions about people and subsequently miss out on opportunities. Just because someone isn't in your field doesn't mean he or she doesn't know and can't connect you to someone influential who is. Just because someone in your field is of a different ethnicity doesn't mean he or she is less likely to want to help you. Be open to having polite conversations with strangers and having real conversations with people who seem interesting. Don't discount anyone.

Now You Tell Me?

Putting your best self forward the first time is a must, and joining your local Toastmasters club can help you do so. Through the organization, you can improve your speaking and presentation skills while networking with people in different fields.   —Yvonne Chase, dating & relationship coach

---

While you are bound to meet people of influence by accident, other connections you make will take place through actual networking events. Walking into one of these events alone may bring back the same butterflies you felt on the first day of school when you were looking for a place to sit at lunch. While it may have seemed like you were the only lonely-looking girl struggling to find a seat next to someone cool, the majority of the girls probably felt the same way.

That's just how networking events are. No one wants to look lonely, unimportant, and bored. Everyone came to mix and mingle, and chances are that if you approach someone they will be relieved that you did. The following are tips to help you be better prepared at your next networking event.

Before the Function:

→ Review your purpose for attending the function. Are you coming to meet a specific person, get some contacts in your profession, or just learn more about the hosts of the function?

→ Plan to arrive on time for the function. If you're attending a meeting that offers networking before it starts, arrive early enough to participate in the networking portion of the meeting. If you arrive on the tail end, people may have already broken off into groups.

→ Create a short introduction about yourself. Example: "I'm a grad student in Emory University's sociology program, and I plan on becoming a sociology professor, hopefully at a school in California, where I'm from. Right now I'm searching for a position within a non-profit that focuses on either kids or health."

→ Have more than enough professional-looking business cards with you, and make sure you have easy access to them.

→ Dress appropriately. Professional networking events normally call for business casual attire.

At the Function:

→ Greet people you know so you can be introduced to others.

→ Introduce yourself to the host of the event. Request introductions to people whom the host recommends you meet.

→ Take the initiative to introduce yourself to other people, especially people who may have seen you once or twice but were never introduced to you.

→ Introduce others to people you've just met.

→ Exchange contact info with the people you meet.

After the Function:

→ Write notes to yourself on the back of the business cards you're given (or put notes in your phone)—something that will help jog your memory about people when you look at their cards/contact info again. Also include the date and name of the function.

→ Contact those individuals who interested you within seven days. Remind them of who you are and where you met, and briefly explain why you're interested in speaking with them further or meeting up.

→ Think about how you could have networked better. Did you miss out on an opportunity to meet someone because you were scared or didn't know how to break into a conversation? Did you neglect to tell people something important about you and your line of work? You did bring enough business cards, didn't you?

Becoming a networking pro may take a little time, but after enough of these events you will be able to work a room of professionals like you worked a room full of your college peers at the parties you miss. The only difference is that working the room now could mean working your way up in your professional career.

12

Finding and Keeping a Career Mentor

No matter what accomplishments
you achieve, somebody helps you.
—Althea Gibson, super athlete

I've been blessed with wonderful people over the years who have served as my mentors. These people, who have included grade school teachers, college professors, employers, and individuals working in and outside of my industry, have helped guide my career path while shaping me into a poised professional.

Make finding a career mentor a priority as you seek to navigate life after college. A career mentor, someone who is dedicated to helping you succeed in your profession, is an invaluable person to have in your life. She or he can help with the following:

- Avoid pitfalls in your job search
- Find vacant positions in your field
- Provide little-known information about your field
- Make a decision regarding choosing between jobs
- Advise you during salary negotiations
- Connect with people to further your career
- Provide a realistic view of what working in your field is like

- Inform you on appropriate business etiquette
- Advise you on how to handle problems in your workplace

Now You Tell Me?

Nearly 1 in 5 women in the United States do not have a mentor, according to a LinkedIn survey of 1,000 female professionals.

Like friendships, career mentor relationships are formed over time. In most cases, mentors are acquired through befriending people you meet who are in a position to help you.

If you haven't met anyone you consider "mentor material" then it's time to start searching. You can seek to be mentored by a successful person in your field at organizational meetings, conferences, career fairs, and other venues. You can even find potential mentors in magazines and newsletters. I found my first New York-based career mentor in the pages of a book review magazine. She was being profiled after having left a wonderful position as a senior editor at a major publishing house to start her own literary agency. I contacted her immediately through email, and although it took about a month or so of polite nudging in the form of more emails and a phone call or two, she eventually agreed to meet with me, and in fact, invited me out to lunch (I paid, as you should insist on doing,

HRinsider Tip: Don't limit your mentor search to people in your geographic area. If there's someone in your industry whom you admire in another part of the country—or even the world—send a short, but sincere email asking for his or her advice. Be respectful of your cyber mentor's time and ask a few specific questions that couldn't be easily answered by Googling. I did this early on in my career, and the people I contacted were flattered to be asked and generously offered support and advice via email. In a few cases, this even led to face-to-face meetings when I or they were on the road.

—Susan Johnston, freelance writer covering career management too). We clicked right away and I was glad I was so persistent. That oͺ email eventually led to an internship with her company and my beiͺ able to learn from someone with years of experience in a field I waͺ just entering.

When you chance upon a potential mentor, introduce yourself as a young professional seeking information from knowledgeable and influential sources like them. Potential mentors can be male or female and any ethnicity. The only thing they must have is a desire to assist you.

Once you've found a mentor, make sure to nurture the relationship by showing your appreciation for the advice your mentor provides. You don't want them to get the feeling they're being taken advantage of. You can show your gratitude by sincere "thank yous" as well as cards, flowers, or lunch. Remember that because career mentor relationships are like friendships, you have to keep in contact with your mentors. Don't just call when you need something. I can tell you from experience that the mentees I have who call, text, or message me on Facebook to check up and apprise me of their successes—and not just when they want advice or need a recommendation—are the ones I find myself promoting to other people. And the rare mentees who call *me* to ask if I need help with anything are the ones I think of first when an opportunity arises that could further their goals.

So, consider and treat mentors as you would a good friend. Do this, and you will have someone in your corner for life.

part two

SUCCEEDING AS A CAREERANISTA

13

Letting Go of
Real World Myths

*If you have a job without any aggravations,
you don't have a job.*
—Malcolm S. Forbes, former publisher of *Forbes*

All college graduates end up asking the question; it's just a matter of when. It may be our fifth month on the job, or perhaps our fifth year, but sooner or later we begin to wonder why someone didn't tell us that life after college isn't all it's cracked up to be.

I began questioning the value of my degree less than one year after I graduated. I wanted my college tuition refunded after discovering that (1) in a tough job market, having two degrees could matter just as much as having two high school diplomas; (2) if I wanted any chance of making $60,000 a year in an entry-level position, I had better go back to school and major in computer science; and (3) a "great" job can turn into a "bad" job faster than celebrities divorce.

Well, the reason we were not told that life after college can be very difficult is simple: If we knew how frustrating working for a living could be, we might not have focused on graduating. Of course, our parents and professors couldn't have that! So, like pretending there is a Santa Claus because you don't want to take away a child's excitement, they thought it best not to come clean until the last possible moment—when we started our search for that perfect career.

Now You Tell Me?

Some people seem to believe that graduating from college represents the climax of their existence—the end of their toiling. But, if you think of your career like a novel, college is merely the prologue. The real beginning—the real chapter one—begins with your first job. The climax arrives (if it does) many chapters later.   —Luke Redd, career writer for Trade-schools.net

---

Yes, we were told many things about how life after college would be, and some of us were a tad bit misinformed. In fact, in college we may have heard of, and began to believe, many myths about the so-called "real world." Some of these myths can hurt us in the long run if we cling to them because they keep us from looking at post-college life realistically, and carrying ourselves accordingly. The following are six myths that belong in a fairytale.

MYTH #1: YOUR DEGREE GUARANTEES YOU A GREAT JOB

Throughout high school and college, we were told that our degree would guarantee us a great job and career. However, it was also stressed that nothing in life is guaranteed. It's true that your degree will get you into interviews a high school diploma can't, and will make you *more likely* to land a great job and build an impressive career. But a college degree shouldn't be mistaken for a magic wand. Even when the job market is not insane, there are plenty of college graduates who go for months on end waiting for not just that superb job they imagined would be awaiting them, but *any* job in their field. They will be the first ones to tell you that a degree can be overrated. And if a degree is the only thing you've got going for you then you'd better have a dozen of them.

Reality Check: It's your hard work, persistence, ambition, and ability to network *combined* with your degree that will unlock doors for you. Good luck is always nice, too.

MYTH #2: YOUR DEGREE GUARANTEES YOU A GREAT SALARY

Many of us were also shown charts highlighting how much more a college graduate can make over a lifetime than someone with just a high school diploma, excluding Bill Gates. We were led to assume that a degree equated to lots and lots of money. So it's not surprising that some college graduates think they're on a hidden camera show when they're offered a job that pays a little over $10 an hour. They start to feel like they wasted four years of their life, and that's not it at all.

Reality Check: Your salary will depend on the type of degree you earned, the career you choose, the company you work for, the city you live in, your experience, and your ability to negotiate the highest wage possible.

MYTH #3: DO WHAT YOU LOVE AND YOU WILL NEVER HAVE TO WORK

This is a catchy little phrase, but unfortunately, it's just not true. If you do what you love, you will feel that your life has more meaning, your whole focus won't be on how much your job pays, and you will undoubtedly be much happier than people who make six figures but hate their jobs. But honestly, work is work and you're not always going to love it. In fact, most people will tell you that they *like* their job, but *loving it* is pushing it. Even positions we feel blessed to have will irk us sometimes, give us headaches, and possibly make us want to quit. You may be doing what you love in a position and still dislike certain aspects of it. That's life and that's work.

Reality Check: Jobs, like people, aren't perfect. If you start a position you wished on a star for thinking you will feel good about it *every day*, you'll lose the excitement and commitment you had for it when all of your expectations aren't met.

MYTH #4:
YOU CAN HAVE IT ALL

There is no shortage of TV shows in which women seem to effortlessly balance their fabulous career with their husband, kids, extended family obligations, social life, community involvement, and need to pee and get eight hours of sleep. Because of this and the fronts that many real working women put up, we may think our lives are off track when we can't put a check mark next to every "success box." However, you should not expect to have it all, *at the same time, all of the time.*

Reality Check: Sane successful women set priorities based on what is in the direst need of attention at different times in their lives. They don't pretend to be professional jugglers, and thus, they avoid handling more balls than they need to. What's more, they don't beat themselves up when one ball has to be dropped and picked up later.

MYTH #5: WORKPLACE SEXISM
DOESN'T EXIST ANYMORE

Most young and middle-aged men you will encounter in the workplace have grown up seeing and treating women as intellectual equals. They have sat side by side with us in the classroom from kindergarten to college; been educated by countless women; had mothers who worked outside of the home just like their fathers; saw women playing a myriad of professional roles on TV; and have formed good working relationships with many of the strong, smart women they have worked alongside in the office. And of course, plenty of men answer to a woman from 9 to 5. So, unlike the many men our mothers and grandmothers may have first encountered who saw a woman's place as solely in the home, today's working men tend to be more enlightened. However, there are still plenty of stone-agers within companies: men who really do believe we can't or shouldn't compete with them in the workplace, and they will let us know this bluntly or on the sly.

Also, even though women can be found kicking butt and taking names in every field, we still live and work in a male-dominated society. Girls don't quite run the world yet, although by the time someone remakes that hip Beyoncé song we just might. The fact that women have much further to go in terms of workplace equality is reflected in the wage gap that still exists between men and women, the time frame it takes for women to reach leadership positions when compared to our male counterparts, and the lack of support available at most companies to make balancing kids and a career easier.

Reality Check: If you get duped into believing that the playing field is totally level, you will be oblivious to all the fouls and illegal plays committed around you. Don't look for signs of sexism everywhere you turn, but don't ignore obvious signs either.

MYTH #6: WE LIVE IN A POST-RACIAL SOCIETY

The workplaces you will find yourself in will likely be more diverse than ever before, as America truly is becoming the melting pot it has long called itself. However, true equality does not exist throughout America—much less in all American workplaces—as the many people of color who say they have experienced unfair treatment at work because of their ethnicity can attest. Yes, it's true that workplace racism is not as blatant as it was 40 or even 20 years ago. Yes, it's true that minorities have more career opportunities than ever before. And yes, a black man was elected president of the United States not once but twice. But it's foolish to think that everyone judges others based solely on their character and background.

Reality Check: Workplace discrimination takes place throughout America on a daily basis—from people not hiring others because of their ethnicity to people treating others differently once they are hired. If you believe otherwise, you will think it's just your bad luck if you get passed over for multiple promotions you deserved, are getting paid far less than everyone else, and are stuck with menial work on the job that no one else has to do.

14

Fitting In
and Standing Out

Here is a simple but powerful rule:
Always give people more than what they expect to get.
—Nelson Boswell, author

Being the new girl on the job can feel like being the new girl at school. You want to fit in and be liked by your co-workers (the students) and your boss (the teacher) while feeling at home in your new environment.

One of the key ways to fit in is by understanding and adapting to the company's culture. Just as every school you attended had its own way of life and culture, so will all the companies you work for throughout your life. You will find that every company operates differently—has its own quirky way of doing things and rules that reflect the beliefs of the higher-ups. Some companies will take some getting used to while others will automatically feel welcoming and safe. Of course, it's also quite possible that many will leave you feeling as if you are the only sane person in the building. How fast you learn to successfully operate within your company's culture will dictate how fast you will fit into the company itself, how happy and productive you will be in your position, and ultimately, how quickly and how far you will advance.

FITTING IN

The following are seven characteristics that I have found work together to create a company's culture and are important for you to gauge correctly early on to fit in.

1. The employer's expectations: Each employer has his or her own expectations for the company. The employees pick up on these expectations and carry themselves accordingly (or should). Some employers may expect their company to just get by and make a little profit. You will be able to tell this because your co-workers will do just what it takes to get by and collect a paycheck. While you should still strive for excellence, you won't be able to condemn others for their lack of initiative in this type of environment. Other employers will want their company to be the best in the city, state, or nation and be very demanding of their employees. Half-stepping on your job in this company will be frowned upon.

2. The rules and regulations: Each company will have it's own set of do's and don'ts to work by. Rules like stealing, back-talking the boss, lying, and so forth are no-brainer rules, but others might not be so obvious. You may not find out exactly what they are until you break a rule or see someone getting fussed at for committing a "no-no." For example, some companies may not have a problem with employees relaxing on the job when the workload is slow. Other companies may expect you to look like you're working even when they know there's nothing to do. Likewise, dating among employees is a normal occurrence at some companies, while it may be forbidden at others. To avoid confusion, ask whether or not something is against company policy or considered an "abomination" before you do something you're unsure about. And if the company has an actual handbook, be sure to read it.

3. The interaction among co-workers: If you find that people rarely leave their cubicles and like to eat lunch alone at your company, then being Miss Friendly might not score you any points. This isn't to say don't be upbeat and cordial, but don't be upset if other people aren't as amiable as you are. Other companies may be under a heavy spirit of

101

camaraderie that most people wish their company had. In this environment, you will hear people's gossip on your first day and be invited out to lunch the next. If you are more of an introvert, you will have to stick your neck out of your shell a little if you want to fit in.

4. The employees' interaction with management: There's a big difference in the atmosphere of a company where the boss is viewed as a team member and one where he or she is solely looked upon as the head honcho. A team member boss may be treated casually by employees and joked with like anyone else. You can tell when you have a head honcho boss because the room will get quiet when he or she enters. Take cues from your co-workers on how to interact with your boss until you get to know his or her management style.

5. The dress code: Don't expect to fit in wearing business casual outfits when the atmosphere is conservative and everyone sports a suit except on Fridays. Take your cues on appropriate attire from your supervisor and well-dressed co-workers.

6. The pace: If it's a fast-paced, deadline-driven environment you're working in, then you better keep up or you'll be seen as a dead weight. If it's a slower-paced, "take your time" environment, then you might not fit in playing Speedy Gonzalez.

7. The competitiveness: Some companies foster a competitive environment among employees. At companies like this, your co-workers will gloat about who sold the most ads, who sold the most merchandise, which team bagged the most clients and finished the project first, and so on. If you're not a competitive person by nature, this may take some getting used to.

Now You Tell Me?

Avoid lofty illusions that you can change the company culture. You may be awesome and powerful, but odds are against you—the new person—being able to shift the whole corporate culture while doing the job you were hired to do.

—CareerBliss.com

During your first few weeks at a new company, focus on learning by observing and adjusting to the company's culture, doing your job well, and getting along with your co-workers. You will have plenty of time to show everyone you are a super star with fantastic ideas. I wish I had been told this early on in my career. Being a bonafide Sagittarius—meaning I find it hard not to voice my opinion about most things—I often had trouble with keeping my mouth shut about the way a company, or people within it, operate. Like many young professionals eager to prove their worth, I made a bad practice of talking about how things could and should be done more efficiently as soon as I got my foot in the door. However, no one, especially those in management, wants advice from a newbie who hasn't even learned all the aspects of her own job.

I was pretty much told exactly that when I worked as an assistant editor for a book publishing company. After being there for just a few weeks, I saw that many of the processes in place were pretty inefficient and led to mistakes. When I asked a co-worker about one backward-seeming process we used to make book revisions, she told me everyone knew it wasted a lot of time but that was how the manager wanted it done. As I advise in the chapter on managing your boss, you should do things the way your boss likes it, but I didn't quite get that back then. I asked my manager numerous times if we could try a different process and then finally she yelled at me, "This is how we do it here! You need to learn to stay in your own lane." Well, my feelings were of course hurt, but I should have considered where she was coming from early on. The process she had set up made her feel comfortable, and since she was ultimately responsible for the success of the books published, it made sense for her to want to do things her way. Who was I to come in critiquing a process that had long been in place?

"Stay in your own lane" is now one of my favorite catchphrases. Stay in yours until you are sure you know enough to help someone else drive. This will happen in no time once you have shown that you aren't the new girl anymore but the "go-to" girl who understands the ins and outs of the company.

DEMONSTRATING KEY SKILLS

On your way to becoming the go-to girl, you will also need to prove to your managers that you were a smart hire. While they know there may be much you need to learn, you will impress them early on by showing yourself to be the following:

1. A team player: An employee who is able to relate to and work well with a diverse group of people. Someone who leaves his or her problems at the front door, and shows up to work with a "winning" attitude. A person who can pull his or her own load and doesn't gripe about having to pull someone else's at times.

2. *A self-starter:* An employee who can get the ball rolling alone. Someone who doesn't have to be babied or asked twice to do something. A person who can generate new ideas and is constantly seeking ways to improve.

3. *Multifaceted:* An employee whose skills aren't limited to those needed just for his or her specific position. Someone who can perform a variety of duties with ease and enthusiasm and is willing to learn and teach new skills.

HRinsider Tip: As a general rule, ask lots of questions. Find out what and who makes things happen in your company. Get to know people's happiness and frustration points. The insight that you gain from the answers will give you the beginnings of a great arsenal of tools for navigating any potentially slippery political or inter-personal situations down the road.

—David Gaspin, HR director

4. *Flexible:* An employee who can "go with the flow" and handle assignments as needed. Someone who won't say things like, "There's no way I can work those hours," "I didn't plan on and don't want to work on this assignment," or "I can't believe I have to share an office with three people."

5. *An excellent communicator:* An employee with poise, tact, and something worthwhile to say. Someone with an excellent command of the English language

who can converse with ease and also write as compellingly as she or he speaks.

Among these qualities, I would rate being a good communicator as the most important, particularly when it comes to your writing skills. Employers often complain that today's graduates lack basic writing skills—no matter their alma mater. This is problematic because whether you have a position that revolves around writing or not, your writing skills—or lack thereof—say something about you. It is hard to take a person seriously and consider them a professional when emails, memos, or reports are littered with errors. The good news is that your writing/communications skills, just like every other skill or professional trait, can always be improved.

Your ability to demonstrate key skills—just like your ability to fit it—will require you to constantly assess yourself to see how you are viewed by others, and then to make the necessary changes if you may be perceived as anything other than a model employee who adds value to the company.

15

Building a Positive Professional Image

*The way to gain a good reputation is to endeavor
to be what you desire to appear.*
—Socrates

Building and maintaining a positive image is as important in the professional workplace as it was in college. The only difference is that the stakes are higher now if you get stuck with a bad reputation.

Word can travel fast about the good you do and the bad—the excellent image you project as well as the one that will keep you from advancing in your career. As women, we often have to struggle harder than our male counterparts to be respected and taken seriously; we don't want our own mistakes to add to this. There are also various stereotypes that exist about Gen Y/Millennials, such as they have a poor work ethic and don't respect authority. As a young professional, it's important to avoid perpetuating these stereotypes.

Projecting an image that demands respect and developing a reputation as an industrious, intelligent, and amiable person should be one of your top professional goals. In order for you to succeed in the workplace and your careers, you must be perceived in a positive light by your peers and the person who signs your paycheck. Although it's easy to forget, everything you do and don't do, say and don't say, is picked apart and judged by others. People view your talk, your walk, your style of dress, and the overall way you carry yourself as a reflection of who you are and what you have to offer. Although no one will expect for you to be perfect, they will expect you to be professional.

At this point in your life, you have probably been exposed to various types of unprofessional people one can find in almost any work environment: bossy people, manipulative people, brown nosers, etc. There are also certain types of unprofessional women who seem common in workplaces, or ones who, while professional, still do themselves or others a disservice in some way. I have found that knowing "what not to be" or what doesn't work is just as helpful as knowing how one should operate. Please do all that you can to ensure you aren't labeled as being like one of these women:

COMMON COMPLAINTS ABOUT GEN Y/MILLENNIALS

- Poor work ethic
- Lazy
- No respect for authority
- Feels entitled
- Can't take criticism
- Dresses and talks too informally
- Depends too much on technology
- Poor writing skills

Ms. That's Not My Job

"That's not my job" is her motto, but the real problem is that no one can figure out what she does anyway. All her peers wonder why she hasn't been fired yet and resent her because she doesn't pull her own weight. The word "teamwork" is not in her dictionary, and neither is "diligence" and "competence." Ms. That's Not My Job spends most of her day pretending to work and thinking about what she's going to do with her next paycheck. She sees her job as just a stepping-stone to something greater, so she never really puts much effort into anything she does. When she gets passed up for promotions or fired, she thinks it's because she didn't brown nose the boss or because he or she just didn't like her.

How *not* to be Ms. That's Not My Job:

- Be willing to work on behalf of the team.
- Assist and train co-workers.
- Be eager to learn new skills.
- Give your best effort on both small and big tasks.

Now You Tell Me?

Employees who provide co-workers with social support, such as through picking up slack for others, inviting co-workers to lunch, and organizing office activities, are much more likely to be engaged at work and to get promoted than those who keep to themselves, according to study conducted by Shawn Achor, author of *The Happiness Advantage*.

Ms. Carrie Bradshaw

Her co-workers wonder if she has thousands of dollars of credit card debt, or a sugar daddy, because they know she doesn't earn enough to sport all those expensive clothes. It's like this woman comes to work for the sole purpose of working her outfit. Everything she wears has its designer label in plain view and she'll find some way to tell you how much the outfit cost her. And while she can name every hot fashion designer in the industry and tell you when a new line is coming out, she draws a blank when you ask her anything about her industry and line of work. She doesn't realize that clothes don't make the woman and she'll never make it out of a cubicle with her present mind-set.

How *not* to be Ms. Carrie Bradshaw:

- Realize that style doesn't have to have a high price tag.
- To avoid jealousy, don't discuss how much money you spend or how much your car, house, etc., cost you.
- Cultivate non-work interests—shopping doesn't count!— and stay abreast of industry news so you don't seem like an airhead.

Ms. I Have a Cause

Whether it's gay rights, ending sexism, vegetarianism, or saving the whales, everyone at the office knows exactly what Ms. I Have a Cause stands for because she's constantly talking about it. Her desk is also littered with paraphernalia promoting what she believes in. While a few co-workers appreciate her enthusiasm for something greater than herself, most find her irritating and try to avoid her—in case she wants to give them another button or invite them to another organizational meeting. No boss will ever put her in a position of authority because her co-workers feel uneasy working with her, especially those who hold beliefs counter to her own. Worse, she could be out of a job if she continues using company time and resources to promote her cause.

How *not* to be Ms. I Have a Cause:

- Respect other people's beliefs and values by not forcing yours upon them through handouts, emails, and conversations they didn't initiate.
- Educate co-workers about your cause if you think they might be interested, but do so after work.
- Only share your views on controversial topics with co-workers with whom you have developed friendships.

Ms. Loud Chatterbox

Ms. Loud Chatterbox talks way too much and much too loudly. When she laughs, you can hear it down the hallway and around the corner, and she tends to laugh often. She never learned how to "use your inside voice" and even if she did, she thinks what she has to say is so important that everyone should hear it. Just as bad, because she's loud, she often comes off as obnoxious and even somewhat aggressive because people feel like she's shouting at them. The co-workers sitting closest to her have taken to wearing earplugs, and others have privately asked the manager to move their workspace. While Ms. Loud Chatterbox may be a good worker, she's in jeopardy of not growing within the company or losing her job altogether. Upper management takes behavioral traits—even like being too loud and talkative—into consideration when it's time for promotions and layoffs.

How *not* to be Ms. Loud Chatterbox:

- Understand that talking louder than normal doesn't help get your point across, it makes people not want to hear it.
- Practice keeping your sentences short and to the point, particularly in busy work environments.
- Respect your boss and co-workers' time. If something isn't urgent, always ask if someone has time to talk—be it in person or via phone.
- Respect other people's workspaces—especially if you work in a cubicle-type environment—by speaking lower than normal when on the phone but with the volume turned up.

Ms. Booty Call

Men's eyes widen and jaws drop when they see Ms. Booty Call approaching. She looks like she is auditioning for a music video or trying to be the next Snooki with her too-short skirts, cleavage-baring shirts, seductive make up, or break-your-ankle high heels. She purposefully draws too much attention to herself and thinks the other women in the office haven't befriended her because they're just jealous. And while the men flock around her, none respect her. She tricked the person interviewing her into offering her a job by wearing a three-piece suit, but now she thinks her job at work is to sit back and look cute. Her career will be ruined if she doesn't make a dramatic change in her appearance.

How *not* to be Ms. Booty Call:

- When in doubt, if something may be too short, tight, or just plain odd for a work environment, don't put it on.
- Learn to dress according to your body type so your clothes will look better on you.
- Aim to wear "conversation pieces," not loads of jewelry and accessories.

110

- Unless you're working at a Mac counter, keep your makeup natural-looking, and avoid obviously fake eyelashes.

Ms. Congeniality

Everyone in the office loves her and doesn't know what they would do without her, which is probably because she does everything. She is the nicest person anyone could work with, but she's just too nice. Ms. Congeniality gives "turn the other cheek" a whole new meaning, and people take advantage of her timid and sweet nature. She's the go-to person when co-workers need someone to cover for them or "just help out" with tedious projects that are past due. Because her boss knows she's so dependable, he or she tends to give her more and harder work than other employees, which wouldn't be so bad if she was rewarded for her extra efforts. Because Ms. Congeniality is afraid of being disliked, she never questions anyone or anything and finds it hard to say no. Because she is afraid to ask for what she wants, like a raise or promotion, she'll likely stay stuck in the same position making the same amount of money she did when she was first hired.

How *not* to be Ms. Congeniality:

- Swap "Yes, of course" with "Let me check. I'll get right back with you" when co-workers ask if you can assist them with something that could be time consuming. Then really think about if you have the time or the desire to take on extra work. If the answer is no, just tell them you would like to help, but your own plate is full.
- Follow the "it takes a team" philosophy, but don't constantly take on other people's responsibilities unless you know you can count on them, too.
- Check your schedule before you volunteer for extra assignments so you don't become overburdened.
- Don't wait for employers to bring up raises and promotions. If you know you deserve one, set up a meeting so you can initiate the conversation.

Ms. Woe Is Me

There is always something wrong with this woman and nothing is ever okay with her. She would complain about winning the lottery if she hit the right numbers. She's the one in the office meeting who brings up 10 baseless reasons why something isn't a good idea, and complains about things that most people wouldn't think twice about. When people aren't trying to avoid her, they're tuning her out. Despite the fact that co-workers have hinted she should try being more positive, she still can't figure out why no one gets along with her and why her employer said the company can no longer afford to keep her.

How *not* to be Ms. Woe Is Me:

- Save tirades about your personal business—possibly cheating boyfriend, overbearing mother, bad drivers—for drinks with the girls.
- Voice concerns you have about office issues with the people who have the ability to solve them.
- Bring problems up in office meetings only when you have solutions.

HRinsider Tip: A common stereotype of the Gen Y generation is that they've been babied by their parents and now have trouble making decisions or solving problems on their own. Don't perpetuate this stereotype by involving your mom or dad in your work life! Having a parent talk to your boss to help solve a conflict is a sure sign of professional immaturity.

—Francina Harrison, founder of Harrison & Associates, TCEnow.com

Ms. Praying Mantis

Ms. Praying Mantis intimidates everyone, including her boss. Her drive, intelligence, and hard work have made her very successful, but she is disliked because of her mean, abrasive attitude. She acts likes she has something to prove to everyone—especially her male co-workers—and people generally know to stay out of her way. She's also prone to backstabbing and questioning co-workers' ethics when she sees them as a threat to her career success. When that doesn't work, she breaks out all of her intimidation techniques. Yet after her boss finally gets tired of everyone complaining about her, she will find herself declawed and unemployed.

How *not* to be Ms. Praying Mantis:

- Don't view or treat your co-workers as competitors; you're not on a remake of *The Apprentice*. Even in competitive environments, such as sales, make it your goal to surpass the company's targets—not specific people.
- Let your good work speak for itself. People who brag about what they have accomplished—or dismiss others deeds— appear insecure.

Ms. You've Got To Be Kidding

"You've got to be kidding" is what the person interviewing this woman said when she walked through the door. Her makeup was all jacked up, her clothes were wrinkled and very out of style, and she may have forgotten to comb her hair. Still, she had impeccable credentials and a great attitude so she was hired. Now she's on the job and both women and men try to hint that she may want to get a make over if she expects the boss to let her meet and greet customers. People just can't figure out how she can be so smart but not see that her sloppy appearance is preventing her from getting ahead. If she takes just a few tips from Ms. Carrie Bradshaw (who calls her "Ugly Betty" behind her back), she will go further at her company and in life.

How *not* to be Ms. You've Got To Be Kidding:

- No matter what notch you are on the totem pole, don't try to get away with dressing below company standards.
- Have a girlfriend with a flair for fashion go through your closet and tell you which clothes and shoes should not be worn to work. Then head to the mall with her to find some basic clothes you can mix and match.
- Get a free makeup consultation at the mall and ask the makeup artist what color base, lipstick, blush, eye shadow,

etc. goes with your skin tone and features. Stick with these colors.

- Google "how to dress for your body type" and keep the tips in mind when shopping for new clothes on your own.
- Get a simple haircut and hairstyle that you can keep up on your own so there's little excuse for bad hair days.
- Buy a full-length mirror and don't head out the door for work without being able to say you look put together.

Ms. Low Self

Ms. Low Self is hard working and extremely smart. Her only problem is that she has very low self-esteem, which doesn't make sense because the girl has it going on. However, because she thinks so lowly of herself, she constantly criticizes herself in front of others, doesn't share her ideas for fear of being rejected, and never takes credit for her accomplishments. She also tends to slink around and avoid eye contact. While Ms. Low Self has much to offer, her self-defeating actions keep her from truly being valued at her company and moving up.

How *not* to be Ms. Low Self:

- Do not downplay your accomplishments when you're given a compliment by pointing out mistakes you made or saying things like "anyone could have done it." Simply say "thank you."
- Put your ideas in writing if you have a hard time verbalizing them.
- Recognize you have a right to be where you are and deserve the career you desire. Seek help from a counselor if you suffer from serious self-esteem issues.

As you can see, these are women you don't want to emulate. Furthermore, you shouldn't even hang around women like Ms. Booty Call and Ms. Praying Mantis. Of course, on the more positive end of the spectrum are women who make you very proud and want to strive to get on their level. Ms. Now That's What I'm Talking About, aka Ms. Michelle in honor of First Lady Michelle Obama, embodies these women.

MS. MICHELLE

She has everyone's attention from the moment she steps into a room. Men are in awe of her because she possesses both beauty and brains. Women can't help but feel a tinge of jealousy because she looks and acts like she has everything together. She is an employer's dream—a poised, confident, cordial, hard-working, dedicated employee, who does more than just get the job done. She checks her attitude at the door, and no matter how much her boss and co-workers ruffle her feathers, she's yet to break a sweat. Ms. Michelle will succeed whether she is trying to climb the corporate ladder, thrive in a small business, or show the world what a real First Lady looks like because she recognizes that image and professionalism are important.

The catch is that you can't just wake up one day and become Ms. Michelle. You have to *work* on becoming her.

Becoming Ms. Michelle

- *Critically analyze the image you're projecting:* Most of us know the negative behaviors we need to work on, but we make excuses for trying not to change. I, for example, am much too open with people. If I'm in the right mood and I feel particularly comfortable, I could share my entire life story with a person I just met. While I generally like that I have such an easygoing personality, I have to remember that there is a thin line between being easygoing and unprofessional. I don't want to appear ditzy in the workplace and become labeled as someone who tells all of her business.

- *Consider the personality traits you have that could possibly annoy, anger, or make people feel sorry for you:* Do you tend to run off at the mouth and constantly find people telling you they'd love to chat with you a little longer but they have to get back to work? Are you somewhat absentminded and frequently reminded by your boss about assignments he or she is afraid you might forget? Do some co-workers avoid

115

you because they are afraid you will go off on them again? You should be aware of at least some of the things you must work on to sharpen your image.

- *Ask someone you trust about what you can do to sharpen your image:* Talk to someone you feel comfortable confiding in about how you want to maintain a professional image. Ask them if there is anything about your personality that might make others think negatively about you. Ask them to be truthful with you, and resist the urge to counter anything they say with an explanation as to why you behave a certain way.

- *Take notes from other people:* Carefully watch how the most respected people at your company carry themselves. The type of people who are most respected differs from company to company. At some places, people who are strictly about business and act like workaholics are deemed the perfect employees. At other companies, people with warm and outgoing personalities are publicly praised. Pick out people who are generally liked and admired and take a mental note of everything they do and don't do that wins the approval of others. If there are certain things a person does that you can easily add into your routine, such as making a point to always speak to people, then do them also. If some things are a little bit harder, such as dressing immaculately, but will really give your image a boost, then try, try, and try some more to emulate that person.

Once you have identified the areas you want to work on, you should write them down. I suggest writing a sentence on two sticky notes, such as "I will avoid gossiping," or "I will avoid giving unconstructive criticism and being snappy when I'm in a bad mood." Put one sticky note inside your desk drawer at work and the other on your bathroom mirror so that you will see the sentences often. Then really try to work on improving in your problem areas.

PRESENTING YOUR IDEAS EFFECTIVELY

Many of us have brilliant ideas but find ourselves unable to communicate them in an effective manner. As part of building your professional image, use these five tips to make your boss and colleagues tune in when you start talking.

1. *Speak with authority: How* you say something is just as important as *what* you say. Avoid phrases that make you seem unsure of yourself, such as "I *think* my plan *may* work."

2. *Show you've done your research:* Decision makers are more apt to appreciate your idea/opinion if it is backed by credible research instead of just your gut feeling. When possible, present findings from key sources that suggest your idea has merit.

3. *Be concise:* Make your idea easy to grasp by explaining it as simply as possible, and try to be brief. People may begin to tune out if you are long-winded or seem to be purposefully using unnecessary jargon or flowery language.

4. *Explain how the idea/plan benefits everyone:* Using concrete examples, show how your idea benefits everyone listening, not just the people who are able to approve it. Your goal is to build consensus and demonstrate that you are looking out for the best interest of everyone in the group or company.

5. *Watch your body language:* Your body language should exude confidence. Maintain eye contact and good posture when you are presenting your ideas, and do not fidget with anything.

Diary of a Careeranista

LISA QUAST ON
LOOKING THE PART

*C*limbing the career ladder is not just about what you know and whom you know; it's also about your appearance. I once worked with someone at the beginning of my career who was incredibly bright, had several college degrees, excellent work experience, and was highly professional. But she never seemed able to get promoted. Puzzled, I had a discussion with our manager. The manager's comment? "Good grief, Lisa. I understand her business strengths, but there's just no way I could put her in front of the management team or customers for a presentation—they wouldn't take her seriously. Have you actually *looked* at her?"

So I did take a good look at her. She mainly wore slacks and a blouse to work each day, her hair was long and straight (think late 1960s/early 1970s) and she rarely if ever wore makeup or jewelry. At the time, I was working in the medical industry for a Japanese firm. The industry, as well as the company, was very conservative. I wore a suit to work every day of the week and for trade shows, the appropriate attire for employees was a black, navy, or dark brown suit.

"Allie," as I'll call her, didn't want to wear suits to work every day, and she didn't like having to take the time to apply makeup. She wanted to wear comfortable clothes and had the attitude that no one could make her do any differently—and she had apparently told this to our manager several times when he had discussions with her about her attire.

In Allie's case, I watched as she sacrificed career promotions for what she felt was comfortable clothing at work. It was a lesson I learned quickly: To hold a certain position—and secure the one after it—you not only need the knowledge, skills, and experience, you also need to look the part. It's pretty simple: While your work ethic might show that you're a super star, your attire might imply laziness and sloppiness. A polished, professional wardrobe that clients and colleagues respect will send the message that you should be taken seriously for new opportunities, promotions, and pay raises.

This is what I wish more women starting out in their careers understood. It's vital that you consciously think about the persona you want to project at work and then dress the part from head to toe. The four most common problems I see with women's appearance are:

Wearing clothes that are inappropriate for the company/industry: A client I once coached was having problems obtaining promotions at an advertising company, so, among other things, I evaluated her work attire and overall "look." Her typical outfit was a gray or navy pantsuit, with minimal makeup and jewelry. Unfortunately, her image projected her as dull and unimaginative—yet the company wanted creative employees who were on top of current trends. By overhauling her wardrobe, hairstyle, and makeup, we were able to update her persona to someone who looked stylish and unique—fit for a job in advertising. This got her the attention she needed from management, and eventually, that much-coveted promotion she wanted.

When dressing for work and shopping for new work clothes, remember the industry you're in. While you don't need to "look like everyone else," you certainly don't need to look like you don't belong. If you feel lost on how to start building a professional wardrobe, ask for help! Go to a large department store and request a personal shopper, or hire a personal stylist. Once that is done, assess your hair and makeup. Spending time and energy to update both conveys that you take pride in yourself and that you stay on top of current trends, which are both important qualities to employers—no matter what the industry.

Wearing clothes that are inappropriate for the geographic area/season of the year: If you move from a colder climate to a much warmer location (or vice versa), you'll need to re-think your work wardrobe. The typical dark clothes you wore almost year round in New York or Seattle won't be appropriate in Phoenix or Atlanta. And don't forget about your outerwear coats. It's not acceptable to wear a leather jacket or your ski coat over your business suit, and sorry ladies, but showing up at a client's office wearing a silk blouse, wool skirt, and heels paired with your winter fleece doesn't create a very pulled together look that instills confidence in your skills.

Taking casual Fridays way too far: Casual Fridays can mean different things to different companies, but no matter the company, it *doesn't* mean you can show up at the office in your gym workout clothes. Wearing tight black leggings with a jog bra underneath a T-shirt will never allow you to project a leadership image. Step up casual Friday. Even when you're given the option to dress casually for work, take it up a notch from your weekend wear. If wearing jeans, choose a dark wash with a trouser cut and a chic shirt with jewelry. Instead of t-shirts, opt for a silk blouse, and always have a third piece like a blazer or cardigan handy, which helps give your outfit that extra bit of polish when needed.

Under-dressing: I nearly gasped when a young woman who I and several other colleagues were interviewing showed up looking like she had stepped right off the set of a trashy reality TV show. Unfortunately, a tight black mini-skirt, a blouse showing lots of cleavage, high heels with no nylons, and five earrings in her ears made it difficult for the interview panel, especially the men, to concentrate on her assets—and not those other "assets" she was so proudly displaying.

I wish I could say this was a rare occurrence, but I find myself constantly amazed by the club-like clothing women wear to work. If you want to advance in your career, then avoid wearing anything remotely skimpy, suggestive, or too tight in a professional office environment. Don't take your work attire cues from reality TV shows; take them from real life by conducting research to ensure your wardrobe is appropriate for the company and industry.

Now that you know what an employer looks for in terms of appearance, apply these suggestions and watch how your boss—as well as everyone else at work—responds to you. Looking the part may just help you obtain that new position you've been hoping for or the promotion you covet.

Lisa Quast is a certified executive coach and mentor, successful global corporate executive and business consultant, and award-winning non-fiction author. Lisa founded Career Woman, Inc. in 2005, a Seattle-based international career coaching and consulting company dedicated to the advancement of women in business and the achievement of their personal and professional aspirations.

16

Managing Your Boss

The most important single ingredient in the formula
of success is knowing how to get along with people.
—Theodore Roosevelt

I have always despised the word "boss." It sounds so controlling, so weighty, so self-important, so . . . bossy. Needless to say, I have never liked the idea of having a boss either. That's why I have always tried to choose jobs that give me a high level of independence. But it's always been clear to me that unless you own your own business, there is no way around having someone who plays the role of head honcho at work. So, when I was a bit younger, through trial and error I learned how to get along with my bosses. And later, when I saw that just "getting along" with my bosses wasn't exactly the smartest thing to do, I started learning how to "manage" them. And I'm still learning.

A ton of books have been written on the sole subject of managing your boss. From *Managing Your Boss In a Week: A Teach Yourself Guide* to *Monster Boss: Strategies for Surviving and Excelling When Your Boss Is a Nightmare*, there are Amazon.com pages, bookstores, and library shelves stacked with reading material dedicated to these people. It's funny that thousands of pages could be written on one aspect pertaining to a person's working life. Yet, there is a reason for this anomaly.

Beyond being the individual who lets you get your foot in the door, your boss also determines what happens to you once the door closes. Whether you get a raise, important assignments, move up in the company, and sometimes whether you're able to move on to bigger and better things, are to a large extent determined by the person to whom you answer first thing in the morning. And, as if bosses weren't influential enough, studies have found that direct supervisors have a huge impact on our happiness. I have certainly found this to be the case in my own life.

Given the role bosses will play in your overall career, you can't afford to look at them as nuisances anymore—tolerating them as you may have during positions you held in college. Your boss is now someone you have to pay attention to. More important, your boss is now someone you have to manage.

An entire book may not be needed to key you in on how to best interact and deal with your supervisors, but everyone starting out in their career can benefit from some pointers. The following advice is devised to help you manage those strange people we call bosses, and to advance your career in the process.

BOSSES 101

No matter how cool certain supervisors are, and no matter how chummy you are with them, you can be sure of two things: they know who's in charge and they're watching you. In fact, they're grading you. Don't let them catch you slipping. When your boss thinks of you, you want him or her to think about how wise they were to hire you and what an asset you've been to the company. You help create and sustain this good image through two ways: your performance on the job and the way you treat your boss. Think about it. You can't succeed at a company if you're a great employee but your boss hates you. And you can't succeed if you're a dead weight but loved by your boss. Your boss has to love you and your work. The following are ways to ensure both.

Loving Your Work

Do your best 24/7: Don't just do your best on assignments you feel matter the most. Treat every assignment, from filing papers to entertaining notable clients, as important. Your boss won't feel comfortable letting you work on major assignments if you act like you can't or don't want to handle the simpler ones.

Show initiative: Your boss expects you to do what's asked of you, so being able to take and follow orders won't get you more than a thank you. Look for ways that you can help your boss or department meet key goals, be it cutting costs, boosting productivity, simplifying a process, or better serving customers.

Bring ideas to the table: Present yourself as knowledgeable, creative, and proactive by offering your boss suggestions and solutions (once you have proved yourself at a company and gotten to know your boss). In doing so, your boss will then think more highly of you, ask your opinion more often, and hopefully come to rely on you for help when problems arise.

Help others: Don't lose out on an opportunity to help other employees by offering advice or training them. This demonstrates your team-player mentality and management skills while showing that you are not out to just better yourself.

Finish assignments ahead of time: Remember how pleased your teachers were with students who turned in assignments *before* they were due? Same thing goes for bosses. Completing projects or little tasks before your boss remembers to ask about them makes you look industrious and thoughtful.

Volunteer for extra assignments: Bosses give extra credit just like teachers. You can earn extra credit from your boss by doing more than what's asked of you. Take on additional assignments when you have the time. This shows your commitment to the company and your enthusiasm.

4 HELPFUL QUESTIONS TO ASK YOUR BOSS

1. "Did you hear about . . .?"

Bosses need information, and they value people who share it. Because managers make many decisions and deal with lots of people, they need to stay up to date with both business developments and changes in the political climate.

2. "What are your most important goals this year?"

Although people are usually clear about their own work goals, they often don't know much about their manager's objectives. If you know what your boss is working toward, then you can spot opportunities to be helpful.

3. "How am I doing? What could I improve?"

Many bosses practice "psychic management"—that is, they have opinions about employee performance, but fail to share those thoughts. Initiating an occasional feedback discussion will let you know what your manager is thinking.

4. "Want to go to lunch or grab a coffee?"

Having lunch or coffee with your manager gives you a chance to talk about something besides work and get to know each other a little better. It's a well-known fact that sharing a meal tends to promote positive feelings.

—*Marie G. McIntyre, founder of Your Office Coach,*
www.yourofficecoach.com. Used with permission.

Loving You

Do it how the boss likes: We all have a certain way we like doing things, which we think is the best, of course. However, so does your boss. Adopting the simple work habits your boss seems to prefer, or swear by—be it following up every phone call with an email, scheduling certain tasks first thing in the morning, or formatting a proposal using a certain font—will make your boss know you're paying attention to him or her and are aiming to please.

Compliment your boss: If you like your boss's hairstyle, outfit, car, presentation, or newly decorated office, then say so. Everyone likes and remembers compliments. However, please note that the word was "compliment," not "kiss up." The difference is that one is sincere and the other is not. Your boss knows the difference.

Make your boss look good: A surefire way to gain your boss's approval is by telling that person's boss or peers how much you admire his or her work ethic or other positive traits. By relating how much you like your boss, how hard working or innovative he or she is, you demonstrate your loyalty and gain more brownie points than you can count.

Be honest: Bosses, like everyone else, despise liars; don't let your boss catch you in a lie! You should be recognized as a person who is honest and sincere. Also, when your boss asks your opinion, state your thoughts truthfully and tactfully, even if you disagree with him or her. Your boss will appreciate your honesty and trust you more.

Be enthusiastic: Smile when you arrive to work. Act like you're glad to be alive and glad to have a job. You don't have to run around with a fake smile on your face, but you should definitely not sport a frown and constant yawn. You want your boss to think that you are glad to be in your position and enjoy working with him or her—not like you're at work just for the money and have to tolerate your boss (even if that's the truth). If you are enthusiastic, your boss will feel likable and in turn treat you well. And funny enough, acting enthusiastic when you really don't feel that way can make you feel better.

Try practicing those tactics to create a better working relationship with your boss and anyone else to whom you report. After working with your boss for a while, you should be able to devise some of your own original tactics. To do this, pay attention to what your boss considers both good and unprofessional work. Take note of the employees your boss seems to favor and dislike. In general, find out what makes your boss tick and then set your clock to the right time.

KNOW YOUR MANAGER'S . . .

Communication style: Does she prefer to communicate in person or primarily by email or phone? Does she like to chit chat before getting down to business or dive right into the issue at hand?

Decision-making style: Does she need a sheet full of facts before making a decision, or is she willing to go with her gut—or that of someone she trusts? Does she usually seek the opinions of others before choosing an option, or does she keep most everyone shut out of the decision-making process?

Pet peeves: What habits annoy her and are sure to cause someone to get on her bad side? What does she consider the height of unprofessionalism?

SWIMMING WITH THE SHARKS

If you're lucky, you'll be blessed with a string of bosses who want to see you succeed and will do everything they can to help you. You'll find that these bosses require little management. However, they also are very rare.

If you're like the majority of working Americans, you'll simply end up with someone who is just a boss—nothing more and nothing less. In their mind, they are there to manage other employees, keep the peace, and help the company stay afloat. If they can help make you into a better person and a better employee then that's great. If not, then that's okay because that's not their job anyway. Managing these bosses is not a very hard task. You can get them to help you by using the strategies given combined with your own.

But then there are the other bosses. The bosses that spawned the creation of "managing your boss" books. The bosses that inspired movies like *The Devil Wears Prada* and the cult-classic *Office Space.* The bosses that help make psychiatrists rich, and occasionally push some employees to go postal. The crazy bosses. If you've never had to work for a boss you thought was hiding a mental illness, then count your blessings because they're out there. The weird thing about crazy bosses though is that you can work for them for months without realizing who and what you're working with. They hardly ever strike you as odd during the interview. They may even appear normal during the first days and weeks on the job. But then you start to notice that your boss is a tad bit different from the ones you're used to. And then it dawns on you . . . my boss is crazy!

Now You Tell Me?

The #1 reason people quit their jobs is a bad boss or immediate supervisor, according to a Gallup poll of more than one million U.S. workers.

I've had my fair share of crazy bosses, and one or two of them made me question my own sanity. So what's a sane girl to do when faced with a boss who might have escaped from a psychiatric ward? Short of quitting your job or transferring to a different department, there's nothing much you can do but learn how to manage a crazy boss, too. However, managing these bosses requires a different set of pointers. Read on for how to best recognize and manage each type of crazy boss.

The Jekyll-Hyde Boss

I know it sounds mean, but I had a boss who I just knew had an undiagnosed split-personality disorder. He could be the most supportive boss on the planet and then turn right around and tell me he wasn't going to help me with anything, that I was doing everything wrong, and that if I didn't like the way things were I could pick up my last paycheck because I was expendable. Sometimes I would cringe when the phone rang in anticipation of a verbal beat down.

Jeckyll-Hyde bosses have mood swings that knock you over. They are prone to fits of rage that include cursing and threatening people. You never know whether they're going to promote you or fire you. In fact, they can do one right after the other. These bosses make you walk on eggshells because you can never guess how they are going to react to anything you or anyone else does. Even the simplest things like accidentally closing a door too hard can upset a Jeckyll-Hyde boss on the wrong day.

Management Tactics:

- *Stay out of their way:* If you can get away with a minimal amount of contact with them, then do so.
- *Anticipate their mood swings:* After watching them do the Dr. Jekyll/Mr. Hyde transformation enough, you may begin to see it coming. Get all you can out of them when they're feeling great, and be on your p's and q's when they're feeling foul.
- *Remind them of your worth:* Jeckyll-Hyde bosses tend to forget how much they like you when they're in a bad mood. Gently remind them of their affinity toward you, stating how just the other day (or past hour) they were very pleased with you.
- *Develop a tough skin:* Learn to just deal with their personality, expecting some really great days and some stank ones.

HRinsider Tip: *Provide solutions, not problems.* Your boss works under extreme daily pressure, so if you have a problem that needs fixing, come up with a suggestion to solve it before you go to speak to him or her. Handle what you can and only enlist your boss for the stuff that requires his or her influence in the organization.

—Rosemary Parr, international trainer & coach

The Hissy Fit Boss

A friend who worked for the same company I did, but had a different boss, once told me that she had a nightmare about answering the work phone on the third ring instead of on the second ring like she was supposed to, and her boss saw this and had an asthma attack. I could almost see it really happening; her boss was notorious for going berserk over lesser things. She started nearly every sentence with "Did you remember?" or "I hope you didn't." She also acted like her duty was to check everything my friend did for errors, which totally negated my friend's work since her job *was* checking for errors.

Always looking over your shoulder, the Hissy Fit boss thinks he or she is the only person who can do something right. On top of that, these bosses tend to be nitpicky, whiny, and busybodies. These bosses act like they're your parents and they treat you like a toddler. What's worse, they expect everyone else to be as overanxious and anal as they are at work.

Management Tactics:

- *Help your boss trust you:* Point out all the great things you've done on your own when your boss tries to micromanage, and ask if you can handle this or that by yourself so you can prove you're skilled and dependable. It may take a while, but once your boss sees that you are fully capable of taking care of business, perhaps he or she will loosen up a little.
- *Become a little obsessive-compulsive yourself:* Make your boss feel like he or she isn't the only anal person in the office. Pay closer attention to the things your boss really cares about and talk to him or her about it. Seeing that you're concerned will relax his or her fears about you.

Now You Tell Me?

Don't wait until your annual review to receive feedback. Hold quarterly meetings with your supervisor to discuss your progress. This will keep you engaged with your supervisor, and you will know in advance if your performance can be improved.

—Carla Jenkins, program analyst for the federal government

The Sticky Note Boss

I had a Sticky Note boss, and to this day, I don't know how I worked with him without pulling out my hair. I felt like I was his mother after having to constantly remind him of things he said he would do, and so

I actually began leaving him sticky notes. At other times, I felt like his personal assistant from doing things he should have been doing.

With a Sticky Note boss, you'll be unable to figure out what intelligent person hired him or her, much less promoted the person to a supervisory position. Besides being entirely too forgetful, Sticky Note bosses just don't know what they're doing. You'll find them asking you for advice, missing deadlines, messing up projects, and goofing off on the job. This displeases you because there's stuff they're supposed to be teaching you, and you can't get your work done because you rely on them.

Management Tactics:

- *Make sure you're on the ball:* One day upper management is going to figure out what they hired and the Sticky Note boss will be fired. You don't want them thinking you were playing around, too. Make a list of all your accomplishments and document your work because you can't rely on a Sticky Note boss to remember anything you did. Also, get to know your boss's boss, and if possible, create opportunities to work with him or her.
- *Make decisions for your boss:* Sticky Note bosses tend to not like making decisions, so attempt to make them for them. Politely tell them what you're going to do instead of asking like you normally would. If they disagree with your decision, then they're forced to make one. This keeps you from waiting around for them to make up their mind.
- *Emphasize your deadlines:* Sticky Note bosses have to be helped to remember everything, from you asking for a specific day off to giving you information you need to complete a project. Emphasize every important deadline and send email reminders.
- *Get help from someone else:* Go to someone else for assistance if you're supposed to be learning specific skills on the job and your boss isn't helping. Don't let Sticky Note bosses keep you from growing on the job.

The Nothing's Right Boss

One of my old roommates had a Nothing's Right boss. Every other day she would come home saying how she was going to quit. Her boss constantly threatened to fire people and got upset about the weirdest things like her employees taking lunch breaks together or meeting each other after hours. She did not understand what "camaraderie" meant and definitely did not promote it.

Grumpy and argumentative, these bosses walk around with a boulder on their shoulders 24/7. They argue for the sake of arguing, and will disagree with you about anything. When they find out you're right, they don't apologize; they get even more ignorant. These bosses are unclear about everything, except that they're always right.

Management Tactics:

- *Avoid disagreements:* Disagreeing with them is pointless; don't even try. If they want to say they wrote the Bible then nod your head and keep working. If they ask you a question and you know there's a specific answer they want to hear, then smile and give it to them.
- *Be specific:* When you talk to them, state what you have to say clearly and concisely. Leave no room for assumptions or questions. This way, they will have a harder time twisting your words around and won't have too much to say or ask afterward.

The Sadistic Boss

Kevin Spacey played this type of boss in *Swimming with Sharks*. My mother wanted me to watch the movie so I could see that my Jekyll-Hyde boss wasn't so bad.

While the other bosses may get on your last nerves, this boss might actually scare you. In fact, it's suspected that the sadistic boss isn't crazy at all. No, this type of boss may actually be evil. How else can you explain why they embarrass their subordinates in front of clients, demand that employees stick to deadlines superwoman couldn't meet, smirk as they disapprove raises without giving a reason, and assign super smart employees to the most menial of tasks? They like being mean and enjoy seeing people below them squirm.

Management Tactics:

- *Quit:* Quit before you get used to being treated like dirt and let everyone else run over you, too.
- *Quit:* Quit while you still have good self-esteem because a sadistic boss will strip you of it.
- *Quit:* Quit while you're still sane and don't need to see a psychiatrist.
- *Quit:* Quit before you end up in jail for hurting your boss.
- *Quit:* Quit while you're still breathing because you don't know just how sadistic your boss really is.

If you'll notice, confronting your crazy boss about his or her behavior was not one of the management tactics listed. This is because confrontation seldom works with crazy bosses. In a perfect world, you would be able to calmly and delicately explain that there are certain behaviors your boss exhibits that trouble you. And in that perfect world, your boss would be appalled that he or she was perceived that way and would promise to make an effort to change. But this is the real world. It's likely that your boss's personality is as set in stone as yours. And no boss will probably like being told that you feel he or she is obsessive, childish, domineering, or ignorant—no matter how nicely you put it. If you truly want to keep your position, your best bet is to change the way *you* act to fit what your boss believes is normal and appropriate. If you can't do that while working for a crazy boss, then do the sane thing and find another job.

HRinsider Tip: Don't get into a power struggle with your supervisor. You won't win. Even if your supervisor is weak, ineffective, and known company-wide as a poor leader, you must not agitate against him. The way to gain authority in a workplace is to earn it through your good work and to make sure your supervisor and others are aware of it.

—Meg Houston Maker, writer & communications strategist

Handling Conflicts
with Co-workers

Whenever you're in conflict with someone, there is one
factor that can make the difference between damaging your
relationship and deepening it. That factor is attitude.
—William James, author

I had barely been working two weeks at my first job after graduation when I found myself about to have an anxiety attack over a
co-worker. You would think that getting along with her would be easy,
considering we only had to interact via the phone and Internet, but
she has been the hardest person I have ever had to work with. Those
simple interactions, which took place every day, left me upset and frustrated at least twice a week. I was serving as the managing editor of a
newspaper in Houston that had the layout done in an entirely different
city—by her. She was accustomed to putting the articles on any page
she desired, and now I was supposed to tell her which should be the
main stories and so on. Well, nearly every time I got the paper it looked
nothing like I expected. To solve this, I eventually worked it out so
that I could see the layout before it was printed and ask her to make
adjustments. Beyond that problem, I felt that she tried to undermine
my relationship with my boss, whom I seldom saw because he worked

in the same office as she did. Instead of calling me about any problems she saw caused by a story, such as one she was having a hard time laying out because of its length, she would complain to him about it and blow the problem out of proportion. He would in turn call me all perturbed, asking me about a problem I had never even heard about and thus hadn't been able to solve.

After talking with her about going straight to him with problems I could easily fix, she stopped doing it—as much. I continued to have other problems with her, however, which I felt were mostly caused by a misunderstanding of job duties, her feeling like I took away some of her decision-making power, and a general personality conflict. Every time the phone rang, I prayed it wasn't her. And we were always somewhat short with each other when we spoke—as if we both could not wait to hang up the phone. It got to the point that we stopped trying to hide our irritation with each other and became downright rude. When we didn't feel like being rude to each other, we would have other people relay our messages, which was childish and unproductive. While I did handle all the major work problems we had as they arose, I never took the time to acknowledge and discuss the obvious tension between us. Had I done so, perhaps work would have been less stressful for both of us.

There have been other co-workers I wanted to wish away too, as sharing air, an office, and work with people of varying personalities 40-plus hours a week isn't always easy. No matter how nice or non-confrontational you are, you are also bound to have conflicts with your co-workers. Knowing how to prevent conflicts or diffuse them before they get out of hand is crucial to succeeding in your career, not to mention guarding your mental health. Work can be hectic enough without the added pressure of mounting problems with your co-workers.

When you find yourself in difficult situations with co-workers, it may help you to reflect upon these very basic truths:

Your co-workers aren't you: Sometimes we forget that we aren't the only one with an opinion. Other people may not see things exactly the way we do. What you find unacceptable and rude at work may not faze the next person. What you believe is a wonderful idea may be ridiculous to any number of people at your company. You can't expect your co-workers to think or act the way you do because they're operating from their own point of view. What you can do is learn to adapt to your co-workers' personalities, and try to understand where they are coming from in any given situation. By recognizing the differences you have with your co-workers (from your work styles to pet peeves), you'll be better able to work with them and handle conflicts when they arise.

Your co-workers have issues just like you: Your co-workers have lives outside of work and you never know what they're going through. They have money problems, relationship problems, self-esteem problems, health problems, and a multitude of other personal conundrums you will never know about. They aren't going to be able to come to work every day in their very best mood, just like you aren't.

Your co-workers want to be liked just like you: As hard as it may be to believe sometimes, few of your co-workers ever intentionally do or say things to cause conflicts in the workplace. Hardly any of them will ever "be out to get you," and most don't come to work to make your life or anyone else's miserable. They want to be liked and respected just like you. They don't want to be thought of as a backstabber, idiot, brown-noser, or mean-spirited person. When a co-worker does or says something that upsets you, try giving him or her the benefit of the doubt that he or she didn't mean to, instead of assuming that something was said or done on purpose. Thinking in this frame of mind will take you off of the defensive and allow you to openly and cordially discuss the issues you feel should be addressed.

HRinsider Tip: If a topic is complicated or sensitive, don't send an email if you can make a phone call, and don't make a phone call if you can have an in-person conversation.

—Judith Pollock, founder of Language at Work

PET PEEVE OR REAL PROBLEM?

The key to handling conflicts with co-workers is to attempt to make amends with the person you are having difficulties with as soon as you realize there's a "real problem." A real problem is one that keeps you from doing your job effectively or seriously upsets your sense of well-being. Someone "rubbing you the wrong way" is not a real problem. You not liking the way someone talks, walks, or dresses doesn't qualify as a real problem. A co-worker who has stolen your idea, one who has lied about you, or a constantly rude and domineering person is someone with whom you may have a real problem.

When faced with what you feel is a conflict at work, take time to calm yourself down and write down exactly what this person is doing or not doing that is driving you batty. This can help you determine if they have broken one of your quirky pet peeves or if they have really over-stepped their boundaries.

Once you have decided that you do have a real problem with this person, get out that piece of paper on which you wrote down his or her faults and write down your own. Be honest with yourself. Have you done anything to provoke this person to act unfriendly toward you? Do you know this person was talking behind your back because you were talking behind his or hers and found out? Think long and think hard. The person may be reacting negatively to your negativity. But regardless of who started acting funny first, you should be the bigger person and end the drama.

ENDING THE DRAMA: FIVE SIMPLE STEPS

Step 1: Approach the person at the end of the workday or when you both have some free time. Make sure no one is around to hear the conversation. If you are constantly around other people, politely and discreetly ask if you could discuss something with him or her in private.

Step 2: Get to the point immediately by tactfully telling the person what you want to discuss. Example: "I didn't want to interrupt you, but I feel that there is tension between us and I was hoping we could talk about what we can both do to work better with each other." Or, "It seems there has been a misunderstanding between us and I want to clear it up so we can work comfortably around each other." Note: When you begin the conversation, keep in mind that your end goal is to have the issue resolved, not to put someone in his or her place. Never start the conversation with a rude question or statement. Example: "Do you have a problem with me?" Or by blaming the person for something. Example: "I know you've been talking behind my back." The person may have been wanting to clear up the problem as much as you. Approaching the person in a negative manner will make the situation worse.

Step 3: Whether the person acknowledges that there's a problem ("Yes, I feel like there's tension between us, too") or plays dumb ("Don't be so sensitive. I call everyone stupid"), be specific about the problem and give recent examples while stating your case. However, avoid accusatory phrases. Say that you are offended because it "seems like" or "appears" or you "feel like" something has happened.

Right: "For the past two weeks, I've felt like you've purposefully belittled me in front of our manager. For example, last Monday you told our manager that the last junior analyst caught on much quicker than I did, and just yesterday I heard you whisper to her that 'it would probably take too much of her time to teach me our new software, from the looks of how slow I've been on other jobs.'"

Wrong: "I don't know if you're trying to make yourself look smart in front of the boss by talking bad about me all day long, but it's getting on my nerves."

Right: "When I first started working here, we seemed to get along great, but for the past two weeks it seems like you've been giving me the cold shoulder by ignoring my questions, or cutting me off when I'm talking to you. Have I done something to offend you?"

Wrong: "You've been acting funny toward me for a long time and I know I haven't done anything to you."

Step 4: Give the person time to respond to what you've said. It's likely that your co-worker will acknowledge that there is a problem, but the reason for it may be far different from what you were thinking. As stated before, the co-worker may feel that he or she was just reacting to an offense *you* committed. On the flip side, the person may deny that a problem even exists. If so, at least your co-worker will be more mindful of how he or she interacts with you. Regardless of what is said, take care to watch your body language and tone of voice.

Step 5: If the person acknowledges that an issue does need to be cleared up, be sincere when you tell him or her that you would like to work out the problem. Attempt to come up with a solution that you both feel is appropriate.

Here's how Carla handled a conflict she encountered.

Carla's Confrontation:

Carla, 23, works as a marketing assistant at the corporate headquarters of a major electronics retailer. She has a conflict with one of her co-workers, Tory, that has been brewing since she started working there a month ago. She's not sure why, but Tory just doesn't seem to like her, as her rude and hurtful comments indicate. She has to work closely with Tory, who happens to be one level above her as a marketing associate, so she's decided to talk to Tory about the conflict they seem to have.

Carla: "Excuse me, Tory. Would it be possible for us to discuss something during our lunch break?"

Tory: "Like what?"

Carla: "Well, I feel like there is tension between us and I'd like to talk about it."

Tory: "We can talk now."

Carla: "I'm unsure if I've done anything to offend you, but sometimes it seems like you are trying to belittle me in front of our manager. For example, last Monday you told our manager that the last marketing assistant caught on much quicker than I did, and just yesterday I heard you whisper to her that it would probably take too much of her time to teach me our new software, from the looks of how slow I've been on other jobs."

Tory: "Well, when you first started working here you acted like no one could tell you anything and like you were smarter than everyone else."

Carla: "Really? When?"

Tory: "I can't pinpoint all the times, but that is the way you have been coming off. And the only reason I said that to the manager was because you acted like you knew everything in front of her, but asked other employees a lot of questions when she wasn't around."

Carla: "I'm sorry if I came off that way to you. That's not how I feel or how I want to be perceived. This is my first real job out of college and I'm trying to do my best. Still, I wish you would have told me how you felt instead of saying those negative things to the manager."

Tory: "Well, that was wrong of me. I apologize."

Carla: "Well, it's cool. I'm glad that's behind us. I hope that we can get along better now. When we first met, I was very hopeful that we would end up being friends. I'd still like that."

Tory: "We did get off to a bad start and I feel bad about that. And I actually thought the same thing about you because we're the same age and both new to the city. Let's just start fresh from here."

Maybe Carla was acting a bit snotty, maybe not. At least she tactfully confronted Tory before the tension built up further. This scenario was played out in a win-win fashion, but many confrontations don't go nearly as smoothly. What is Carla supposed to do if her confrontation with Tory is played out like this?

Carla's Confrontation Revisited:

Carla: "Excuse me, Tory. Would it be possible for us to discuss something during our lunch break?"

Tory: "What is it?"

Carla: "Well, I feel like there is tension between us and I'd like to talk about it."

Tory: "You're right—there's tension and it's not my fault."

Carla: "Excuse me? I'm unsure if I've done anything to offend you, but sometimes it seems like you are trying to belittle me in front of our manager. For example, last Monday you told our manager that the last marketing assistant caught on much quicker than I did, and just yesterday—."

Tory: "I never said that."

Carla: "I was right there when you said that and everyone else heard it, too."

Tory: "Well, maybe I did, but it's only because you act like you're better than everyone else and so smart and pretty. The only reason you got this job is because my friend quit."

Carla: "What do you mean, 'like I'm better than everyone else'"?

Tory: "You acted like you were ready to run the company when you first stepped in, and you brown-nosed the manager. I guess you think you're all that because you graduated from Georgetown.

Carla: "I'm sorry if I came off that way to you. That's certainly not how I want to be perceived. This is my first real job out of college and I'm trying to do my best. Still, I wish you would have told me how you felt instead of saying those negative things to the manager."

Tory: "Oh well, I wouldn't have said those things if you didn't act so prissy. Is that all you wanted to talk about? I'm busy."

There's not much of a chance that Carla will want to be in the same room with Tory after this incident. Carla may have to have a small talk with her manager if Tory continues acting ignorant and a second conversation doesn't lead to a resolution. Sometimes all you can do is try. When it appears that your co-worker just doesn't want to act right, there are still other ways to end the drama.

Now You Tell Me?

Don't expect to like everybody. And don't expect everybody to like you. As with any group of people, you're going to get along with some better than others, and there may be a few you just can't stand. Be tolerant. Pick your battles. Sometimes it's just enough that the work gets done.

—Karen Burns, author of *The Amazing Adventures of Working Girl: Real-Life Career Advice You Can Actually Use*

WHEN ALL ELSE FAILS

Involve your supervisor: It may temporarily create more tension, but getting someone with some authority to handle the conflict may be the only way to stop the madness. You should approach your supervisor about the conflict and just lay it out plainly and calmly. Explain how you tried and failed to resolve the issue on your own, and how you really want this conflict resolved as soon as possible. This way you will cover your butt (in case the other person talked to your supervisor first) and you will be closer to working in peace.

Steer clear of your co-worker: If you can work on a different team or in another room or office without inconveniencing yourself, then it may be wise to do so. Don't view this as running away—you're saving yourself from more drama.

Regardless of what happens in situations with your co-workers, you have to stay cool. Never allow anyone to turn you into a yelling, cursing, crying, or fighting person on the job. You will disgrace yourself in front of your boss and fellow co-workers, even if everyone knows you're not the one with the problem. Remember that part of working in a professional position means being a professional.

Working Around
Office Politics

As far as possible, without surrender,
be on good terms with all persons.
—Max Ehrmann, poet

I learned a long time ago that the word "grown-up" simply refers to someone who can be considered an adult, not necessarily a mature or professional person. If you haven't discovered it yet, this fact is apparent at most companies.

When I was a teenager changing minimum-wage jobs frequently, and even when I took my first semi-professional position as an editorial assistant, I learned that so-called grown-ups could be just as immature, irrational, and simple-minded as the children they were raising. However, unlike their kids, they can also be vindictive and messy, especially when they are given a little power at work.

It is nearly inevitable that you will work in an environment that will remind you of your old college yard or high school cafeteria. You will quickly notice that certain people don't like each other and entire groups of people seem pitted against one another. And somehow, at some point in time, you will feel as if you're in the middle of them. One of your co-workers will pull you aside to tell you to "watch out for so and so" and how horrible a person he or she is. People in a team or department you are working in will badmouth another group they feel aren't doing their jobs effectively. Your boss might even whisper that you should avoid a couple of people he or she happens to loathe.

Of course, you want to avoid being sucked into all of the drama some of your colleagues seem to thrive on. You find the secrecy, back-stabbing, and unprofessional behavior they exhibit to be appalling. But it is hard to stay out of office politics because you work closely and depend on so many of these people. So, short of jumping into all of the ongoing frays, what do you do? More important, what do you *not* do? I have found that you can't avoid office politics, but you can work around them. Rules to remember:

Observe your environment: Take careful mental notes of who doesn't like who, and why, through the unasked-for stories your co-workers will tell you. Don't ask any of them to elaborate—just listen. It's important for you to know about the co-worker conflicts and power struggles at play in the workplace so you can keep yourself out of them.

Judge people for yourself: You should already have learned that you can't believe everything you hear—this is especially true in the workplace. People will have motives for telling you certain things about others, and you will probably find that most of what you're told are half-truths or outright lies. You can listen to other people's warnings, but reserve your judgment. It would be a shame for you to dodge interacting with a potentially fantastic co-worker because of someone else's opinion.

Don't sip from the water cooler: Keep your lips locked during "water-cooler" type conversations, especially those that involve people's private lives. Otherwise, your feedback may be a part of the next water-cooler meeting.

Keep confidences: Secrets abound in the workplace, and your colleagues and boss will likely share all types of private information with you once they feel you can be trusted. Don't break their trust. In addition to losing the respect of the person whose secret you told, the person you blabbed to will know that you can't be trusted as well.

Don't take sides: You are likely to feel that someone is in the wrong in certain situations; however, unless you are directly involved in it, you shouldn't deliberately show whose side you are on. Don't write any letters stating your views on a personal work dispute; don't talk to your boss about your views; and don't tell the co-worker you feel is behaving badly that you think he or she is wrong. Showing that you are on one person's side automatically puts you on other people's bad sides, and you may not even know it.

Avoid playing the mediator: Unless you work in the HR department, you shouldn't attempt to help co-workers solve messy work disputes. You should even stay out of conflicts between people you consider good friends. Once you put yourself in the middle of them, you will find yourself taking sides.

Minimize your interaction with troublesome colleagues: Befriending co-workers who are always at the center of office politics will reflect badly upon you and create automatic enemies. Avoid people who seem to strategize about how to make others look bad or who use their influence to get people in trouble. Once you accidentally piss off these types of people, they may devise schemes to ruin your reputation as well.

Keep quiet when involved in a conflict: Colleagues will flock to you to get your take on a messy situation. Resist the urge to state your case, gain sympathy, or badmouth other people involved in the conflict because doing so will only worsen the chance of it getting resolved quickly and peaceably.

Diary of a Careeranista

TALIA NYE ON
CHECKING YOUR PROBLEMS AT THE DOOR

I once had a dear friend with whom I worked in El Paso, Texas. He was several years older than I, had been in the business a lot longer than I had, and was someone for whom I had a great deal of respect. He gave me several nuggets of wisdom during the years we worked together, but one of them has always stayed with me.

I occasionally was in the habit of letting my personal emotions surface at work. "How's it going, T?" they'd ask. "Oh, okay, but I have a headache," I'd say. Other responses were, "My boyfriend and I are fighting," or "My mother is driving me nuts," or "I can't stand this outfit I have on . . . " You get the picture.

However, I truly wasn't in a bad mood, nor was I at the point of needing crisis intervention. My flip answers were my way of humanizing myself, trying to make myself seem more like a "regular human being." Unfortunately, I was being perceived as a whining, self-indulgent priss who never felt good about herself. What I learned was that folks at work don't really want to hear about your personal life; they all have problems of their own. So, my friend's advice to me, advice I am happy to pass along, is to take a deep breath at the front door before you enter your place of work. Free your mind of whatever troubles you've left at home, put on your "work face" (or your "big-girl panties" as I have told my girls on occasion), and wear it with a smile! I know it sounds a little hokey, but this tactic has worked for me for the past 23 years.

If you want to, you can even make this a sort of ritual before you start work. For many years now, I have chosen to park a good distance from my job. I welcome the walk to and from the office for the brief solitude it gives me as I gear up or wind down from my day. I've found that often, I must consciously work to lose the attitude or the depression or the anger or the anxiety or the stress that hitched a ride with me to work that morning, and that this brief stroll gives me a bit more time to do so.

Once I enter the building, I know that I have to bring my A Game.

Hanging on to the handle of the door that leads to my office, I'll take a few cleansing breaths and tell myself, "Okay, time to focus. I'm at work now and I have a reputation to protect, a job to do, a career to advance," or words to that effect. Your mantra will be different from mine. We're different people and we have different problems. But remember, we all have problems and we all have to check them at the door.

Talia Nye is a former U.S. Air Force sergeant, television news journalist, and public relations professional. Presently, she is an assistant criminal district attorney in Bexar County, Texas, where she has worked since graduating from St. Mary's University School of Law in 2008. Talia lives in San Antonio, Texas, with her two daughters—Chelsea, who is studying stenography, and Courtney, a high school senior with an eye toward attending the United States Military Academy at West Point.

19

Succeeding
in Corporate America

America, be placed on notice. We know who we are.
We understand our collective power.
Following today we will act on that power.
—Maxine Waters, congresswoman

The term "corporate America" means different things to different people. To some individuals, corporate America creates thoughts of multinational corporations housed in sky-high buildings with more employees than can be counted. Others define corporate America by the environment it often fosters: competitive, demanding, and money-driven. Yet to women, the term corporate America may bring to mind even less appealing images. When many of us envision corporate America—particularly its upper echelons and boardrooms—we visualize an environment that's dominated by men. And we think of it as a somewhat unwelcoming place—a place that has traditionally been harder for us to enter and succeed in than our male counterparts.

Nevertheless, as a larger number of big companies have begun to embrace gender diversity and proactively attract, hire, and promote women, more of us have gravitated toward working in a corporate environment, or one in which few female faces can be found. And in the many cases in which it was clear women still weren't wanted, our more daring sisters busted their way in.

Working for larger businesses can provide more money, more prestige, and more opportunities to have a greater impact in one's chosen industry than working for smaller and less recognized companies. However, despite the positives, there are still aspects of working in corporate and male-dominated environments that women may find disheartening, particularly those eyeing positions ranging from manager to CEO.

Issue 1—It Gets Lonelier as You Work Your Way Up

If you walk inside the building of most major U.S. corporations, you are bound to be greeted by many smiling women, possibly leaving you to think they run the place. Yet appearances are truly deceiving—unfortunately, they will more than likely be support staff and junior management. A sea of male faces is what you will likely find should you make your way past the receptionist desk and small offices and into the boardrooms and big corner offices, where the company's leading executives dwell.

It's just a matter of numbers. Although women make up nearly half of the labor force and comprise 51 percent of management and professional positions, they hold only 14 percent of executive officer positions at Fortune 500 companies, according to a study by Catalyst, a research and advisory organization working to advance women in business. As a result, there are fewer and fewer women the higher one looks up a company's totem pole. So, once women get to a coveted top spot, they often find it's a lonely spot too, as the majority of their peers are now men. And African-American, Latina, Asian, and virtually all non-white women may find themselves feeling totally isolated when they arrive to the C-suite because of the lack of racial diversity.

Issue 2—Women Receive Less Rewards & Recognition

The notion that women have to work harder and smarter than their male counterparts is considered a fact of life for those working in corporate America and male-dominated fields. According to the Center for American Progress, the wage gap widens with age and accumulates over time, thus women in upper management are even less likely than those starting out to be making what their male peers earn. In fact, female chief executives are paid only 69 percent as much as male executives, on average, according to a study conducted by the Institute for Women's Policy Research. Other studies have found that women on executive management paths don't get promoted as fast as their male counterparts—which helps to explain why it's lonelier at the top.

Racism, like sexism, is also still an issue in corporate America. African-American women, Latinas, and others from historically disenfranchised racial groups tend to feel even more overlooked and disrespected than their white and Asian female peers. Despite their education and status in the company, they may find that their intellect and ability to perform are always under question, as if affirmative action or a bad hiring decision is what landed them the job. For example, in a study conducted by The League of Black Women, 48 percent of black female respondents said negative stereotypes of and prejudice toward black women continue to have a profound negative impact on their well-being and global positioning. Findings such as this demonstrate that it can be even more difficult for women of color to obtain the level of success they desire.

Issue 3—It Doesn't Embrace Gender & Cultural Differences

Ever wonder why there aren't more women's stalls or restrooms in the buildings you enter? I am totally guessing here, but I bet it's because men dominate the architecture and design industry and it just doesn't occur to them that we use the restroom more frequently than they do. Well, much more than extra restrooms are missing from male-dominated workplaces, including norms and policies that acknowledge gender and racial differences. Researchers have found that one of the reasons it is harder for women to succeed in male-dominated industries and corporate environments is because of the extra responsibilities we have during motherhood and the lack of company policies in place to support working mothers. Many women actually report feeling guilty when they become pregnant and worrying about their jobs because of the negative impact it may have on their career progression. They fear that they will be seen as less productive and company-focused than their male peers and non-mothers and are scared they might get kicked off the corporate ladder should they need to take extra time off during pregnancy, choose to stay home with their child longer than company policy allots, or need to rework their work schedules. And unfortunately, women have reason to be apprehensive: studies have found that mothers are less likely to be promoted than non-mothers. Surely if men were both the primary caregivers and breadwinners—and more women were in leadership roles to set company policy—there would be a company-wide understanding at businesses everywhere that people should be able to take care of their families and business too, and policies would exist to make juggling both easier.

In regard to cultural differences, because corporate America is largely controlled by white males, they define what is acceptable regarding everything from speech, to dress, to hairstyles. Some can appreciate cultural expression, but others feel that if they don't speak it, if they don't wear it, and if they can't comb it a certain way, then you shouldn't either. Even some women feel that way. An editor for *Glamour* magazine once came under fire for saying that locs and afros were a "real no no" in a corporate environment, a comment she made during a presentation to female lawyers titled "Do's and Don'ts of Corporate Fashion." Opinions like this can pose a problem for African-Americans and other people of color who want to fit in without forsaking their cultural backgrounds.

Issue 4—It's Too Money Driven & Competitive

While all businesses are in some way money driven, larger corporations tend to place an even higher importance on earning certain figures given that they are responsible to so many people, especially investors. Thus, the bottom line may be the only line employees are expected to care about, which can result in an even more stressful environment. And as women, we tend to want to know that our work—no matter what it is—is meaningful in some way. Yes, we go to work to make money, but that's not the driving force.

A money-driven environment combined with a male-dominated environment almost can't help but be über competitive, another possible turn off. Many of us have been raised to compete against ourselves, do the best we can, and of course, to share. Men, however, don't receive these messages. Instead, through team sports, parental raising, the media, and, some would argue—their male makeup—men are taught that if someone is going to win, it better be them.

The problem is, in very competitive, male-dominated environments, everyone is trying to climb the success ladder at the same time, and some people will pull you down to beat you to the top. This leads to tension among employees, who feel like they always have to be ahead of the next person. Work-life balance then becomes impossible as they toil themselves to exhaustion to do so. This is problematic because the "anytime, anywhere" performance model is irreconcilable with women's double burden as children's primary caregivers, as McKinsey & Company, a global management consulting firm, stressed in a report titled *Women Matter: Gender Diversity, A Corporate Performance Driver.*

Lastly, for women and minorities working in competitive, mostly male environments, there is yet another conundrum: they may feel pitted against each other. Women may assume their main competition is other women given that there are so few opportunities for them to advance, and the same goes for people of color. So, instead of being able to confide in and be encouraged by those who share their same gender or ethnicity, women and minorities may adopt a "crabs in the barrel" mentality that actually works against their advancement.

SWIMMING IN THE CORPORATE ENVIRONMENT

As a woman, you can't afford to be oblivious to the fact that corporate America's environment basically

HRinsider Tip: Pursue and be willing to move into corporate line positions with profit and loss responsibilities. These positions are most valued by companies because they directly contribute to the bottom line.

—from the report *Risk and Reward: Black Women Leading Out on a Limb* works against you, not for you. This doesn't mean you can't climb the corporate ladder, shatter the glass ceilings you may face, and do as well or better than your male counterparts. You can do this and more, as countless women have already proven. However, you will need a bold, driven mindset and an excellent career strategy to match. As part of your career strategy:

Have a Plan

If your goal is to climb the corporate ladder at the company you're working for then you'll need to know how to climb it. It may not be a typical straight ladder—parts of it might be broken off and it may zig-zag. So have a plan before you start climbing. You'll first need to know what rung on the ladder you're starting from and how many steps you need to climb to get to where you want to be. Find out what the people in the positions you desire did to get to where they are. Where did they start on the ladder? How many years did it take them to get the position they have? How many times did they get promoted? What was special about them? To whom are they connected? What advice can they give you? Knowing these things will help you map out a plan to get you to the rung on the ladder you desire. Even more important, through finding the answers to these types of questions you will learn more about what it takes to succeed in your company overall.

As part of your plan, also:

HRinsider Tip: The best way to stand out is to take on the more challenging, perhaps less attractive, projects. If you show success completing them, senior personnel at your company will take notice and consider you for future important work.

—Terri Tierney-Clark, founder of TheNewCareerist.com

Further your education: Focus on increasing your skill set and industry knowledge by taking additional courses in your field or earning an advanced degree—if having one in your field is truly valuable and won't put you deeper into debt. Doing so will better position you for upper management opportunities at your present company. It will also make you more competitive should you decide to lend your talents to another entity.

Improve your leadership abilities: Apply for your company's leadership development program, if one is available. Beyond improving your management capabilities, this will put you on the company's radar and in touch with potential mentors and sponsors.

Make company leadership aware of your accomplishments and ambition: Too often, women hope that higher ups will see their good work and thus keep them in mind for promotions and leadership opportunities. However, you can't afford to wait to be noticed. Keep your managers updated on your accomplishments and inform them of the career path you have planned. This doesn't mean saying, "I intend to be the CEO one day," but just that you desire to grow with the company in your current position and subsequent ones, and that your ultimate goal is to be a key decision maker.

Now You Tell Me?

From kindergarten on, girls are taught that if they do a good job, they will be recognized for their work and be promoted accordingly. Unfortunately, success in the business world doesn't work this way. The right people need to know about your accomplishments if you want get ahead.

—Connie Glaser, women's leadership expert

Expressing your desires will keep you on management's radar should big or small opportunities arise. However, it's not just your immediate supervisors who should know you're the one to watch. Managers in other departments should know your name and so should the company's top executives—even if the only time you get to give your name and share your aspirations is in the elevator. Asking to be a part of cross-functional teams, attending networking events, and just introducing yourself to company heavyweights can get you noticed. Once someone notices you and asks what your ambitions are, don't be shy. And if they don't ask, tell them anyway!

DEVELOPING THE EXECUTIVE MINDSET

Researchers for McKinsey & Company, a global management consulting firm, conducted interviews with 200 female executives to learn more about what it takes for women to "make it to the top." The women shared a common set of foundational strengths that fueled their growth:

Robust work ethic: Willingness to consistently go above and beyond to get the job done.

Results orientation: Relentless focus on performance and improving the bottom line.

Resilience: Perseverance in the face of adversity and tremendous grit to stay the course.

Persistence in getting feedback: Working to continually improve their own performance by actively seeking out their blind spots and regarding feedback with a growth mind-set.

Team leadership: Being able to inspire, motivate, and lead teams.

—*Used with permission*

Adapt to the Environment

It can truly seem as if men are from Mars and women are from Venus in the workplace too, not just the romantic world. And unfortunately, because men often control the environment, you may find yourself having to slightly adjust the way you act and the things you say in order to excel. For example, men are more likely than women to share their accomplishments and state their desires. This places women at a clear disadvantage. According to research from McKinsey & Company, one of the keys to success lies in the ability to promote oneself and to be assertive about one's performance and ambitions. Women, notes the organization, tend to minimize their own contributions. For example, in a survey of MBA students McKinsey & Company conducted, 70 percent of female respondents rated their own performance as *equivalent* to that of their co-workers, while 70 percent of men rated themselves *higher* than their co-workers. It's not as if the male MBA students actually performed better than the female MBA students; as men, they were just not shy about tooting their own horn and saying they were better than their competition. Another disadvantage: Women tend to be less competitive than men, less willing to take risks, and uncomfortable handling conflicts head-on—traits needed in corporate, male-dominated environments.

Of course, just as the sexes have been found to communicate and think somewhat differently in romantic relationships, so have they in professional relationships, as shown in the table "Gender-Based Perceptions in the Workplace" at the end of this chapter. To understand your male colleagues better, you should seek to understand gender differences and adjust your habits as you see fit.

Another way in which you may have to change your *modus operandi* is by being less sensitive. If you are perceived as being a "cry baby," this can further alienate you from your male colleagues. This can equate to you not being placed in positions of leadership, as the people you will most likely be leading are men. To be clear, being less sensitive does not mean putting up with sexist or discriminatory jokes; it means not taking everything so personally. Show that you can accept criticism without being offended, be sarcastic with the best of them, and handle a joke—no matter how lame.

Now You Tell Me?

Eliminate caution when you are getting ready to speak up, when you're in a meeting, when you're talking one on one to somebody. Too often, women don't speak up if they don't think they have the right thing to say or if they don't think what they're saying is significant. The result can be that they don't say much of anything and then people assume they don't have anything to say and they lose credibility.

— Kerrie Halmi, founder of Platinum Exchange, a women's leadership program

---

If you are a woman of color, you may find yourself feeling pressured to adapt to predominantly male corporate environments in other ways as well. Given that corporate America does not generally embrace cultural differences, you may feel you have to "leave your culture at home" to make your co-workers and management more accepting of you. For example, for Latina women who speak Spanish, this may mean not speaking in Spanish to other Spanish speakers on the job. For black women, this may mean not wearing your hair in certain natural styles. This is not to say that you have to or should change anything about yourself in an effort to make others more comfortable. I personally won't work for a company that makes me hesitant to say the word "black" aloud, or makes me feel the need to straighten my hair. Whether you choose to conform in such ways is a personal choice.

Now You Tell Me?

A sponsor adds legitimacy to you as he or she puts her reputation to work for you. You normally do not spend a lot of time with a sponsor; it is not needed. You only need to make sure that your sponsor knows what you are accomplishing and that he or she feels comfortable and secure in "vouching" for you.

—Wilka Toppins, former Fortune 100 VP & founder of Ask The Corporate Latina

---

Get Sponsored

While having a career mentor—someone who advises you about your career—is critical to your success, having a sponsor will put you on the fast track to that success. A sponsor is an individual of influence within your company who is able to help guide your career through creating opportunities for you. As the Center for Work Life Policy described them in a press release about women's lack of sponsorship: "Sponsors advocate and facilitate critical career moves. Just as President Obama did for Elena Kagan, and John McCain for Sarah Palin, sponsors go out on a limb for their protégés, providing stretch opportunities, forming critical connections, and promoting visibility." A study published in the *Harvard Business Review* on the subject, "The Sponsor Effect: Breaking Through the Last Glass Ceiling," found that one of the reasons men get promoted at higher rates than women is because they have some one higher up looking out for them. And, as other research has found, while women tend to have plenty of mentors, they rarely have sponsors.

To find a sponsor, you should consider with whom within your company's leadership will be the most appropriate person to align yourself. Obviously, the company president will likely be way out of reach, but what about VPs, assistant VPs, and division managers? You can put yourself in their path by attending corporate functions, volunteering for assignments they are working on, or being bold and contacting them directly via email or phone. However, there is no need in your introduction to mention the word "sponsorship," as this somewhat new term may throw them off or be construed as something else. Instead, discuss your desire to be mentored by a higher-level exec because of your ambition and career aspirations. As the mentorship develops, it can be shaped into a sponsorship in which you are able to ask for direct help in achieving your goals.

Look and Act the Part

If your goal is to be a vice president, then you don't start dressing and acting like one the day you get hired for that position; you start now, regardless of how far down the totem pole you are. Looking polished and exuding confidence is key to being considered as someone with leadership potential, and you just never know who is watching you.

In regard to attire, it is worth it to invest in quality professional clothing that complements your shape and makes you feel good. While you don't have to go to work wearing a two-piece suit, you should never be ashamed to be seen should you be introduced to an executive. This also means checking to make sure your clothes are not too tight or skimpy. Women often have to work extra hard to gain the respect of their male peers, and wearing sexually suggestive clothing doesn't help our cause. When in doubt, always err on the conservative side and look to women who are respected within the company for clues on how to dress.

In regard to projecting confidence, there is no use in looking like an exec if your attitude and mannerisms reflect someone unsure of herself. People are naturally attracted to those who are comfortable with who they are, know what they want, and aren't afraid to go out and get it.

Gather Support

Being one of a few women or people of color can lead to feelings of alienation, in turn, stressing you out and making you perform poorly. And no one wants to spend hours of their day feeling vulnerable and lonesome. However, chances are that your situation isn't half as bad as you think. Feelings of alienation are strengthened when you assume that your male colleagues or those within a different racial group will be less friendly and supportive of you because of your gender or ethnicity. However, when working in a predominantly male environment, or one dominated by a certain ethnic group, you may have to go out of your way to reach out to your co-workers, and that's okay. Through asking colleagues to lunch, attending networking and team sporting events, and even dreaded office parties, you can be proactive about getting to know your colleagues on a more personal level, thus opening the door for good working relationships.

If you don't find enough support on the job, then seek it after hours. Build up a support network of other professionals, family, and friends that reinforce your sense of adequacy and make you feel more secure about your position at work as a woman.

GENDER-BASED PERCEPTIONS
IN THE WORKPLACE

	FEMININE	MASCULINE
Organizational structure	participative (see colleagues as complementary)	hierarchical (see colleagues as potential competition)
Focus of interpersonal attention	process (care about how people treat each other in carrying out work)	outcome (care about "where they stand" in relation to others)
Operating style	interactional (interact to connect, arrive at understandings)	transactional (interact to pass information and give directions)
Problem-solving style	intuitive (trust instincts; will provide proof/ explanation as necessary)	linear (based on methodical thinking; will not trust intuition until proof is presented)
Individual work style	collaborative (see work as part of a whole; discuss and review with colleagues)	independent (see work as a separate piece; complete work without the "help" of others)
Management style	supportive (seek to aid, support, facilitate, and provide comfort, meaning, and rewards)	directive (seek to test, direct, organize, and provide challenges, goals, and incentives)
View of work-related conflict	disruptive (seek to create harmony; view negative comments as unproductive)	normal (accept a level of conflict as inevitable; view negative comments as normal part of work)

—Used with permission by Dr. Anne Litwin, first published in *Managing in the Age of Change: Essential Skills to Manage Today's Workforce*

20

Attaining
Work-Life Balance

You cannot really be first-rate
at your work if your work is all you are.
—Anna Quindlen, journalist

I t was 1 a.m. on a Wednesday, and I was wide awake. My eyelids were heavy but my mind wouldn't rest. I kept thinking about all the work that had to be done, how much my boss was counting on me, and how good sleep would feel when it finally came. But my problem wasn't insomnia; it was actually much worse. I was employed by a company that repeatedly had me working until the wee hours of the morning—despite my 9 to 5 schedule. So, I drank another cup of coffee, realizing there was little chance I would be counting sheep before sunrise.

During this period of my life, I experienced what can only be described as "work-life imbalance," and so did my co-workers. We went into work not knowing when we would get off, skipped lunch or scarfed down something at our desks, and spent the workday trying our best to avoid looking at the time because it just didn't matter. We had tons of work to do, not enough people or resources to do it, and the expectation that regardless of these and other problems, we would figure it out. And we did, during regular work hours, evenings, and weekends.

I was getting paid hourly at the time (unlike some of my very peeved salaried colleagues), and at first I was happy to clock all those extra hours. However, I soon realized that a fatter paycheck was lousy compensation for the mental and physical stress I was experiencing. I arrived home each day exhausted, hoping that tomorrow would not be so bad. I talked much less to family and friends because I wanted to go to bed early, and when I did speak to them it was primarily to complain about my job. While once I had exercised five times a week, I couldn't find the time most days to fit it into my schedule—without swapping exercise for more sleep, that is. So, like many cubicle warriors whose butts are tied to a chair all day, I began packing on pounds from a lack of physical activity.

The situation my co-workers and I found ourselves in would have been easier to understand or tolerate if our workload and hours were not consistently heavy, or if we had been given any indication of this before being hired. We could have even made sense of our predicament if abnormally long hours were normal for companies like ours, but we were producing books, not saving lives like nurses or police officers. Patient but proactive, we addressed the issue with our manager individually, whom we expected was also tired of burning midnight oil, paper, and wood. But she, a workaholic by nature, was actually half of the problem. While she acknowledged that the way we operated wasn't exactly "normal," she basically told us to suck it up because "that's just how things are at this company."

Now You Tell Me?

Nearly one-third of 1,714 employed adults surveyed by the American Psychological Association in 2012 reported having difficulty balancing work and family life.

After my own fruitless conversation with my manager, not one week went by in which I didn't think about quitting. However, I stayed with the company for eight months. It wasn't so much because I absolutely needed the job or couldn't find something else; I actually felt bad for wanting to quit. Quitting seemed like an indication of ungratefulness, inflexibility, laziness, and a lack of perseverance and ambition. After all, I knew that employees throughout the United States worked crazy hours, so there wasn't a conspiracy at my company. But what really kept me from leaving sooner is that like many professionals, the American work ethic had been deeply ingrained in my psyche. My family, teachers, other professionals, and the media taught me that real go-getters prove themselves on the job by coming in early and staying late; by putting the company before themselves and doing what is asked to get the job done, no matter what; and by making as many sacrifices as necessary to have a successful career in which they bring home the big bucks. However, I've learned that there truly is such a thing as working *too hard* and sacrificing *too much*. The question is, when do you cross the line from working for a living to living to work, and what can you do about it?

4 SIGNS OF WORK-LIFE IMBALANCE

1. *You are mildly or all-out depressed:* This is a sure sign that your work-life balance is out of order, unless something else is giving you the blues. Trouble is, when people think of depression, they imagine someone crying uncontrollably all the time, contemplating suicide, and being unable to get out of bed, much less to work. But most people are quite functional when they are depressed (I am), and go to work with fake smiles on their faces. So forget about the movie-like signs of depression (but if you have them, seek help immediately!). Instead, check this list culled in part from the Mayo Clinic and CDC:

- Feeling "empty," anxious, and/or irritable
- Feeling helpless and/or worthless
- Sleeping too much or too little
- Having no interest in activities you used to enjoy when you do have the time for them
- Feeling fatigued
- Experiencing physical symptoms like headaches and digestive problems that started after work became a huge drag

2. You feel and/or look awful: The demands of your job leave little time for exercise or not enough energy for it. You also rarely have time to cook dinner or prepare lunches for the next day, so you find yourself making bad food choices or not eating enough. Your lack of exercise and poor diet are making you lethargic, and you're either gaining or losing too much weight. Worse, the stress of work is causing headaches, insomnia, joint pains, or other seemingly minor health problems that you hope are temporary. If you check your blood pressure—and you should—it might be higher than 120/80, or whatever reading is normal for you. You also find yourself looking a mess. Whereas once you would not have stepped out of the house without appearing at least somewhat polished, now you just throw on clothes and head out the door without checking a mirror.

Now You Tell Me?

Women whose work is highly stressful have a 40 percent increased risk of heart disease compared with their less-stressed colleagues, according to findings from a Harvard University health study.

---

3. Your social life sucks: It has been ages since you went to a happy hour, much less had a chat longer than 10 minutes with a girlfriend, and you haven't talked to your parents in so long that they think you're mad at them. Because of your hectic schedule—or lack of a regular one—you avoid making definite plans for evenings or weekends because you know you may have to cancel them. You find yourself telling people "I'll let you know" about everything from weddings and birthday parties to dinner and the movies. And lunch? Forget about it.

4. Your love/family life sucks: If you're single, the only men you see are in the office and you don't have time for online dating, so your boyfriend search has been put on hold. If you snagged a boyfriend or tied the knot before your life became imbalanced, then you are begging your sweetie not to get sour with you. On the rare occasions when you are not working—or going on a tirade about how much you hate your job—you just want to watch something funny on TV or sleep. If he complains about never seeing you or says you are obsessed with your job, you take out your frustration on him and retort that he just has a problem with successful women. If you have kids, you feel utterly guilt ridden about the lack of quality time you are spending with them, and your mouth hurts from constantly saying, "Mommy has to work."

Once you have confirmed that you suffer from work-life imbalance, you have to find the appropriate treatment. As with any malady, various treatment options are available and the one you need will depend on how ill you are. Unfortunately, a combination of treatments are often needed to find and sustain relief for this particular affliction. Also, remember that it takes time to see if your treatment program works, and treatment may have to be started up again just as you think you are all better.

WORK-LIFE IMBALANCE TREATMENTS

1. Stop overextending yourself: Work-life imbalance is often self-imposed because of our desire to prove to others—and ourselves—that we have the drive and work ethic needed to excel at our company and/or in our careers. Thus, you may be taking on much more than you can handle or taking the whole "arrive early, leave late" mantra too seriously. This inadvertently creates the expectation that you can be called upon to work *whenever* and with a crazy workload. From time to time, *when you truly have time*, offer to take on additional work. However, do not get into the habit of volunteering for extra assignments every time you have a bit of free time, or always saying yes to an extra project or

HRinsider Tip: If you realize you've got a serious threat to your work-life nirvana on your hands, it's time to speak up. Your boss isn't a mind reader, so neither mental messages nor passive aggressive emails are going to work. This doesn't mean you need to walk in, guns blazing—this just means you need to have your facts checked and laid out.

—Megan Broussard, founder of ProfessionGal.com

duty. Focus on your regular work and do it exceptionally well. Your aim is to be a super woman, not Superwoman.

2. *Manage your time better:* It may be that your own processes are causing you to work longer and harder. A tell-tale sign of this is if you are the only one who constantly has to work late to finish assignments. Consider your workday and responsibilities, and see where you may be wasting time. Do you surf the web half the day in between daydreaming, texting, and chatting with co-workers? Do you tend to procrastinate on projects and then find yourself behind the eight ball to get them done? If so, focus on working faster and more efficiently so you can get home at a decent hour. If you admire a particular co-worker for his or her ability to "get in and get out," ask about the strategies he or she employs to achieve work-life balance.

3. *Request that your time be managed better:* The people we report to are often in charge of how we spend our time, dictating when and how certain things should be done. Sometimes the systems they have set up are colossal time wasters. You should speak up if this is the case. You will be doing yourself, your co-workers, and probably the person toying with your time a huge favor; however, you must have a solution or two ready when you address this issue. Obviously, if the person thought there was a better way, he or she would be using it. Ask to speak to your supervisor in private and express your concerns, be it repeatedly having to work later than anticipated or having a consistently heavy workload.

During this polite conversation, you will explain that you are more than willing to do what's necessary for the team or company to excel—as you hope your hard work has shown—but you believe that work life could be made easier *for you and others* if a few practices were adopted. Then, outline your proposed solutions, making sure to stress how they can be used or tweaked to also help others, and in turn promote a better working environment.

4. *Ask for re-clarification of what's expected:* Chances are that you were told you would be working 9 to 5 but have never been able to leave before 6 p.m. Or, what was described as the "typical workload"

is anything but. This is because during the interview, employers often tell you what the position should be like instead of how it actually is. If what you were expecting the workload or hours to be is nothing like your current reality, then discuss this in private with your supervisor. Perhaps adjustments can be made.

Example of what to say: "I'd like to get clarity about my expected work schedule. I know that while my schedule and those of my colleagues is 9-to-5, things often come up that make working later a necessity. However, I wanted to know if working past 5 p.m. is now the expectation because we're frequently asked to work to 7:30 p.m. and sometimes much later. I ask because I had planned my schedule around a 9 to 5 workday and I keep finding myself having to cancel other important commitments."

If you don't have a new schedule that you knew nothing about, then your supervisor will likely just explain the need for the extra hours—either apologetically or with an attitude. In either case, you should then repeat your desire to have the schedule you expected, and ask if you can both brainstorm ways in which you can get all your work done within the regular timeframe. And again, reiterate that you have no problem working later on occasions when it just can't be helped. In the case of an overflowing workload, follow the same strategy for reducing extra hours.

5. *Set and stick to boundaries:* As a friend of a good friend once said, "Boundaries are freedom," and this is certainly the case with work. While boundaries should be set as early as possible, it's never too late to draw a line in your work sand that shows supervisors and co-workers that a happy work/life is important to you. Your boundaries are created by letting people know this, both verbally and through your actions.

To get this point across, as needed, politely but unapologetically say things like, "Barring the occasional emergency, I need to leave the office by 7 p.m. so that I don't break my other commitments"; or "I can work weekends as needed, of course, but in general they are full of personal commitments and activities I've planned."

If you will notice, all of those sample sentences used to create boundaries have the word "commitment" in it. This is because you don't want to downplay all the commitments you have outside of work—even if they are just sleeping, eating, and watching TV (which you would never say, of course). Just as your supervisors expect you to honor your agreed-upon work commitments, so should your commitments outside of work be honored.

When it comes to your actions, you have to have guts. If your workday is supposed to end at 5 p.m., then leave no more than 20 minutes after that unless you have been asked to stay or something just can't wait until tomorrow to get done. Don't wait for other people to leave before you so that you don't look bad. No one wants to be the first person out the door but somebody has to. Do everyone a favor and go!

Just as important, there should be no reason why you're answering work phone calls and emails outside of regular work hours (unless your job specifically demands it). So, ignore both and then only respond if the voicemail or email indicates there is an emergency, and even then let some time pass if you can. You don't want to create or feed the expectation that you can be easily reached on your off days and will drop what you're doing. When and if you're asked why you didn't respond, say you weren't checking emails or voicemails because it was the evening or weekend. And, going back to strategy three about getting re-clarification, ask if this is now something that is expected of you. If it is, explain that you would like to find a way in which you can do everything needed of you during your regular work hours, barring emergencies or periods when the workload is unusually heavy.

Now, I know you're scared. You're thinking you run the risk of being looked upon as inflexible and not a team player, which is true. However, just as likely, you and your time will be respected more. If your work is top-notch but the boundaries you set are held against you, then you may need to look for another job, which brings us to treatment number 6.

6. *Quit after all effort has been made to improve work-life balance:* It's quite possible that the culture of your company works entirely against work-life balance, or your boss is a workaholic and seriously expects

everyone else to be, too. Unless you are in a leadership position or pals with your boss, there will be virtually nothing you can do to remedy this. Employers and HR are the ones who set formal and informal policies that affect work-life balance, such as the ability to telecommute, vary work hours, and call in sick without fear of being fired. And your boss sets the workload and expectations. If it's clear that everyone works too much, and there is nothing that will ever to be done about it, then you can choose to suck it up or seek to work for a company that will let you have a job and a life. It's less stressful to look for a job when you have one, so start looking now. As part of this job search, pay attention to what the company says about work-life balance.

Now You Tell Me?

Commit to doing just one thing this week or weekend to begin to put balance back in your life. Call a friend, go to a movie with your family, buy a book, sign up for that course you've been putting off, or spend the day working on your favorite craft. Do this every week for a year and you'll be amazed at all the life you've put back into your days.

—Shari McGuire, author of *Take Back Your Time: 101 Simple Tips to Shrink Your Work-Week and Conquer the Chaos in Your Life*

As you start and try out your treatments, you will inevitably be reminded that you are not the only one struggling to achieve work-life balance. Americans work harder and longer hours than professionals in most other industrialized nations. However, unlike the majority of unsatisfied and tired Americans, you don't have to accept this as normal. Your company and boss do not own you, and your mental, emotional, and physical health should not be compromised at the expense of a paycheck. You deserve to and can construct a work life that, while not perfect, makes you feel good about yourself and gives you the means to enjoy life more.

WORK-LIFE IMBALANCE FLAGS
YOU MISSED DURING THE INTERVIEW

- The employer insinuated that it is great you are young and single.
- The employer had mounds of paperwork on his or her desk and the phone wouldn't stop ringing.
- The employer stressed that the workload is heavy.
- The employer asked if you could work weekends, even though they wouldn't be in your normal schedule.
- The employer asked if you mind working late.
- Your potential co-workers looked like the walking dead and there were empty coffee cups on their desks.
- Your potential co-workers looked extremely busy and talked insanely fast.
- The potential co-workers you talked to hinted or told you outright that the workload or hours are ridiculous.

21

Losing Your Job Without Losing Yourself

As we drive along this road called life,
occasionally a gal will find herself a little lost.
And when that happens, I guess she has to let go of the
coulda, shoulda, woulda, buckle up and just keep going.
—Carrie Bradshaw from *Sex and the City*

The first job I was ever "relieved" from was as a concession stand clerk at a one-dollar movie theater. I was 14 and technically was not old enough to have the job. But that's not why I got fired. I was let go for eating a hot dog. I was closing with my co-workers and we were supposed to throw the leftover hot dogs away; we were forbidden to eat them. Back then, I couldn't stand to abide by rules that didn't make sense to me, so, at my co-workers' urging (who said they wouldn't tell), I ate one. Of course, the same co-worker who said she ate them all the time told the manager the next day and I was fired as soon as I got to work. I was stunned about losing my job over a piece of meat and bread, but not really upset. After all, I didn't really have to work, and I wasn't supposed to be working anyway. I went home and enjoyed the rest of my day.

Eight years and probably a half dozen retail, clerical, and telemarketing jobs later, I was fired again. Yet this time I nearly wrecked my car as I went home because I couldn't see through my tears.

I was fired for asking my boss, publisher of the newspaper I edited, for money to pay for a root canal. I know it sounds weird, but it's true. My former boss, however, has always insisted that I quit, and I think he honestly believes this. So, to be fair, I'll just say that I got fired/quit, though the story behind why this happened still sounds far-fetched and we don't agree on that either.

After going to the dentist, I discovered that I needed not one, but two root canals, and very soon or else both teeth would need to be pulled. Now, why I let it get that bad is another story, but two root canals is what I needed.

After contemplating how I was going to pay for two root canals totaling about $1,000, I decided that I should ask my boss for the money. Here was my rationale: My boss was not providing health insurance; it seemed like I was due a raise (which I was sure my boss couldn't afford, but I thought he might be able to afford two root canals); and I had just been nominated for a national writing award. After convincing myself that my logic was sound, asking him to pay for two root canals, or even one, didn't seem like such a big deal. I couldn't have been more wrong.

One day, my boss called from the sister office in a different city. He sounded all chipper, which everyone knew could change at any moment, so I decided to ask him while he was in a good mood. After explaining how my teeth ached and how I needed a root canal (I had decided to ask for just one initially), I asked him for the money as sweetly as I possibly could. Well, he laughed at me and then asked what made me think he should pay for my root canal with his money. I looked at the phone kind of funny when he said that because I couldn't tell whether he was being serious or playful. My boss was known for helping employees out with personal things, from paying their rent to getting a car (the latter he had done for me). So, I decided he was being playful.

After explaining my rationale to him, he became very quiet. Then he asked how much of a raise I wanted. I told him I was asking for money for a root canal and not a raise, at which point he just asked me again about the raise. I let out a sigh and decided to play along just in case he really was considering giving me a raise. Before we hung up, he said he'd talk to his wife, co-owner of the newspaper, about it and call me back.

Early the next morning he called me at the office and he didn't sound upbeat like the day before. He sounded pissed, and I knew that when he sounded like that I wasn't going to have a very good workday. He started half-yelling at me about how he couldn't believe I had the audacity to ask for a raise when he was already paying me more than he should (which was so not true, by the way!). Halfway through the one-way conversation I felt nauseous. Was I losing my mind, or had I just asked him for a root canal? I tried to explain that I had never asked for a raise, but he told me that he knew what I had said. At that point, I knew there was no point in arguing.

Next, I unfolded the latest newspaper onto my desk like he asked me to and began going through it page by page as he told me what a bad job I was doing and why. Now I was nauseous and speechless. Less than two weeks ago he had been bragging on me to all of his colleagues about how good I was and how I was nominated for this special award. And now I wasn't even worth the money he gave me?

After berating me for a few more minutes, he said he'd have to think about whether he wanted to even "keep me" now, and then he hung up the phone. I stared at my computer and started crying. I didn't know what was going on.

Later that day the newspaper's co-manager told me my boss had called him the night before sounding all upset and saying that I had demanded a raise. The co-manager said he was probably just having a lot of money problems right now, and that my just saying the word "money" had set him off. My boss called a couple more times that day to talk to the co-manager about me and the "raise I demanded." He didn't want to talk to me at all, so I sat by helplessly as he went on and on about my lousy work and how he couldn't afford to give me a raise, much less the salary I was already receiving. Not wanting to get himself snapped at, the co-manager didn't do anything but listen as he went on with his verbal rampage.

When the last phone call from him came in that day, I was exhausted from worrying and wondering how this had happened and why. My boss had gone left field on various people, but I never dreamed that he'd be like that toward me. The co-manager told me he was pretty sure my boss was going to let me go, and he asked me what I wanted to do. I told him that I really couldn't see myself working there anymore after the unprofessional way I had been treated.

Still, when I left work I expected my boss to call me on my cell phone and talk the matter out with me. Or, I expected his wife, who had been like an adopted mother to me, to call me and ask what was going on. But I got a call from neither of them. The next morning the co-manager came into my office, sat in a chair with my last check in his lap looking all sad, and told me that my boss wanted me to pack my things and leave immediately. He had told him what I said about not being sure I wanted to work there anymore. I was angry at the co-manager, who I thought could have done or said more to save my job and who had further thrown me under the bus by relaying something I thought I said in confidence. I was also dumfounded, and so was the rest of the staff. They thought it was a joke at first.

After the initial shock wore off, depression set in. A man who had given me my first real job out of college, and whom I had known and worked for since my senior year in high school, had just had someone else tell me I was fired. This was a man who I also loved and respected and who I thought loved and respected me. And to top it off, his wife, who I just knew would straighten things out, didn't call me or return my phone calls. I just didn't get it. And even though I have since made amends with them both, and found out the situation was just as confusing and frustrating to them, I still can't figure out how that whole ordeal ever happened.

As you can tell by my story, getting fired or laid off can be a very traumatic experience. The ordeal is hard to shake off for individuals starting out in their careers, as well as those who have been working their way up in their chosen profession. Psychologists acknowledge that losing a job can cause as much stress as losing a loved one because people tend to define themselves by their occupation. Jobs provide more than just a steady paycheck. Along with the money comes a sense of belonging, security, and pride. Those special intangibles can be lost in a matter of moments. The added financial stress that job loss puts people through only makes matters worse. But despite this, you can't lose yourself to job loss. People from all walks of life have taken this bullet, survived, and even been better off because of the experience— you can too. The following are suggestions for dealing with job loss and getting your career and life back on track.

Now You Tell Me?

You may have lost your job, but you have not lost your skills, capabilities, and potential along with it. Remember, in these moments of transition, to remove the shame, blame, guilt, or meaning around this momentary pause in your career trajectory. Success is rarely a straight line; rather, it's a series of jagged ones, up and down and often slow-moving. However, when viewed from beginning to end, we see major progress, even if the road has not been clear of obstacles.

—Laura Labovich, founder of The Career Strategy Group

LOOK AHEAD

The best way for you to bounce back is to look ahead. You lost your job, but while doing so, you have gained a chance to seek other opportunities—opportunities you never would have known existed had you not lost your job. So resist the urge to feel sorry for yourself, dwell on whatever you've lost, or be angry with the company or your former boss for the situation you're in. You have to concentrate on making a comeback and you can't do this if you're filled with regret, anger, or sadness. Remember that the only person who can turn your career around is you. And the only person standing in your way of success is you. Once you've surveyed what you've lost, discover what you have to gain. Make the decision to make your job loss one of the best things that ever happened to your career.

I felt like a failure and as if the world was coming to an end when I was let go. But as I was surfing my computer for newspaper jobs a week later, a thought popped into my mind from out of nowhere: *You always wanted to get into book publishing; why don't you pursue a career in that? Hmmm,* I thought, as I remembered how in college I wanted to edit books. *That's not a bad idea.*

That random thought of actually pursuing a career in book publishing, which I eventually did, would never have entered my mind or been taken seriously if I had been at work editing news articles that day, and not unemployed and miserable at home.

FOCUS ON YOUR FINANCES

Unemployment takes many people by surprise as they realize that they aren't prepared to go without a steady paycheck. Give yourself an applause if you have money in the bank to pay your bills for a couple of months. If you don't, like most people, you're going to need to do a lot of maneuvering, especially if you are living on your own. Chances are, you'll have to seriously scramble to pay your bills for a while. You may have to borrow money from your relatives or a bank until you can get yourself together. Do what you have to, but try to avoid taking on credit card debt. Also, find out if you are eligible to collect unemployment compensation and if so, file for it immediately. You also have to cut back on spending, even if you have money saved. Now is not the time to go shopping, out to eat, or spend your cash on any form of entertainment.

I had been promising myself to save up for a rainy day since I received my first post-college paycheck. When the rainy day finally came in the form of job loss, I had less than $1,000 in the bank and I needed some of that to pay bills. Likewise, a friend of mine who lost his job right after I did had recently purchased a new car and signed a new apartment lease. We were so unlucky it was almost funny. He ended up having to break his lease and share an apartment with a friend, and I had to break my lease too and move home to claim my old bedroom.

Although we eventually made it out of "brokeness," we both vowed never to be stuck in that kind of predicament again.

BE PATIENT

I know it's hard to be told to be patient when you're deciding how to spend your last twenty dollar bill, but impatience just adds to the stress. It takes most people months upon months to find a job close to the one they had, or one they will enjoy. Commit yourself to searching for a job every weekday, and do not let your ego keep you from telling others who can help you about your job loss. You aren't the first person and you won't be the last person to lose her job. Nearly every working person has been fired or laid off at least once. Use all possible avenues to search for another job, which includes networking, not just scouring job sites. Don't feel like a bum if two months go by and you haven't been called in for an interview; search harder and try harder, something will come through. In the meantime, you can search for a part-time job in any field just to pay your bills, and get a roommate to reduce your rent, if that's plausible.

I became somewhat obsessive-compulsive after a month went by and I hadn't been called in for an interview. I checked job sites every half hour for new postings. I also became somewhat of a grump, as I would get irritated at friends who called me between 9 and 5 because I was hoping they would be an employer. I was feeling particularly horrible one day, when I drove by a person on the street selling framed poems. My eyes fell on one titled "Don't Quit," and I laughed because I felt like I was supposed to see it. I realized then that it was only a matter of time before I got the job I needed, and worrying incessantly wasn't going to make it come faster.

GET OUT OF THE HOUSE

Take advantage of all the extra free time you have to avoid being stressed out about your job loss. Read, exercise, do some of the things you couldn't when working 40-plus hours a week. Do not allow yourself to stay in the house pigging out, sleeping, watching television, or being depressed.

Barnes & Noble became my best friend when I was looking for work, and so did parks. I also took advantage of the many free activities and events my city offered. And of course, when I eventually secured a job, I missed all that time to myself, not to mention sleeping late.

Now You Tell Me?

Poor attendance, a poor work ethic, and poor time management skills were the top three shortcomings managers said were likely to get a new college graduate fired, according to a poll conducted by the Center for Professional Excellence at York College of Pennsylvania.

LEARN FROM THE EXPERIENCE

Whether you were laid off or fired, there is a lesson to be learned from the experience. Perhaps you learned what kind of company you don't want to work for ever again; situations with co-workers or your boss that led to your firing that you should avoid next time; or maybe losing your job made you realize how lucky you were to have it and you'll be more grateful and humble working on the next job. Everyone takes away something different that can help them be more successful. Whatever lesson you've learned, remember that your job loss can be a major turning point in your life—a positive turning point. Take time to reevaluate what kind of career you truly want, the direction you want to head in, and what you will need to accomplish to help you achieve your career goals.

After being fired/quitting, I spent months agonizing over what I could have done to save my job. But had I kept my mouth shut, I would have also shut myself out of experiences I have been very fortunate to have. I truly believe that losing that one job set me on a totally different life path—a better path. The truth is that I probably never would have left that company on my own because I was just too comfortable. Sometimes you have to be kicked out of someplace in order to go where you need to be. As *Wall Street Journal* career columnist Hall Lancaster once wrote, "Getting fired is nature's way of telling you that you had the wrong job in the first place."

BECOME MORE EMPLOYABLE

To make unemployment your stepping stone to a better job and career, you should focus on becoming more employable *while* you're unemployed. Doing so will set you apart from the millions of other job seekers who spend hours each day sending out resumes but do little to *add* to their resume. Possible steps to take:

1. Learn a new industry-specific skill

Unless you have kept abreast of the latest technologies and changes within your field, it's likely that you still have the same skill set or use the same computer programs and equipment that you did when you were hired in your previous position. Through looking at the job requirements for positions you are interested in, you can see which skills you might be lacking. Set yourself apart from other candidates by having the skills that are in demand right now.

2. Secure an internship

While internships have largely been considered a smart way for college students to increase their chances of landing a job, unemployed entry- and mid-level professionals have also found interning to be beneficial. Look for an internship that will allow you to apply the knowledge and skills you have gained thus far while networking and learning something new.

3. Teach a class

No matter what industry you are in and how long you've been working, you have likely gained skills and knowledge that could be invaluable to others. Teaching a class in your area of expertise not only positions you as an expert in your field, it is an excellent tool for networking and is sure to impress a potential employer. Anything you feel comfortable teaching could be suitable for a class. For example, if you are a pro in Word, Excel, or any other computer program, you could teach others the basics. Of course, in order to teach a class, students are needed. Consider going to your nearest community center or library and offering to teach a class for free.

4. Start an industry-focused blog

Just like teaching, creating an industry-focused blog is an interesting and effective vehicle to display your knowledge. But even more important, blogging provides a tremendous opportunity to broaden your network and put you in touch with potential employers.

5. Begin learning a new language

If you are one of the millions of people who have been promising yourself to finally become fluent in another language, now is definitely the time. Beyond making you more well-rounded, learning a new language will give you a definite edge over other job seekers.

ILLEGALLY DISMISSED?

Sometimes it seems like it's easier to get fired than it is to get hired. Most firings never seem fair or just to the person getting dismissed, and many times people are fired for reasons that are hard to comprehend. What's worse, employers can virtually fire someone at-will because they know their employee is not protected by the law in most instances. You forgot to type that letter? Bye! You refuse to put your hair in a ponytail? See ya! You think our company policies are outdated? Go start your own company! Getting fired really is that easy. So, while many people's first thought is to sue their company for giving them the boot, the chance that they will win a lawsuit is very slim simply because the law is not on their side. Oftentimes, battling an employer is just not worth it because most people wouldn't opt to go back to the company that fired them anyway.

Yet the law is on the employee's side in certain situations. State and federal laws protect employees from being fired because of their ethnicity, age, national origin, religious beliefs, gender, or because of a handicap. And although as of this writing there is not a federal law prohibiting firing employees because of their sexual orientation, at least half of all states have made it illegal to discriminate (which often includes termination) against employees because of their sexual orientation, though most laws just apply to public employment. In regard to weight discrimination, Michigan is currently the only state with laws that include height and weight as protected categories under anti-discrimination law.

You may be fired because of someone else's prejudice during the course of your career because racism, sexism, ageism, and all those other uncool "isms" are still a problem in the workplace. If you feel that you were discriminated against and fired due to prejudice then you may have a case worth fighting for. Contact your local Equal Employment Opportunity Commission to discuss your case with a counselor, or seek advice from a lawyer who specializes in employment law.

22

Getting Your
Finances in Check

I have enough money to last me the rest of my life—
unless I buy something.
—Jackie Mason, comedian

Remember when your eyes lit up after you found out how much your salary would be? If not, then please play along. They told you $44,259 a year! (the average salary for 2012 graduates, according to the National Association of Colleges and Employers). You quickly divided that by 12 and got giddy thinking about what you could do earning $3,688 a month.

You could finally visit Paris and Jamaica, move into that beautiful apartment that had seemed above your means, afford a new car, get your hair and nails done every week, and even take your mom shopping once in a while. You had it all figured out, and what's more, you were going to have money to save!

But then reality hit you. You forgot about Uncle Sam, and you know he has to have his money. Okay, okay, you said. I'm lucky to be an American. I can work with $29,742 a year. But then reality pimp slapped you. You also had to pay a Social Security and Medicare tax, and you worked in Massachusetts, so that meant a state income tax as well. This is crazy, you whined. No wonder Republicans focus on high taxes. But still, $25,010 a year—2,084 a month—isn't too bad, plus I'm lucky to even have a job. But then reality pushed you on the ground and dragged you to the mailbox, where three bills were waiting. This is getting scary, you thought. Then you sat down and calculated how much your rent, car note, insurance, utility bills, school loan payments, and credit card bills totaled. That left $210 and some change. Okay, you said . . . I can save up and then go to Jamaica (forget Paris) when I find a good deal on Expedia.com, get my hair and nails done once a month, and take mom shopping when there's a sale at Macy's.

But wait a minute! What about spending money for the trip? What about gas to get to the beauty salon? And what about food and toilet paper?

Budgeting. It seems like the simplest task. Save some money here, put some money there, but budgeting is hard for most people because they think it's that simple. Budgeting takes time, effort, and a heap of discipline. And if you're going to learn how to do it effectively, your best bet is to start now—not with next week's paycheck or next month's.

So go get a piece of paper, a trusty calculator, and some tissues . . . in case you start to cry. Budgeting can be painful, too.

First, you have to understand the reason why budgeting your money is so important. The main reason is that you can waste every hard-earned dollar you take home if you don't take control of your finances. Devising and sticking to a budget will also help you reach your monthly goal of paying all the bills, your short-term goal of having nice things, and your long-term goal of having peace of mind because you are financially secure and don't have to worry about money. Those are your goals, aren't they?

For the most part, your money should be directed into the following categories:

1. Expenses: All the bills you have to pay and things you must have to live and work: food, gas, toiletries, and miscellaneous items you pay for often.

2. Emergency fund: Money is put into this category (normally into a savings account) for when your money isn't quite right. You will use

182

this if your transmission goes out, you must take the next flight out of town for an emergency, or if you lose your job for some reason, etc. You never know what circumstance will have you digging in your pockets for a large sum of money. But you will be able to financially handle those rainy days that inevitably come if you prepare for them now. Experts recommend that you save an amount equal to *at least* three months of your living expenses. Unfortunately, only about half of all Americans have more emergency savings than credit card debt, according to research published by Bankrate.com.

3. *Debt:* Money in this category goes to all the companies or people you owe.

4. *Savings:* Most financial advisers recommend saving at least 10 percent of your monthly income, although more is always encouraged. The money can be divided into two categories.

Short-term savings: Money put into this category goes toward saving up for expenses you feel are important and desire in the near future, such as a trip, car, or wedding.

Long-term savings: Money is put into this category so you can move out of your apartment one day and into your own home, and live comfortably when you're no longer working.

Now get a notebook and sharpen a pencil—you're about to do your budget. Using Naomi's sample budget, fill out the following on a separate sheet of paper as best as you can. First, determine how much you actually take home every month by looking at your last paycheck stub. If you get money from another source that comes regularly, such as a second job or child support, figure out that net amount, too. Now add all the figures up. This is your total monthly income.

Next, estimate how much each of your monthly "must be paid" expenses are, using the list I have provided as a guide. It's better to overestimate than underestimate how much you spend on expenses that vary each month, like electricity, gas, and groceries. Once you have calculated all the expenses in this category, add them all up and deduct the figure from your total monthly income.

NAOMI'S SAMPLE BUDGET

Salary per month (after taxes)	$2,500
Monthly "Must Be Paid" Expenses	
Rent (utilities included)	$1,000
Car Payment	$300
Gasoline	$200
Car Insurance	$100
Cell Phone	$80
Community Transit	$0
Groceries	$200
Health Insurance	$125
Laundry	$0
Other Insurance	$0
Personal Hygiene	$50
School Loan Payment	$200
Total Credit Card Payments	$50
Total Monthly "Must Be Paid" Expenses = $2,305	
Income minus Monthly "Must Be Paid" Expenses = $195	

Now move on to the "I could live without it" expenses. These expenses are the ones that keep many people from budgeting effectively and saving. Instead of spending money frivolously on things you don't need, you need to budget them into your budget. You must decide how much money you can afford to spend on clothes, eating out, and personal care to be within your budget and have money left over to save each month. So, if you decide that you will only spend $50 a month on clothes, then according to your budget, you will have to wait two months to buy a $75 jacket. If you said you'd only spend $25 on movies and it's the middle of the month and you've already used up $24.99, then according to your budget you'll have to watch it later on video. You have to take your budget seriously.

One of the biggest expenses that is hard to keep up with falls under "miscellaneous," such as ink for your printer and speeding tickets you didn't deserve. You never can tell what you will unexpectedly need or have to pay for on a monthly basis. Therefore, you should have at least $100 under miscellaneous.

Once you have set aside money for each expense in the monthly "I could live without it" expenses category, calculate the total. Then deduct the total from your total monthly income and the total from your monthly "must be paid" expenses category.

NAOMI'S SAMPLE BUDGET (CONTINUED)

Monthly "I Could Live Without It" Expenses	
Beauty Salon	$60
Cable/Internet Access:	$80
Clothes	$100
Dry-Cleaning	$30
Eating Out	$150
Other Entertainment	$0
Movies	$25
Nail Salon	$60
Deli Work Lunches	$40
Miscellaneous	$100
Total Monthly "I Could Live Without It" Expenses: $645	
Total Monthly Income ($2,500) **minus** *Total Monthly "Must Be Paid" Expenses ($2,305)* **minus** *Total Monthly "I Could Live Without It" Expenses ($645) = –$450*	

According to this sample budget, Naomi has a negative balance of $450 each month. Unfortunately, there are plenty of real women and men who find themselves in this situation and end up living off of their credit cards and/or constantly borrowing money from family and friends. Like Naomi, people who don't make enough to support their lifestyle will need to change it ASAP. In this case, Naomi barely makes enough to pay her "must be paid" expenses. She would need to look into sharing an apartment to reduce her rent. Carpooling to work would also be wise, and she should be calling her student loan lender to see if she can pay less each month through one of their plans. Of course, there are plenty of items that can be slashed under her "I could live without it" expenses, starting with spending $150 a month eating out and a combined $120 on hair and nails.

How much money do you have left? If you don't have at least 10 percent, you need to go back and see if you gave yourself too much of an allowance for things you can do without or if you are really just living above your means.

Here are four expenses that drain people's bank accounts, and a list of budgeting tips.

MONEY DRAINERS

Unaffordable apartments: Your rent is the largest expense you have each month, so doesn't it make sense to be economical when choosing an apartment? Shop around for the very best deal when looking for a new residence, and remember that an apartment is something you don't own. The extra money you spend to stay in a premier apartment could be saved to put money down on a premier (but affordable) house. What's more, if you are single then you should seriously consider getting a roommate. I know you are grown, but having a roommate can actually make life more fun, and at the very least, affordable.

New cars: One of the first things many people do when they get a new or better paying job is run out and buy a new car. This usually means a higher car note than they had and more expensive insurance. Think wisely before opting to get a new ride, especially one that you know is too expensive. The money you spend on a higher car note can go into your savings, toward paying off your debt, or toward investing in something that won't depreciate the moment you buy it. Think cute but used.

Clothes and shoes: No one expects you to walk around naked, but it's likely you are overspending on your outfits. Before you buy another new thing, go into your closet and survey what you actually have. Do you see a lot of clothes and shoes that you still like but don't wear, and just as many that look alike? Those are two signs you have not been shopping with sense. You probably can go without buying new clothes all year, if you are honest. If new clothes are needed then head to a discount retail shop with a list of exactly what you require. Or, even better, be flexible on what the word "new" means. Check out a clothing consignment or thrift store and then give yourself praise for finding so many name-brand items at insanely low prices.

Restaurants: Happy hours can actually make you sad if they leave you hungry at the end of the month. And lunch specials aren't so special if they add onto your sense of "brokeness." Let's not even talk about regular dinners. While you need food to live, it does not have to come from restaurants to the extent it currently does. Until you can really afford to go out to eat more than twice a month (and not with a credit card), then you simply should not do so.

My money waster has always been food because I love restaurants' ambiance. After graduating, I struggled with making sure all my bills got paid in full each month, but still found a way to spend at least $40 a week at restaurants or small eateries. When I moved to New York, I made less money than I did after graduating but still usually spent at least $60 a week because I had more restaurants, delis, and bakeries to choose from. I have since made a point to eat out no more than once a week, or when someone else is paying. I also religiously use Groupon and Living Social, so I end up paying at least half price on most meals.

MONEY SAVERS

Instead of . . . going out to lunch every day during your work break . . . *You could . . .* go to the grocery store and buy food to make salads, sandwiches, or soups for the week. This will help you save money and stay fit.

Instead of . . . buying coffee from Starbucks each morning . . . *You could* . . . . buy a coffee pot and great-tasting coffee from the supermarket, make it yourself, and take it to work.

Instead of . . . paying for cable . . . *You could . . .* cut it off, watch shows via Hulu or Netflix, and commit to reading more.

Instead of . . . paying for gym memberships . . . *You could . . .* find some people to work out with outdoors or buy some workout videos.

Instead of . . . getting your hair done every week . . . *You could . . .* find a style that you can do yourself and limit your trips to the salon.

Instead of . . . driving to work every day . . . *You could . . .* car pool with employees who stay close to you or use public transportation.

WHERE TO DIRECT YOUR DOLLARS

One of the best ways I have found to save cash is to have a set amount of money electronically taken out of your bank account each month and transferred into a savings account that pays interest.

To start saving for retirement, take advantage of your employer's 401(k) plan and/or research opening a Roth IRA (individual retirement account) with an investment management company. Have the money you're saving for retirement electronically taken out each month and put into your retirement account. And then don't touch it!

I found it nearly impossible to save money consistently until I opened an online savings account and Roth IRA. I foolishly depended on myself to transfer a set amount of money each month into a savings account. The problem was that the savings account was tied to my checking account. I ended up dipping into my savings account nearly every month or putting in less than what I was supposed to. A year after I started "saving," I had less than $1,000 in my savings account; I had planned to have $4,000.

Once I opened an online savings account and Roth IRA, my money immediately began to grow. I had a set amount of money electronically transferred from my checking account to the new accounts every month on the same day I got paid. This way, I never saw the money I was trying to save, and thus could not spend it. I check both accounts every other week to see how much more money I've earned and to give myself something to smile about.

As you work on getting your finances in check, congratulate yourself for every dollar you save, because it really does add up. Also, please don't let anyone tell you that you're cheap for creating and sticking to a budget. The same people who complain when you say you can't afford to do something will be the same ones asking you for money in the long run.

Now You Tell Me?

We need to let go of our inner desire to please others, which is where most of our purchases come from. Outside of reasonable accommodations, food, transportation, and clothing, there isn't anything else that should be a priority in our lives while we climb out of debt and change poor money management behavior.

—Bonita Vinson, author
of *Purses, Pearls & Pumps: Straight Talk About Women & Finances*

SIMPLE WAYS TO SAVE MORE $$$$

Master the thirty-day rule: Whenever you're considering making an unnecessary purchase, wait thirty days and then ask yourself if you still want that item. Quite often, you'll find that the urge to buy has passed and you'll have saved yourself some money by simply waiting.

Don't go to stores or shopping centers for entertainment: Doing so is just an encouragement to spend money you don't really have on stuff you don't really need. Instead, find other places to entertain yourself— the park, a museum, a friend's house, or even in your own home.

Write a list before you go shopping, and stick to it: Make a careful plan of what you'll buy before you go, then stick strictly to that list when you go to the store. Don't put anything in the cart that's not on the list, no matter how tempting, and you'll come out of the store saving a bundle.

Invite friends over instead of going out: Almost every activity at home is less expensive than going out. Invite some friends over and have a cookout or a potluck meal. Everyone will have fun, the cost will be low, and the others will likely reciprocate not long afterwards.

—Trent Hamm, founder of TheSimpleDollar.com
and author of *The Simple Dollar: How One Man Wiped Out His Debts
and Achieved the Life of His Dreams*

23

Reducing
Post-College Debt

Credit buying is much like being drunk.
The buzz happens immediately, and it gives you a lift.
The hangover comes the day after.
—Dr. Joyce Brothers, psychologist

As college students, many of us did some very curious things with our money that we pretended made sense. I convinced myself that putting new bedroom furniture on credit cards was okay because I'd be able to pay it off in full when I graduated. Going on little shopping sprees with Express and Macy's cards was okay too because I'd pay those bills off when I got my student loan refund. Now, I couldn't reasonably argue why asking for more money in student loans than I needed for tuition and bills made sense, but that didn't matter. I felt I'd have the rest of my life to pay it back.

Well, the rest of my life came too soon! I nearly fainted when I received the first statement showing how much I owed the federal government. And that was before I went to grad school. If you're like me and most recent college graduates, you're pinching yourself for not listening closely to your financial aid advisers and for not reading those anti-credit card signs on campus. What's worse, you're getting bills in the mail that all say the same thing: It's payback time!

Being stalked by debt after graduation is not uncommon. According to the Institute for College Access & Success' latest findings, two-thirds of college seniors who graduated had student loan debt, with an average of $26,600 per borrower. Just as problematic, the average college student graduates with around $4,000 in credit card debt, according to financial services company Sallie Mae.

Basically, a lot of us owe a lot of companies money—including the federal government, the biggest company of all. Yet, while it's often a struggle to pay all the bills fresh out of college, don't overlook the importance of paying off the debt you've accumulated. It has to be done, even if it takes until you are in your 40s like it did for President Obama and First Lady Michelle. Too much debt can eventually mean your lack of a car, house, important future loans, and wealth.

It's best to start reducing your debt as soon as you've got money coming in on a regular basis. If you're budgeting your money effectively, then digging yourself out of debt will be much easier. The following are steps you can follow to begin to pay off your existing credit card and school loan debt.

DIGGING YOURSELF OUT OF CREDIT CARD DEBT

1. Determine how much credit card debt you're in: Gather up all your credit card statements and write down the balance of each card, the interest rate, and the minimum amount due each month.

2. Keep your two major credit cards with the lowest rates: Cut up the others and close their accounts immediately. Also cancel department store cards no matter how often you shop there. To stay out of debt you should purchase goodies with cash or your debit card.

3. Analyze your spending habits and see where you can cut costs: This goes back to budgeting. Think of all the things you waste money on and don't really need. Instead of spending $15 a month getting a fill-in, you could show off the beauty of your natural nails and add that $15 to the $10 you were going to send The Limited. Do you have to go out to eat thrice a week? Isn't it time you learned to cook a real meal anyway? Why are you buying another pair of black heels?

4. Start paying off the card with the lowest balance and work your way up: Tackle the smallest balance first so paying off your credit card debt won't seem like such an impossible task. As shown in step 3, see where you can cut unnecessary expenses and then pay as much as you possibly can each month on the card with the lowest balance. It's okay to pay the minimum on the rest; however, paying as much as you can on the first card you've chosen to pay off is extremely important. There is no way you can beat credit card debt by paying just the minimum balance on all of your cards. Mailing off checks for $10 may seem sweet and simple, but you don't want to be 50 years old and still sending in that same amount on those very same cards.

For example, if you owe $2,750 on a credit card with an 18 percent interest rate, and you only pay the minimum monthly payment of $68.75 (2.5 percent of the balance), it will take you about 21 years (254 months) to pay it off. Your total payment for this credit card would be $6,490.66 because you will have paid $3,740.66 in interest, which is more than you initially borrowed. Scary, isn't it?

Once the first card is paid off, don't spend the extra money you now have. Instead, add the amount you used to pay off the old card to the money you plan to use to bring the next card to a zero balance. This will help you quickly pay it off.

5. When you've paid one card off, start paying off another: Use the same strategy with all of your cards. After you've paid off the card with the lowest balance, start paying off the next card with the lowest balance.

Now You Tell Me?

Inquire about automatic repayments—it's the single best way to ensure you don't miss a payment, and you won't have to think about it again once you've set it up. Added bonus: Many loan companies deduct half a percentage point or more from your loan if you opt to make automatic payments.

—Tushar Mathur, founder of EverythingFinanceblog.com

DIGGING YOURSELF OUT
OF STUDENT LOAN DEBT

Paying off your school loans is much trickier than credit cards and a lot harder because of all the money you may owe. If you were like many undergraduates, once you got the bill each semester showing what you owed, you looked at it once and filed or threw it away. At the end of your final semester, you received the total bill and almost cried.

The grace period the government and private lenders give you comes much faster than expected. But if you can, once it's over you should start paying what is rightfully theirs. The amount they ask for each month under a Standard Repayment Plan can seem outrageously high, but it's the amount you need to pay to be finished before retirement.

Under the federal government's Standard Repayment Plan, you repay your loan in equal monthly installments over a period of no longer than 10 years. This ensures a quick payoff and minimizes your total interest costs. If you can, find a way without borrowing money from someone else to pay the amount asked, and try to pay even more than that. If you can't, here are your main options:

1. *Graduated repayment:* This option is designed for borrowers whose salary starts out low, but is expected to increase over time. Payments start out lower and increase according to a set schedule. Interest payments will be higher than under a Standard Repayment Plan. This plan requires you to prove your income to your lender and payments are made for up to 10 years.

2. *Extended repayment:* This plan stretches the loan repayment term for up to 25 years, depending on how much you borrowed. Payments are still fixed each month, but will normally be less than under a Standard or Graduated Repayment Plan. You will pay more interest because the loan term is longer.

3. *Income-based repayment:* This option also lets borrowers begin with low payments and progress to higher payments. However, instead

of increasing according to a set schedule, payments under this plan increase or decrease based on your income and family size. You have to qualify for a partial financial hardship to qualify for this repayment option, which allows you to make monthly payments for a maximum of 25 years.

4. *Pay as you earn plan:* To qualify for this relatively new plan, you must have a partial financial hardship. You can claim this if the monthly amount you would be required to pay on your eligible federal student loans under a Standard Repayment Plan is higher than the monthly amount you would be required to repay under the Pay As You Earn Plan. However, once you qualify for the plan, you can continue to make payments under it even if you no longer have a partial financial hardship. Your payment amount may increase or decrease each year based on your income and family size, and payments can be made for up to 20 years.

5. *Income contingent repayment (ICR):* This plan is as tricky as its name. When you barely have enough money to buy ramen noodles, you can qualify for this plan, which allows you to make monthly payments for a maximum of 25 years. Your ICR payment is based on your adjusted gross income, family size, and the total amount of your Direct Loans. The trouble with the ICR payment is that it may be even less than the monthly interest accruing on your loan. So, if you're supposed to be paying $200 a month ($140 for the principal and $60 for the interest) and you are only paying $40 a month, you would not be paying all of the interest, much less the principal amount. This plan can waste your money and keep your loan growing.

6. *Deferment:* A deferment is a temporary suspension of your monthly loan payment. If you have an unsubsidized loan, your principal payments will be postponed but interest will be charged and added to the principal balance of your loan. Principal payments are postponed and interest is not charged on subsidized loans. The lender will require proof that you qualify for a deferment, which may be because you're

in school at least half-time, are unemployed, are a working mother, or are in the armed forces.

7. *Forbearance:* A forbearance is also used to temporarily suspend or reduce your monthly school loan payments. However, you can only qualify for it if you are not eligible for a deferment, and interest will accrue on both your subsidized and unsubsidized loans. Forbearances last for up to 12 months at a time.

Lenders advise that you call them before the grace period is up to discuss your options. If you have more than one loan, you may want to look into consolidating them so you only have to worry about one company and can perhaps get a lower interest rate. As you look at your options, please remember that not paying back your loans is *not an option.* Unlike a car or house, lenders can't repossess your education, but they can make it hard for you to get a car or house by destroying your credit.

part three

QUESTIONS OF
A CAREERANISTA

24

Where Should I Live?

Toto, I have a feeling we're not in Kansas anymore.
—Dorothy, from the *Wizard of Oz*

Choosing where to live is yet another decision graduation may demand that you make. If you're still job searching, do you stay put for a while, head back to your hometown, move to a city you're familiar with, or relocate to one you have just seen on a map?

Moving from San Marcos, Texas, to Houston after I graduated was not something I really had to think about. I had a great job awaiting me there, friends, family, a boyfriend, and it was a major city. So I was 100 percent confident that Houston was meant to be my home after finishing college—if only for a while.

A year later, I was in a U-Haul truck headed from Houston to Fort Worth, Texas, where I grew up. I was not especially happy about having to move back because of job loss, but the move had advantages, and I had a plan. By living with my mom, I could save up money to move to New York—a move I felt compelled to make. Also, most of my family lived in Fort Worth, including a soon-to-be born niece. So, while I was not anxious to move from "H-Town" back to what I thought was appropriately nicknamed "Funky Town," I knew that the move made sense.

Yet when the time came for me to move to New York, my stomach was doing tap dances. Even after all my plans had been finalized and I was sitting on a plane bound for the East Coast and a new life, I couldn't help but wonder if I was making the smartest decision. I was heading thousands of miles away from my family to a place notorious for cold weather, an exorbitant cost of living, rude people, crowded streets, and where the worst act of terrorism on American soil had recently taken place. What's more, I only knew one person who lived there. But, I reminded myself over and over again, it's also the publishing capital of the world; it's the most diverse city in America; there's tons to do at nearly all hours of the day; it's home to artists, singers, and actors; and I'm also going there to get my master's degree. So, in spite of my ambivalence, I decided not to ask the pilot to turn the plane around.

I lived in New York for three years, but I was only really comfortable living there the last two. I almost packed my bags and headed to the airport once or twice in the first few months that I was there. I was appalled at having to pay $950 for a 1 ½ bedroom apartment that was worth $450, seeing rodents in my super clean kitchen, and going grocery shopping and to the laundromat with my own store-bought cart. But I found strength in the knowledge that "if I could make it here, I could make it anywhere," and my certainty that New York was where I was supposed to be. By the time I was ready for my next adventure—to teach journalism at a university in Oklahoma—I felt like a bona fide New Yorker (Brooklynite, to be exact) and loved the city that never sleeps.

If you are thinking about moving to an entirely new location for career-related reasons, applaud yourself for your bravery. It takes guts and a lot of faith to move somewhere new. Apparently, the United States is filled with lots of brave people. According to the Census Bureau, more than six million people move each year for career-related reasons.

There will be pros and cons to any move you make, whether it is to a city 30 miles away or across the nation. Make sure you've done your research on a city before giving the postal service a change of address form. Consider the following factors:

1. Cost of living: If the salary you're offered in a certain city seems unusually generous, the chances are it's not just because they like you—the cost of living may be exceptionally high. This means that the salary you receive may have less spending power than that offered by another company in a different city. Before moving to a city you know little about—be it because of a job offer or to seek a job—compare the prices of certain things you know you'll need and have to pay for. Consider the following information:

- The cost of housing, including hotels and motels
- The cost of car insurance and gas
- Tax rates, including state, local, and property taxes
- The cost of utilities, including electricity, water, gas, and phone service
- The cost of food at grocery stores, fast food places, and restaurants

Also, visit PaycheckCalculators.org to see how much you would actually bring home based on a certain salary. Some states have a high state income tax, while others don't have one at all.

2. The job market: How long you will stay with a particular company is uncertain. If you move to a city just because of a job offer, it's important to know that there will be other job opportunities in that same city should you decide to quit that job but stay in the same location. Conduct a simple Google search or call the city's local Chamber of Commerce to find out the following information:

- How many companies like the one you may work for are in the city
- The average salary for your occupation in the city
- The unemployment rate, and the rate in your field in that city
- If there is growth in your field in that city

3. Housing: Whether you have your own place or share a residence, housing costs can take a huge chunk out of your salary. The average cost of a one-bedroom apartment can vary by more than $1,000 depending on what city and neighborhood you live in. The salary you receive should allow you to afford a low to moderately priced apartment or house in a relatively safe neighborhood, preferably no more than 30 miles from your job. You can use Craigslist.org to quickly determine the average prices of apartments and houses.

Now You Tell Me?

Consider making your first home in your new state temporary. Instead of committing yourself to a one-year lease before you've even started your job, think about staying with some friends or a relative for a month or two. You can save money and make better long-term decisions for yourself if you're lucky enough to find a way to get your feet wet before diving in.

—Kristen Gomez, writer for the Cappex.com College Insider Blog

---

4. Climate: Think about your climate preferences and the city's average climate. Luckily, most U.S. city climates follow the normal pattern of having a spring, summer, fall, and winter. But think about how happy you would be if you moved to one of those cities that stays extraordinarily cold, hot, or rainy for longer than just three months, or suffered from droughts, hurricanes, tornadoes, or earthquakes.

5. Crime: You don't want to be a single woman living in a city or neighborhood where people tell you to stay inside after dark. Before you move into a particular neighborhood, talk to people in the community about how safe they feel living there. At nighttime, visit the neighborhoods you are considering living in. You should also find out the following information from the police department or a website they can direct you to:

- The crime rate in the city and in the neighborhood you plan to live
- What types of crimes occur most (check out Spotcrime.com)

- The number and percentage of crimes during the last year against women

6. *Education:* You never know when you will get the urge to get another degree or just take some interesting classes. You might hate having to commute to another city to do this. Check to see if there are colleges or universities in the city that you can afford and would want to attend.

7. *Recreation/entertainment:* You don't want to be bored out of your mind in a city, regardless of the money you're making. While you don't have to live in a major city that has tons to do at all hours, residing somewhere that has enough recreation and entertainment spots to fit your needs is important. Find out if there is an adequate amount of malls, movie theaters, museums, night clubs, restaurants, parks, and libraries to fit your taste. If there are any particular activities you enjoy, such as going to dance classes, find out how many places offer them.

8. *The people:* It doesn't make much sense to move to a place where you will feel like a lone duck. Find out the following information from the city's official website before you start packing your bags:

- The racial breakdown of the city
- The male-to-female ratio
- Age demographics
- People's primary political affiliation

Now that you have taken these factors into consideration, you should be well on your way to choosing your next place to call home. It's a big decision, but be confident in knowing that you've done the research. More important, take pride in giving yourself the chance to experience something new, somewhere new.

25

Can I Skip
Paying My Dues?

*As we speed along this endless road to
the destination called who we hope to be,
I can't help but whine, "Are we there yet?"*
—Carrie Bradshaw from *Sex and the City*

Wouldn't it be cool if we could just click our heels three times and be where we wanted to be in our careers? We could then sidestep the unpaid internships; bypass the entry-level job; get a master's degree without having to master anything; skip the climb up the corporate ladder; and find ourselves suddenly in a position that would have taken us years to secure by any other means than pure magic. All that matters is that we got to where we wanted to be anyway, right? Well, not quite.

The thought of success, fame, and fortune makes many people's hearts beat faster, but the hard work, patience, and discipline it takes to acquire what we want often slow it down. During college, many of us said we were going to be lawyers, doctors, famous writers and such, and halfway expected for those titles to just be bestowed upon us after graduation. It's no wonder that we're taken aback when the full realization comes that it will be six years before we're a lawyer, eight years before we're a doctor, and perhaps actually dead before we are regarded as a prolific writer. All that in-between time is looked upon as a nuisance.

Sometimes we even treat the in-between time as a nuisance, and that's not good because we could be bothered for years. Turning our nose up at internships, assistant positions, and more school, we act as if these are things we must endure. We might even feel that the work is beneath us. Take notes? Answer the phone? File that? Assist you? I didn't take out $40,000 in loans for this, we scream.

I was indignant when the director of my master's program in publishing suggested that I get an internship when I couldn't find a job I wanted. *I was the managing editor of a newspaper and he wants me to get an internship?* I fumed. But that was the problem. I had experience in newspaper publishing—and not that much, if we're being honest—and virtually none worth bragging about in books. I soon told my ego to be quiet and started applying for internships, ultimately landing an unpaid one through networking. It was at a small literary agency and I loved it. No, I didn't have my own office, much less my own cubicle. And yes, I had to do administrative-type work that I loathed by nature. However, I was schooled on another aspect of the publishing business, treated with respect and like an actual associate at the agency, and was mentored by the owners. Had I decided I was too good to have to "pay my dues," I would have been hurt by more than just my ego.

Even since then, like countless other mid-career and senior-level professionals, I have often found myself having to backtrack to get to where I want. When I stopped teaching college and decided I wanted to pursue book publishing *again,* I had to take a position much lower on the publishing totem pole than I expected from having been out of the game for so long.

Because of the recent high rates of unemployment and increased number of layoffs, even those who were at the top of their game have found themselves having to accept positions that are really for less experienced professionals. And, when people decide to change careers, it's almost expected that they will be starting from near scratch, despite the wealth of experience they've accumulated in another industry.

As a recent grad, you are the least immune to having to pay your dues. The reality of the situation is that graduating from college, even with a master's or doctorate degree, usually marks the beginning of our careers. This often means proving ourselves over and over again and working for not-so-great pay. Regardless of what degree you've earned, what school you graduated from, or your title, you'll likely be looked upon as a rookie.

It's just like being a freshman in college again. You had to take all those boring prerequisites before you could get into your major. You had to be a contributing member of an organization before you could run for president. And you definitely had to be inducted into a sorority before you could call yourself a soror. Likewise, you won't be able to stride into a new company, name your price, ask where your office is, start working on major-league deals, and put up a "Head Careeranista in Charge" sign. "What are her credentials?" "What has she accomplished?" "How many years has she been in the business?" your unimpressed co-workers will ask. They will expect to be shown more than a degree.

If you find that you have lots of dues to pay, then just roll up your sleeves and put on a smile. Having a good attitude about the hard work ahead will make the months go by faster. Humbly accept what is required to progress in your career, realizing that your work is not in vain. You can learn career-enhancing knowledge on any job if you go in with the right mind-set. And while you're at it, you can learn more about this crazy adventure called life.

I once called to check up on a friend who I knew was struggling somewhat in his career as a poet/business owner. Always the optimist, when I asked what he was up to, he replied, "Oh. Just working on my story." "Your story?" I asked, confused. "Yeah, all the stuff I'm going through now will make good story material for when I'm rich and famous and am being interviewed by reporters!" he said.

Like him, you're working on your story. No one will want to hear about how you graduated from college and were handed all that you wished for. However, your future mentees won't mind listening about how you patiently busted tables and babysat while holding down a full-time job to pay for graduate school. Your children will want to hear about the faith you had in yourself that helped you work your way up in a Fortune 500 company. Colleagues will want to learn how you went from delivering coffee to delivering paychecks you signed. Ironically, after recounting your adventures you can smile and say, "You know . . . success is a journey, not a destination. It's all about paying your dues."

WHAT IF THE DUES ARE TOO HIGH?

Paying your dues does not mean putting up with nonsense. You might be young and you might be a rookie, but you are still a professional. Older co-workers and managers should treat you as such. Here are signs you aren't getting the respect you deserve.

People:

- Constantly make references to your age.
- Call you "baby," "honey," "sweetie," and other endearing but unprofessional terms of endearment.
- Have you run errands or perform work that someone less experienced would normally be responsible for.
- Keep saying that you need more experience to perform certain job functions, but won't teach you how.
- Micromanage you while never giving you the opportunity to prove you can handle things on your own.
- Expect you to work longer hours than older or married workers, insinuating that you have more time on your hands because you are young or single.

If it's clear you're being taken advantage of or treated differently, you should politely tell the offending parties that while they may mean well, they are making you feel like an outsider. Let them know that age differences and lack of experience aside, you would like to be treated like the professional you are.

26

Should I Quit My Job?

The return from your work must be the satisfaction which
that work brings you and the world's need for that work.
With this, life is heaven, or as near heaven as you can get.
Without this—with work which you despise, which bores you,
and which the world does not need—this life is hell.
—W.E.B DuBois

In America, it's now common for people to work for more than 10 different companies in their lifetime, as well as to enter into a different career than what they initially studied for. I, for example, have to use both my hands and feet to count the number of companies I have worked for since college (part time and full time). Even though I have worked as a freelance writer/editor for half of my adult life, that is still quite a lot. When I graduated, I planned to stay in newspaper journalism, but eventually found my way into book publishing and then teaching. Now I am an editor and writer for various types of publications, as well as a business owner and professional speaker. Who knows what I will "be" in my 40s. I have the itch to go back into teaching and I'd love to host a TV show.

Like me, you can almost forget the idea of working for just one or two companies all of your life. Not only will you probably be unable to;

you probably won't even want to. Like many new grads, you will likely bounce from company to company as you try to get yourself together and figure out what you really want to do. Yet, while changing jobs frequently is not looked down upon as much as it was years ago, your decision to change jobs should not be made hastily. Many people just entering the workforce make a bad habit of job hopping in search of that "perfect job." However, before we rush to open every door that opportunity may be waiting behind, we should also take into account the door we are shutting behind us and where we are trying to end up in the long run.

Now You Tell Me?

A poor diet leaves us feeling sluggish and irritable, exacerbating any negative feelings we may have about work. By eating well and exercising regularly, we can increase our energy levels and alertness and lift our mood. You might be surprised at how much these changes can contribute to a more positive attitude about your job.

—Nisa Chitakasem, co-founder of PositionIgnition.com

JOB HOPPING WITH SENSE

Ideally, each position you take should be one that increases your knowledge and skill set, preparing you for bigger and better things. Think of each job as a "career builder." If you jump from job to job without gaining the knowledge needed to further your career, you will always be in the same position you were in when you took your very first job. It's fine to leave once you've learned all you can from working at a company and are ready to move on, or if you determine that a job is not going to further your career goals. However, don't make the decision to quit prematurely and end up quitting the next one just as fast. If you are thinking about leaving your job, you should also be thinking about what you honestly want to do with your career so that your next move will be a smart one.

If you enjoy working at your company but are contemplating leaving because of things that can be changed or improved if given time, such as a low salary or unchallenging work, consider talking to your boss and asking him or her if the company can help meet your needs. You would be surprised at what you can get when you just ask for what you want. When unsure about whether to change jobs, weigh the advantages and disadvantages carefully. Look at Lauren's case, for example.

LAUREN'S DILEMMA

Lauren had always dreamed of being a noted biological research scientist. After graduating summa cum laude from a public university with a degree in biology, she took a job as a research assistant at a prominent university/biomedical research center. She had received offers from several other research centers that offered her more money than the $45,000 she was currently getting paid, but she opted for this center because of its reputation, perceived chance of advancement, and interesting research projects. The center would also pay for half of her graduate school tuition. She was really excited during her first three months of employment, but after working there for six months she got the itch to leave. She determined that she really wasn't getting paid what she was worth and she also wasn't getting the hands-on experience she had expected because one of the center's research projects got canceled. Lauren noted that she had a lot of other opportunities to consider and one seemed particularly exciting. Other fellow biology graduates had told her how she could make more than $100,000 a year pitching pharmaceutical companies' new products to doctors. This job, they bragged, would give her unlimited income earning potential and the chance to travel within the United States and abroad. A scout for one of these companies who was looking for young women contacted Lauren and basically guaranteed her a job.

Before trying to make a decision, Lauren talked to her supervisor about her two needs that weren't being met.

To Lauren's surprise, her supervisor promised her a $5,000 raise in eight months because she knew that Lauren was underpaid, and she said more interesting work would be coming within months. She also told Lauren that she wanted her to stay and would do all that she could to help her career blossom.

Although this news excited Lauren, she still went ahead and weighed the pros and cons of leaving her present job to break into the pharmaceutical sales business.

Now You Tell Me?

The old adage, "Out of the frying pan and into the fire" is filled with wisdom: Often we leave a job because of unhappiness and in our zeal to get away, we fall right back into the same traps, the same situations.

—Teri Lucie Thompson, senior VP of university relations & CMO at the University of Arizona

---

DO I STAY?

Advantages

1. Excellent research facility.
2. Chance to meet top-notch influential doctors and research scientists.
3. They'll pay for half of my graduate school tuition.
4. Promise of professional advancement.
5. More money in about eight months.
6. Stay in my field because I still want to be a sought-after research scientist.

Disadvantages

1. Not making as much money as I could right now.
2. Have to be bored for a while.

DO I GO?

Advantages

1. Chance to make major money!
2. Opportunity to travel.

Disadvantages

1. Might not make a lot more money because the job is commission-based.
2. May hate the career (I'm really not a sales person).
3. May not get to travel to the places I want.
4. Won't get the experience I need to become a sought-after research scientist.

After actually reviewing all that her present job had to offer, Lauren decided to stay. It was pretty clear that she had a good thing going even if the work was kind of boring at the moment. While waiting on the new research project, she volunteered to help out in another department and decided to get an easy part-time job at night until she got the raise she was promised.

Of course, there will always be opportunities and offers elsewhere that we'd be foolish not to accept. And time is too short to waste our potential at a job we don't enjoy, or in a career that we know is wrong for us. So, when you've looked at all your options and feel in your heart that it's time to leave, just do it and wave goodbye to your old co-workers. In the example below, Daina's decision was easy to make.

DAINA'S DILEMMA

After interning two years during college for a small public relations agency in Manhattan, Daina was offered a full-time salaried position as a public relations associate. She was ecstatic. It would have been hard to find anything more than an entry-level public relations job in New York and she was on great terms with everyone she worked with. But after working three more years at the agency, she found herself getting bored. She really wasn't doing much more than she did when she interned and she wanted to work with the big name clients her company couldn't seem to get a hold of. She had made many contacts while at the agency and was about to start sending out resumes when one of her friends at a larger agency in Atlanta called her and said her public relations director wanted to meet her. Supposedly, she had heard great things about Daina's work and wanted to feel her out to see if she would fit in at her company.

Daina jumped on the opportunity and had an interview set up the next week in Atlanta on the weekend. The public relations director was very impressed with Daina's work and aspirations, and offered her a job as a senior public relations associate—a job that was hard to get among people who already worked there.

Daina would get the chance to work with million dollar clients at a reputable company, travel, and enjoy the freedom of not having to live paycheck to paycheck. Daina was getting paid $50,000 a year, which left her broke every month in New York. This agency offered her $65,000 a year, which could be stretched a long way in Atlanta. Daina didn't have time to weigh the pros and cons of leaving—she was too busy packing to move to Atlanta. She turned in her two-weeks' notice to her public relations director. He was sad to see her go, but he understood that this job could provide more opportunities for Daina to really make a name for herself in the public relations field. Daina left that PR agency for the new one without any doubt in her mind that she was doing what was best for her career.

WHEN YOU KNOW IT'S TIME TO GO!

Now, there are some jobs that we should consider leaving, and then there are others that demand we start sending out resumes immediately. Unfortunately, some positions you take may look good under the "job description" but end up making you sick in the stomach for various reasons.

One position I held for eight months with a book publishing company had me giving myself pep talks in the morning just to get through the day. And my co-worker literally started going to a psychologist to help her cope with the stress at work. Our boss—nice as she was—was the epitome of a micromanager, and a workaholic to top it off. She actually asked us—and we both had professional positions, mind you—

to "cc" her on all emails, and many emails she asked to see before we sent them out. Since she arrived to work later than we did, she also asked that we call to let her know when we got into the office so she could let us know if there was any "mission critical" work to do.

The problem was, although we worked for a book publisher and not for the military, everything was mission critical to her. This meant that we routinely worked 12-hour days and even did overnighters. I, like my co-worker, stayed for longer than we should have because the economy was in the tank and we didn't like the idea of leaving a job before a year was up. However, one morning I woke up and realized that not only was I not getting the experience and respect I needed because of my boss's micromanagement, my health was being compromised. And the only reason I had not gone to a psychologist like my co-worker was because I couldn't afford it. Jobs shouldn't drive you to a shrink, I fumed as I finally wrote my resignation letter.

As I realized, you will probably spend as much time at work as you do with the people you love, so it doesn't make sense to keep working at a place that has you frowning during half of your day. While you are still urged to think wisely before quitting a job, when the following scenarios arise you should think twice about staying.

HRinsider Tip: If you're not ready to quit your job that sucks, get a side job consulting, or consider freelancing. More cash means you're able to create financial padding if and when you do decide to leave. But more important, getting distance between you and your current job is essential for creativity. When you stretch your muscles, your new job will stimulate ideas for your old job, and vice versa.
—Rebecca Thorman, founder of Kontrary.com

YOU KNOW IT'S TIME TO GO . . .

1. When you are ever physically, sexually, verbally, or emotionally abused, and the actions of the abuser go unpunished or are ignored by management.

2. When you feel like you need a drink each morning to get through your work day.

3. When the work you do is utterly boring and unchallenging, or just as problematic, needlessly demanding.

4. When you consistently get denied raises or promotions you feel you've earned.

5. When your boss hints that you may be happy somewhere else.

6. When the only friends you have at work are the office goldfish.

7. When you spend most of your time at work day dreaming about quitting.

8. When you get your check late more than you get it on time.

9. When you're not getting paid anywhere near what you should be.

10. When everyone from the CEO to the secretary's assistant is an incompetent jerk.

QUITTING CORRECTLY

While the urge to run out your employer's door may be strong at times, it's wise for you to quit the "correct way." Most companies expect to receive two weeks' notice from employees so they will have a chance to delegate the work to someone else or replace the person leaving. By giving two weeks' notice, you'll leave with a better chance of receiving a favorable reference and being reemployed if need be. Telling your employer verbally about your decision may suffice for part-time or semi-professional positions, but for professional positions, you should provide your employer with a written letter stating your intentions. In this letter, include the following:

- The last day you will be working.
- Whether you would like to continue health care coverage and for how long.
- How you would like to receive your last paycheck.
- Positive words stating what you appreciated about the company.

HRinsider Tip: It may seem ideal to give your boss a "heads up" that you're pursuing new ventures, but be very careful. Some employers may see your friendly "heads up" as a threat for salary or benefits negotiating power. Your employer may begin to see you as a temporary employee and remove you from important projects, or worse, immediately begin the search for your replacement.

—Sudy Bharadwaj, co-founder of JackalopeJobs.com

Finally, if you find yourself leaving because you can't stand working at the place another day, resist the urge to tell the world about it via Facebook and other social media outlets when you do quit. Posting nasty things about your company, boss, or former co-workers reeks of immaturity. Also, in addition to burning bridges with your former employer, a potential employer who sees negative postings will think twice about hiring you.

Diary of a Careeranista

CHRYSTAL BAKER ON FINDING YOUR OWN WAY

*I*t has been said that the third time is a charm, and ironically, I found this to ring true regarding my desire to find a career that excites me. I have held several positions that slowly but steadily stole my joy. There were times when I cried in the bathroom as I prepared for work because I had no desire to be there. I dreaded the drive to the office, and I hoped for an out at the end of each day. Just as the clock struck closing time, I sprinted out the door. My negative outlook on the situations affected my mental, emotional, and physical well-being in many ways, and also prevented me from being the best worker I could be.

I always tried to suck it up at first, chiding myself for being ungrateful because many of my friends didn't even have a job. I also questioned whether I wanted too much from a career as I reflected on the working lives of most of my elders. It seemed that older generations come from a place where working for a paycheck is the most important thing you can do. You need money to survive, and whether you enjoy the work is considered a moot issue.

Yet try as I might, I knew I couldn't live like that. I was, and am, part of a generation that does not want to spend the majority of our lives working just to pay the rent. We want to enjoy every aspect of our professional lives. Through my own struggles, I have found that questioning our path and the journey we need to take—sometimes over and over again—is the very thing that leads to a fulfilling career.

Ironically, the beginning of the journey often begins with a breaking point. In 2005, I arrived in Los Angeles two weeks after graduating from college ready to work in the television industry. I just knew that I wanted to be a producer. Lucky for me, I had an internship that led to employment within a month of being there. Yet after a year of working full time, I knew that I did not want to pursue that course any longer. Now, this was what I spent four years studying in college. I had even produced and edited a student television drama for two years during school. But here I was, in a job that outsiders envied, and I despised it. I spent one more year in that job, each day disliking it more and more. I had no drive, and I didn't see any change on the way. My heart screamed that I had to get out of there, so in 2007, I hopped into the advertising and marketing field. I had an interest in campaigns and events, and I thought I would be able to pick up some knowledge and learn the ropes.

With the best of intentions, I went into my second post-college job eager to learn and ready to explore. To my surprise, in less than six months I knew that this was not the place for me either. I was not challenged, I was bothered by the cracks in the company management, and I saw no higher-level position that intrigued me. I wanted out. The problem was, I had no idea where I would go after that.

At this point I was frustrated with the world, but even more so with myself. I was even more uncertain about my future than I had been the day I received my diploma. People telling me that my constant job jumping was happening because I was finicky and making decisions too quickly only made me feel worse. However, I now know that "wanting out" is our mind's way of telling us that we need to escape, but in a good way. Further, it is our intuition telling us that something is not right and we are in danger—danger of being perpetually unhappy like the millions of other people going to jobs they abhor. As most people will tell you, you should always listen to your intuition—regardless of what conventional wisdom tells you. Unfortunately, it took a while longer for that message to reach my inbox.

In late 2008, after one year of working for the advertising agency, I told a former college classmate that he and I should start a food blog because we both loved cooking for ourselves and other people. I had been reading other food blogs for a few months and it seemed like an interesting way to document and share our dishes. He loved the idea and within days we were up and running as The Duo Dishes. It was a great outlet to relieve stress and actually work on something I was passionate about. The blog began to introduce me to another world—one that intrigued me—and that was exactly what I was looking for at the time. A little voice in my head tried to push me into researching job options in the culinary industry, but I did not want to risk jumping head first into a third career that could lead to nowhere.

By summer of 2009, I woefully celebrated my two-year anniversary at that dead-end job with a measly and somewhat fictional title bump, and it was around that time when I honestly and truly could see no upside to the situation I was in. I was in the sludgiest mud pit, and there were very few limbs I could grab to pull myself out. During all of my days there, I would work, and at night I would be sad and complain to my friends. And I would cook. I made food for myself, for my friends, and for friends of friends—all documented on my food blog. I also studied recipes online, watched TV shows about food, leafed through cookbooks, and poured through food photography. Soon, the food blog turned into a venue that attracted attention from readers around the world, as well as awards, notable mentions, and recipe development opportunities with international companies. Working on the food blog was fun for me, and after months of telling myself I couldn't really turn my love of food into a career, I finally decided to test this belief by actually reaching out to people who could help me start a career in the culinary arts.

Through my contacts, I learned about an opportunity to volunteer as an assistant for a cooking school. I loved the work, and a few months later I received a call with an offer for a part-time position that would also allow me to teach there. Everything seemed to be lining up and I was ecstatic, but there was a problem: If I was to accept, I would need to give up my advertising agency position, which would translate to a drastic pay cut. My brain and heart battled with each other as I tried to figure out the best decision.

The battle between brain and heart really indicates the battle between your practical self and the dreamer inside you. The practical part of me had a hard time letting the dreamer see the light of day, which equated to me rarely taking real risks. I was still very wrapped up in the "what ifs" of the world: What if I don't make it? What if they say no? What if this fails? But after considering all the time I had spent feeling stifled and bored, I finally understood that playing it safe literally gets you nowhere. Without expending an effort, you are guaranteed to stay in the same place that drives you crazy. That is why I ultimately made the impractical but wise decision to cut my steady paycheck in half and accept the part-time position at the cooking school. And lo and behold, instead of feeling scared and like I had made a huge mistake, the only thing I felt after resigning was the lifting of a weight—a burden—off of my shoulders and spirit. Although the economy was still in a rut, I did not fret because I realized that I would be able to pursue what I really wanted to do, and that would be food.

Of course, my decision to leave yet another job drew criticism from my family. I was—and still sometimes am asked—what my "real" goals are, what my plan is, what I'm doing with my life. I try not to let that discourage me.

I try not to second-guess myself during those days that seem tougher than the ones before it. I know that I am building my own career path. Though it may be the third time that I am pursuing something concrete, it is the first time I've felt comfortable, capable, and happy doing it.

I have since moved on from my position with the cooking school, but it was a stepping stone for me to enter a new place in my career. I am now officially a freelancer, and I have been lucky to be in a flexible professional situation that allows me to do what I enjoy while also providing me with the time to build my own brand. I have been able to partner with national and international food brands, speak at a blogging conference, have my work published in cookbooks, meet world-renowned chefs, interview business owners, collaborate with food stylists, organize culinary events, and explore my world through food in a way that would not have been possible had I not taken the chance.

Since deciding to pursue what I really love, I have grown into a stronger person with increased clarity and purpose. I understand that while my path is still defining itself, my path does not define me. I am not unsuccessful if I do not succeed every time. I am unsuccessful when I do not put in the effort. As I continue to build, create, and lay down a foundation, I see that my way was there all along. It may have taken longer than I wanted it to, but like all good things, it came to light. Now it is up to me to make everything come to fruition.

As you embark on your own career journey—be it the first, third, or fifth time—I hope you give yourself the space and time to go where your heart leads you, to find your own way, no matter how long it takes.

Chrystal Baker is the co-founder and co-publisher of DuoDishes.com, a Los Angeles-based recipe and food events blog that features eclectic and homestyle dishes, mingling Southern roots, West Coast flair, and international ingredients. She is a cook, teacher, culinary consultant, and freelance food and lifestyle contributor to CBSLA.com, BasilMagazine.com, and FrugivoreMag.com. Her writing and recipes have also been published in three cookbooks. In addition, Chrystal manages her own travel and lifestyle site, AnyandEverywhere.com, as well as F2PCulinaryClub.com, an arm of Inglewood, California's Social Justice Learning Institute food equality movement.

Do I Have to
Go Back to School?

An investment in knowledge always pays the best interest.
—Benjamin Franklin

My grandmother once told me that going back to school is never a bad decision, and I believe she's right. There is a marked difference between the average lifetime earnings of those with just a bachelor's degree compared to those with a post-graduate education. According to research published by Georgetown University's Center for Education and the Workforce, those holding bachelor's degrees earn about $2.27 million over their lifetime, while those with master's, doctoral, and professional degrees earn $2.67 million, $3.25 million, and $3.65 million, respectively. Given the general monetary advantage of attaining more than a bachelor's degree, I think a better question to ask is: "When is it a good time to go back to school?"

Certain careers we plan to have, such as a lawyer, pharmacist, or tenured professor, require further education. Generally, people who intend on getting into occupations requiring more instruction should enter their needed program shortly after they receive their first degree. Without the advanced degree they can be stuck in limbo.

Yet most occupations are easier to advance in with a post-grad degree, but certainly aren't off limits without one. For these positions, it may be wiser to work a couple of years before becoming a student again. This way you will have acquired some professional experience, which will make you even more marketable once you receive a post-graduate degree. You may also be able to save money to pay for life's necessities if you aren't able to work full time while attending school.

You should be picky about where you receive your post-graduate degree because all schools aren't equal. You will be investing at least two years of your life getting a master's degree and as many as seven years for a doctorate. Finding a school that will meet the majority of your needs during this time period is crucial.

WHAT TO LOOK FOR

1. A school with a great, accredited program: Find the school with the best program you are interested in that you can afford to attend. Remember, just because the university up the street from you offers a graduate degree like the one you're looking for, doesn't mean that is where you need to go. Find out if the program has been rated one of the best of its kind, or at least is considered a good program to go through by professionals in your field. Before applying, also research the university online or contact the department's academic counselor to find out the following:

- Whether late afternoon/evening classes are offered (in case you will also be working)

- The program's retention rate and the number of students who graduate each year

- If any of the faculty are particularly well known in the field

- How the program differs from other similar ones

- How closely faculty members work with students

- The job placement rate of the program and examples of places recent graduates are now working

- Any recent awards/recognitions the program has received

When you visit the school, ask to speak privately to at least two students in the program to find out their likes and dislikes. Also ask for the contact information of two recent alumni to get their opinion about the program.

2. *A school in a good location:* It's probable that you will have to move to receive your post-graduate degree. While you could attend the same school you received your bachelor's degree from, I wouldn't recommend it. The change of atmosphere will help you better adapt to other environments and you're more likely to meet new and different people. The location of the school you choose should:

- Be some place you will like to live. Even if the program is great, you're not going to spend all of your time in class. Choose a university in a city that you will feel comfortable living in for a couple of years.

- Have many companies that you can work or intern for. Some cities are known for certain industries, like Los Angeles, which is known for its entertainment industry, and Washington, D.C., which is home to many public policy organizations. You want to be able to gain experience in your field while you're going to school, which is easier when the city has a lot of companies you'd be interested in working for.

3. *A school that offers you some kind of fellowship or assistantship:* Increasing your knowledge will likely mean increasing your debt. However, you shouldn't have to pay for all of your post-graduate degree with student loans. Choose a university that offers to pay all or part of your tuition or housing because of your academic background or in exchange for working at the school.

4. *A school where you feel welcome and comfortable:* Take into account your preferences in regard to the size of the school and its racial and gender makeup. Also ask about the culture of the program. Are students

and faculty super competitive or do they make a point of helping each other and have a high level of camaraderie?

5. *A school that has adequate resources and facilities:* Make sure the program is adequately funded so you are likely to get continued financial assistance and other types of support. Check out the library and computer and gym facilities to see if they will meet your needs.

I chose to pursue a master's degree after leaving my first job after college. I had majored in print journalism and sociology but decided that I now wanted to work in book publishing. There are only a couple of cities to go to if you seriously want to pursue a career in book publishing, and New York City is the best one. While I was told that most people didn't have a master's in the field, and I didn't necessarily need one, I still thought earning a master's in publishing would benefit me. I knew very little about the industry, had no contacts, and didn't have enough money to move to New York without a job.

There were two universities that offered a master's in the field: Pace University and New York University (NYU). I was accepted to both. While NYU had more name recognition, I wasn't offered a very good financial aid package. Pace offered me an assistantship that paid my tuition and allowed me to gain experience in the field through working for their university press; my decision was easy.

I learned a lot through the program and made great contacts and friends. My post-graduate degree also allowed me to secure positions I wouldn't have even been considered for with just a bachelor's degree, including as a faculty member at a university.

It is important to note, however, that going back to school may not always be the smartest choice. Rethink sending out applications if you are already burdened by student loan debt; not totally interested in your field of study; planning to start a family soon; or secretly view going to grad school as a way to avoid getting a job or because one has been difficult to find thus far.

Also, keep in mind that you can go back to school for something other than a degree, and save a lot of time and money. Getting a certificate in a course of study could be a fast and easy way to increase your knowledge. There are also any number of adult education classes that you can take. These could be classes directly related to your field or ones that just seem interesting, such as photography or screenwriting. The point is that just as your bachelor's degree has opened doors for you, any schooling beyond that can too.

5 REASONS *NOT* TO GO TO GRAD SCHOOL

1. The "real world" may be more helpful for your career instead.
2. Going to grad school might mean you have to put important life milestones on hold, like getting married or starting a family.
3. You might not have the time or resources to be a full-time grad student.
4. Getting an advanced degree doesn't automatically single you out as a better or more qualified potential employee.
5. A graduate degree no longer guarantees a high-paying job.

—Sydney Nolan, writer for Hercampus.com

WHAT ABOUT AN ONLINE DEGREE?

The number of adults pursuing an online degree continues to grow, including among full-time workers who often find online classes easier to balance and complete. However, an online degree may not be as beneficial as one gained in the classroom. Employers may question how rigorous the coursework was when compared to a brick-and-mortar school, and how much you really learned.

In a study by the Society for Human Resource Management, almost half of HR professionals surveyed said applicants with online degrees were viewed less favorably than those with traditional degrees. Also, only 15 percent indicated that an online degree is acceptable for a job applicant seeking an executive-level position.

However, despite findings like these, because the number of people earning degrees online is skyrocketing, the overall perception about them is changing as a result. If you do choose an online program, opt for an accredited one that is tied to a university that has name recognition. Also, just as you would do with a regular degree program, contact recent graduates to learn what their likes and dislikes were.

Diary of a Careeranista

LOLA BROWN ON BLURRED LINES: THE ROAD THROUGH GRADUATE SCHOOL IS NOT ALWAYS A STRAIGHT ONE

*I*n less than 10 days, I will have a Ph.D. in biochemistry. It's amazing to be able to write that. I really don't even believe it yet. This is a monumental step on a ladder I've been climbing for a long time. My journey, however, was not a straight line.

Since high school, my passion has been to find the cure for sickle cell anemia. It was something that struck me from the moment I was sitting in biology class my junior year, learning how the disease severely impacted the quality of life of so many people, primarily people of color. Even today, it still touches my heart to reflect on the strength and will people with sickle cell anemia have. I felt it would be an honor to use my God-given intellect to help find a cure for this disease. So, after graduating from Brown University with a degree in biology, I entered graduate school at Georgia Tech full of ambition and the desire to make an impact in sickle cell anemia research.

What I didn't realize is that getting a Ph.D. takes much more than intelligence and hard work. Much like in the business world, success can be dependent on your being mentored and assisted by seasoned professionals in the field. Soon after starting the program, I learned how true this was when I began having challenges with my Ph.D. advisor. We had a difficult time communicating, and I soon learned that without a supportive advisor, the likelihood of my obtaining a doctorate wasn't very good. I became very frustrated and depressed about my situation. I was at a point where I needed help desperately, yet didn't know where to turn. I also felt like I was letting down the people who were cheering me on, as well as the people with sickle cell anemia who I could potentially help.

My life hit a low point when I was asked to complete the program with a master's degree instead of a Ph.D. Although I was excited and proud of my accomplishment—very few women venture into the sciences, much less receive a master's in biochemistry—I had not finished what I sought to do.

Dejected and mentally exhausted, I decided to work for a while; "a while" soon turned into four years. However, during this time, I had a chance to learn more about myself and use my talents in other ways. I started a tutoring business, worked as a science teacher at one of the top K–12 schools in the country, and conducted biomedical research with scientists at Spelman College. It was an incredible time in my life during which I spread my wings and realized that I was a success, with or without the Ph.D. It wasn't until making this realization that I felt confident enough to go back to finish what I started.

Shortly after my 30th birthday, I entered a Ph.D. program in biochemistry at the University of Maryland Baltimore County (UMBC). On one hand, this was exciting; on the other hand I thought, "Am I really starting over?" The classes I took at Georgia Tech were not accepted by UMBC so I had to start from the beginning—back to classes, late night studying, and all-night cram sessions. It was challenging at times. Conducting research can be extremely trying and then there are many experiments that are unsuccessful. This felt like a huge weight on my shoulders, and on more than one occasion, I wanted to quit the program. But unlike my experience at Georgia Tech, my Ph.D. advisor at UMBC, Dr. Michael Summers, was extremely encouraging. His support, in addition to the boosts of confidence I received from my family and friends, kept me going. A book I read during my grad school hiatus was also paramount. In his book *Think and Grow Rick: A Black Choice*, Dennis Kimbro writes, "It is not so much brilliancy of intellect, talent, or resources as it is persistency of effort and constancy of purpose that draws greatness to the individual." So I persisted and kept persisting until my Ph.D. was finally completed. Through this experience, I have learned a few powerful lessons that I would like to share:

1. *Your life may not always go according to plan:* I am a planner, I always had a plan for what I wanted to do by a certain age. Some of those things happened, many of them did not. My Ph.D. journey has taught me to be more willing to go with the flow and not be so dogmatic about my own plans. Although the full story has yet to be revealed, I think getting a Ph.D. from UMBC instead of Georgia Tech will work to my advantage.

2. *Spread your wings:* In some cases, you may need to take a break. That's okay! Explore who you are, what you enjoy, what you don't enjoy, and who you want to be.

3.   Get a smart game plan: I believe in working smart, then working hard. You have to know when you have to buckle down and work hard, and when you can rest a little bit. There were moments during my Ph.D. when I was running three experiments at one time and other times when I didn't have a lot to do. But I was constantly asking myself, "Am I doing things in the most efficient way possible?" The last thing I wanted to do was work hard on something just to realize I could have done it quicker or better if I had done it another way. I never skimped on working hard; I just planned where and when I had to focus my energy to get everything done.

4.   Network proactively: Over the years, I have developed an incomparable group of mentors, which I call my personal board of directors. I have different mentors for different areas of my life, including career advancement, work-life balance, and effective communication strategies. I am an introvert, and I still often get nervous approaching a potential mentor. One thing that I find helpful is to always be prepared. I am able to clearly articulate where I need help and how I think that person might be able to help me. It's vital to be clear and to the point with people from whom you want assistance. Most people are very busy. Appearing uncertain or being vague indicates a lack of forethought.

5.   Realize what you are not in control over: Most of us work so hard trying to make decisions that will give us the best opportunity for success. However, in some cases we will find that our efforts simply aren't enough, and there is something that we don't yet possess to achieve the success we're yearning for; in other words, the problem is out of our hands. Once we do everything we can, we must be comfortable in letting it go and moving forward. There were many times I prayed over situations with school. Once I knew I had done everything I could do, I began to have confidence that my problem was already solved and just prepared myself for the next step.

I will soon start a post-doctoral position at Yale University. Never would I have thought that after going through so many challenges, I would have the opportunity to conduct research at an Ivy League university. I am overjoyed to have finally earned my Ph.D., but I am even more proud to have developed the tremendous depth of character this Ph.D. experience has given me.

Lola Brown, Ph.D., is a research scientist, mentor, and educator. You may visit her website, www.lolabrown.org.

28

Can I Be
My Own Boss?

*If you are committed to creating value and if you aren't
afraid of hard times, obstacles become utterly unimportant.
A nuisance perhaps; but with no real power. The world
respects creation; people will get out of your way.*
—Candice Carpenter, founder of iVillage.com

I remember the exact moment I asked myself this question—"Why can't I be my own boss?"—and for the first time felt a good degree of certainty that I absolutely, positively could, and what's more, I was finally prepared to do it. I was 32 and working for a book publishing company in a role I had prayed to the universe for. They say you should be careful what you ask for, and through this job I learned that lesson.

One day, about six months after being brought on board, I was in my boss's office patiently waiting for her to end a phone call so we could discuss a new freelancer she had hired. A smile was plastered on my face, but all I could think about was how much I hated coming to work every day. As she chatted on the phone, I reviewed the freelancer's resume and something in my head literally went ding, ding, ding— if he can freelance full time and earn a living, then so can I! I felt an urge of excitement about this possibility and the next thing I knew I had written a whole page of notes on the back of his resume about the editing/writing/resume writing business I would start. I could hardly concentrate when she finally got off the phone to begin our meeting. Once home, I got right to work planning what would soon be a successful business—one that now includes being the publisher of Careeranista.com. However, I had always had the entrepreneurship bug inside of me. Even if I had not been in a job I disliked at the time, it would not have been too long before I made the move to work for myself. No matter the reason for your desire to be your own boss, although it may not be easy, it is certainly possible.

Now You Tell Me?

If U.S.-based women-owned businesses were their own country, they would constitute *the fifth largest GDP* in the world, trailing closely behind Germany, and ahead of countries including France and Italy, according to the Center for Women's Business Research.

It is estimated that there are more than 8.6 million women-owned businesses in the United States, generating more than $1.3 trillion in revenues and employing nearly 7.8 million people, according to American Express' 2013 *OPEN State of Women-Owned Businesses Report.* Just as inspiring, over the past 14 years, women-owned firms have grown at a rate that exceeds the national average.

If you are like most of these women business owners, your venture into entrepreneurship will likely start while you are still working for someone else. You will have a great idea but want to test it out while you are still employed. This is wise considering that only half of all new businesses survive five years or more, according to the Small Business Administration. However, many women find that they never end up being a bona fide entrepreneur because they are too afraid to let go of their job/safety net. If you truly desire to turn your side hustle into your only hustle, then here is how to get started.

TURNING YOUR SIDE HUSTLE
INTO YOUR *ONLY* HUSTLE

Focus, focus, focus: Your side hustle may be a combination of too many hustles, which keeps you from being successful in any one area. Sure, being a masseuse, website designer, and event planner on the side may keep life interesting, but they don't go together. Plus, it's hard enough to make even one of them your full-time business when you are holding down a full-time job. If this is a problem for you, it's time to let all but one go. Since you are likely passionate about each one of them, keep the one that either is making you the most money now or has shown it has the potential to. Once you know what your true gold mine of a business is, hustle harder on it. The company you work for doesn't wait for customers to come to them and neither should you. Start investing a significant amount of time into marketing your service or product better, as well as finding new ways to earn more income through it.

Now You Tell Me?

Don't start a business simply because it seems sexy or boasts large hypothetical profit margins and returns. Do what you love. Businesses built around your strengths and talents will have a greater chance of success. It's not only important to create a profitable business, it's also important that you're happy managing and growing it day in and day out. If your heart isn't in it, you will not be successful.

—Scott Gerber, founder of the *Young Entrepreneur Council*

Set smart goals and a serious timeline: One of your biggest struggles probably revolves around being more disciplined. However, to be a successful full-time business owner, you have to finally get your act together. Begin by setting realistic but challenging SMART goals to ensure your goals are Specific, Measurable, Attainable, Realistic, and Timely. No more "I'm waiting to feel inspired" or "I'll start networking next week." Inspiration is often driven by action and next week will find your business even more in need of an owner with true willpower.

To kick your business into high gear, create daily, weekly, and monthly objectives that focus on increasing your client base and earnings. Now, since the most important goal is to one day hand in your resignation letter, set a date for when this will happen. To give yourself a confidence boost and make quitting your 9 to 5 seem more real, write the resignation letter today and put it in a place where you will see it often.

Downsize: Don't expect your full-time business to immediately bring in what your full-time job does; it's not likely to happen. You started off making much less than you do now in your regular job, and you had to work your way up to bring in more dough. The same thing goes for your business. Given this fact, start looking for ways to downsize certain things in your life, such as your rent and car note, while living more frugally in general. Cutting costs now will make it easier for you to live, save, and invest back into your business once you can't rely on a steady paycheck. Speaking of a steady paycheck . . .

Ditch the idea that a full-time job equals job security: America's continuing high unemployment rate, hints of layoffs by medium and large businesses every year, and the federal government's past sequestrations and shutdowns show there is no such thing as true job security. What a full-time job does offer is money you can count on each month, and it's understandable that you are hesitant to give that up. It sucks not knowing how you will pay next month's rent. But since you are downsizing, give yourself permission to let your full-time job go once you are consistently earning enough from your side hustle to cover your necessities each month, and have enough in savings should you have some very dry months. Also, keep in mind that you can always get a part-time job to bring in a definite dollar amount each month to make you feel more comfortable.

Now You Tell Me?

The idea that a job is the most secure way to generate income is just silly. You can't have security if you don't have control, and employees have the least control of anyone.

—Steve Pavlina, personal development coach

Enlist support: Running a profitable business is difficult when you lack a support system. Begin networking with both budding and seasoned entrepreneurs through organizations for the self-employed. Fellow cubicle-ditchers tend to be the best people to give you advice and to connect you to the tools and people that can help you achieve your business goals faster. Of course, support from family and friends is also vital. Let them know of your plans and any ways they can help you, which should include helping to market your business through social media and via word of mouth. Unfortunately, you will also find that some people will be downright unsupportive. With a worried expression, they will talk about how hard it is to find a job and question why anyone would want to give one up. However, afterward, these same people will probably talk about how much they can't stand their job. Avoid all types of well-meaning dream crushers—even if it means talking to your own parents a bit less often. Although it's true that entrepreneurship is hard, puts you at a financial risk, and certainly isn't for everybody, there are plenty of success stories. You can be the next one.

Whatever you do, don't give up on your dream of being successfully self-employed, and don't waste another hour just dreaming about it. You *can* be your own boss.

PREPARING TO BE THE CEO (CHIEF EVERYTHING OFFICER)

Developing a small business into a successful enterprise demands more than passion. In order to succeed, you need to understand and to become proficient in a set of fundamental business skills, including these:

Communication Skills to be clear about your expectations and sensitive when dealing with problems . . . *Leadership Skills* to assemble, mobilize, and motivate teams and forge long-term relationships with prospects, customers, suppliers, employees, and investors . . . *Strategic Planning Skills* to effectively define your company's strategy or direction and make decisions on allocation of resources . . . *Analytical Skills* to objectively assess the present state of your business, determine where you want to be in the future, and what to do in order to close the gap . . . *Sales & Marketing Skills* to communicate a compelling message to the right target audience that generates new business, and in turn, builds profitable revenue streams . . . *General Management Skills* to develop and implement a management system that will manage daily operations, nurture stakeholders, and support business growth . . . *Cash Flow Management Skills* to monitor, protect, control, and put cash to work.

—Terry H. Hill, founder and managing partner of Legacy Associates, Inc., a business consulting and advisory services firm, Legacyai.com

part four

HANDLING A CAREERANISTA'S BIGGEST OBSTACLES

29

Overcoming Self-doubt and the Fear of Failure

And the day came when the risk to remain tight in a bud
was more painful than the risk it took to blossom.
—Anais Nin, author

The most powerful and influential barrier to your success is some-one you thought wanted the best for you. She's a woman you have confided all your hopes and dreams to and trusted with your life. If there wasn't anyone else you could rely on when times got tough, you knew you could depend on her. Yet she has still betrayed your confidence time and time again, and if you don't acknowledge the power she has over you she may prevent you from creating the life you desire. Who would do such a thing? You would. A doubtful and fearful you who is so scared to fail that you keep yourself from succeeding.

When you are overcome with self-doubt and the fear of failure, you become a barrier to your own success. That frustrated voice inside your head that tells you the goals you're working toward can't be accomplished, and you're not good enough, smart enough, attractive enough, talented enough, and woman enough to accomplish them anyway, can be more detrimental to your livelihood than sexism, racism, and ageism combined.

Feelings of self-doubt and the fear of failure aren't foreign to anyone.

These two cousins of discouragement strike people at various points in their lives, usually when there is something they're hoping to achieve.

These negative feelings are what kept many of your high school classmates from going to college. They caused some of the people who entered college with you to drop out. Self-doubt and the fear of failure even managed to keep students who stayed in college from majoring in what they wanted to because they felt the classes would be too hard for them. What have the spirits of self-doubt and the fear of failure kept you from accomplishing thus far?

Now You Tell Me?

When you are willing to take responsibility for what you have done or not done, learning from the challenges, obstacles, and difficulties you face, you will grow.

—Dr. Iyanla Vanzant, life coach & author

I still hate to admit this, but my self-doubt and fear of failure led me to leave New York after I had only been there a year and move to Atlanta. I had become engaged to a man who lived there, and I used the engagement as an excuse for me to move. Never mind that I had known him for less than five months; never mind that he had a pretty questionable past; and never mind that I wasn't all that attracted to him. I convinced myself that he was the love of my life and told everyone who would listen. However, the truth was that I was just lonely, I loved the idea of being married, I was tired of paying sky-high rent, and I was frustrated to the point that I didn't see things getting better soon. "Soon" to me then meant within a month, as I can be ridiculously impatient. And I guess that somehow my unconscious reasoned that if I stayed and my situation didn't improve then I would be a failure, but if I left now then I had nothing to feel sorry about. So I left. And leaving New York at that time is the most foolish decision I have ever made. I sold all my furniture, gave up my apartment, and moved to a state where it would be even harder to find a job in publishing.

It took me less than three days to realize what an awful mistake I had made, and why. I was a nervous wreck. When the UPS man brought my boxes to my then fiancé's house, I asked him if there was any way he could just have them shipped back. He looked at me as if I was insane, and I sat right down in front of him in the driveway and started crying. The poor man probably thought I was being beaten.

Luckily, I wasn't silly enough to stay in Atlanta in order to avoid the embarrassment moving back to New York would bring. And I was thoroughly embarrassed. The majority of my family and friends had told me the move would all but murder my career, and this was after they had stressed the fact that I barely knew the man I was engaged to. My grandma was so mad she wouldn't talk to me. My friends called me back-to-back up until the time I boarded the plane to see what I was smoking.

What they hadn't known, of course, was that I had begun doubting my ability to have the life I envisioned. As I surveyed the mess I created, I was finally able to recognize that by moving to Atlanta, I was failing myself, not saving myself. Three weeks later I was back in New York—minus my own apartment, furniture, a job, and a fiancé. I did have a renewed sense of determination, faith, and purpose, however, and I soon discovered that was all I needed.

Now You Tell Me?

Fall down. Make a mess. Break something occasionally. Know that your mistakes are your own unique way of getting to where you need to be. And remember that the story is never over. —Conan O'Brien in a 2000 commencement speech at Harvard

---

If you're not careful you can sabotage your career by letting self-doubt and the fear of failure take control of your mind. They're sneaky and always waiting for an opportunity to do you harm. It doesn't matter whether the opportunity is big or small. Self-doubt and the fear of failure will keep you from applying for a position because "it may be too difficult." Self-doubt and the fear of failure will stop you from trying to move up in a company because "you might not fit in with management." If you allow them to, self-doubt and the fear of failure will talk you out of pursuing the career you dreamed of since you were a child because of your gender or ethnicity. They will come up with a thousand reasons of why you can't and shouldn't attempt something to further your career as they destroy it in the process. Their scheming never stops. So, while opportunity after opportunity may knock at your door, you may never hear it because self-doubt and the fear of failure are clogging your ears with nonsense.

This will undoubtedly happen at various points in your life, as very few people feel imbued with self-confidence all of the time. I certainly don't. Although you likely can't rid yourselves of these feelings forever, you can learn to handle them much better when they do surface and successfully keep them from wreaking havoc in your life. But first, it's important that you understand that self-doubt and the fear of failure don't just fall out of the sky and bury themselves in your brain. These feelings are developed over time or arise as the result of something, making you feel the way you do for various reasons. It's crucial to find out now what they are.

From reflecting on my own life and speaking with women of varying ages, I have found that for most women, our feelings of inadequacy almost always stem from one of three "self-esteem busters": unconstructive criticism from family and friends, media images, and measuring ourselves against other people.

SELF-ESTEEM BUSTERS

Unconstructive criticism from family and friends: The people closest to you play a huge role in shaping who you are and how you feel about yourself. Unfortunately, sometimes well-meaning family and friends can do major damage to our self-esteem. Many may make remarks about the way we look, talk, act, or dress that leave us feeling and wondering if there really is something wrong with us. Others may pick at us, pointing out past mistakes while neglecting to tell us how we can do better next time. Some may suggest that our goals are more like fantasies by saying we need to "be more realistic."

What to remember: The unconstructive criticism loved ones give you normally just reflects their own insecurities, particularly when it is about you being able to achieve something. People can be very unsupportive when they aren't satisfied with what they have accomplished in their own lives.

Media images: Advertising and images in magazines, in the movies, on television, on the web, and even in bathroom stalls bombard us every day and leave too many of us feeling less than adequate. I'm referring to images that tell our subconscious minds we really need to be a certain size to be beautiful; able to afford a certain house and car to have "made it"; be in a certain position by a certain age to be considered successful; and wear certain designer clothes to be fashionable. And then, even if by some chance we fit this image of the perfect woman, media images still make us feel like losers if we don't have a man by our side—and a super handsome man with money at that.

What to remember: The point of advertising is to make you feel incomplete if you don't have whatever is being sold. Also, for the most part, *you choose* what images you see. If you find yourself feeling lousy after reading your favorite magazine or watching rounds of TV, you can choose to read or look at something that doesn't undermine your sense of self-worth.

Now You Tell Me?

The ability to be comfortable in your own skin and to find your own niche is a must for today's competitive world. Learn to embrace and accept your originality, your body composition, the hue of your complexion, your voice, your essence, and your professional style. Once you have accepted who you are, you can begin to share what you bring to the workforce, relationships, and the world.

—Francina Harrison, founder of Harrison & Associates, TCEnow.com

---

Measuring ourselves against other people: Although it's natural for us to automatically compare ourselves to others because we notice differences, measuring ourselves against others involves a whole other process—and one that is very unhealthy. It requires us to spend time thinking about the good attributes or possessions another person has while dismissing or not giving ourselves credit for our own good attributes and what we have obtained. And no matter who we measure ourselves against and what we measure—our shoes against someone else's, our hair, our waists, our cars, our positions, our bank accounts, our ability to make friends, our ambition—we rarely find ourselves at the top of the measuring stick. The result is a supreme sense of dissatisfaction with ourselves, and the false belief that if only we had what *they* had, we would be so much happier and better off.

What to remember: There is always going to be someone who you would consider smarter or a little less intelligent than you, prettier or not as attractive, wealthier or broker, so measuring yourself against others invites you to become either vain or extremely bitter, as the poem *Desiderata* notes. Also, don't be fooled into thinking someone else has everything all together. Although you should not look for flaws in the people whose looks or things you covet, you should realize that it's unlikely that they have everything they want, too. However, they, like you, should focus on what they do have. And, if you truly do aspire to have what someone else has—and it is attainable—then just complaining about it won't get you anywhere. Find out what they did and how they did it to get in a position to have what you desire.

Now You Tell Me?

Comparing ourselves to other people is one of the fastest ways to worsen depression and anxiety. Sure, it can sometimes impel us to work harder or get motivated, but more often than not, we feel inadequate and "less than." Try to focus on yourself, your own betterment, and your own life.

—Dr. Sheenie Ambardar, The Happiness Psychiatrist

Once you have determined the root causes of your low self-esteem, you can look at the way you feel much more rationally and work on changing your negative, self-defeating inner dialogue. As you work on doing this, you can go through these five steps (repeated as often as necessary) to cast self-doubt and the fear of failure out of your life:

CASTING SELF-DOUBT
AND FEAR OF FAILURE OUT OF YOUR LIFE

Step 1—Acknowledge that self-doubt and the fear of failure are sabotaging you: Self-doubt and the fear of failure are often so powerful because we deny they exist. Sometimes we don't want to believe that we're the only ones holding ourselves back. It's much easier for us to place blame on others. After we've run out of scapegoats, we make up lame excuses to explain why we can't do this and that. When you acknowledge that you may be working against yourself—for whatever reason—you're able to start working for yourself.

Step 2—Write down what self-doubt and the fear of failure have kept you from doing: Whether it was applying for a new job or taking one, write it down. Whether it was quitting your tear-producing position and starting that cool business you envisioned, or traveling the world instead of getting a job, write it down. Write down all the goals you have stored away. You will be amazed at all the dreams you've abandoned while plagued with self-doubt and the fear of failure.

Step 3—Write down what your reasons were for not doing what you wanted: Right under each of your abandoned goals, write down why you chose not to pursue them. This is where you will likely notice how much your life has been influenced by self-esteem busters. Then, you may find that what once seemed like good reasons for your inaction now appear unimportant and quite silly. Now imagine what your life would be like had you done what your heart wanted. Imagine the path you would be walking on. It's probably the one you wish you were walking on now. The good news is that it is never too late to change direction.

Step 4—Write down and reflect on your past accomplishments: It's funny how impressed we become about other people's accomplishments. When it comes to ours, we think or say that they don't count because they are in the past. Don't downplay your successes, especially to yourself. Instead, take out a sheet of paper and at the top write "I Did That!" Underneath, write down all your major and minor accomplishments and reflect on them often. For each accomplishment, think about the time when you doubted it was possible and the sense of achievement you felt when you proved yourself wrong. Use your "I Did That!" paper to remind yourself that you are more than capable of setting and meeting goals.

Step 5—Begin speaking positive things into existence: You are smart, you are beautiful, you are creative, you are talented. You are worthy of a life and career twice as awesome as you hope it will be, and it can be yours. What are you talking about? It *will* be yours! Start replacing the put-downs you feed yourself with words of encouragement and praise. As life coach Sonia Croquette once said, "Your own words are the bricks and mortar of the dreams you want to realize." Remember this and talk about what you can achieve and why you are capable of achieving that and more. If you are not feeling that, then you will have to fake it until you make it. When you wake up in the morning, count your accomplishments one by one (which is easy to do with your "I Did That" list). After that, say aloud the renewed goals you have made for your career and life and the qualities you have that will help you achieve them.

Once you've cut self-doubt and the fear of failure loose, you will begin to see opportunities in a new light. What seemed risky will now appear exciting. What appeared too challenging will interest you now because you want to be challenged. You can now sift through all the plans you put in storage—or the garbage—and see which ones can still give your life the boost it needs. The potential you have is enormous if you allow yourself to take advantage of it.

30

Ignoring
the Naysayers

Do not allow people to dim your shine because they are blinded.
Tell them to put on sunglasses.
—Lady Gaga

Your family's and friends' questions seem appropriate enough, but you can't figure out why they have to bombard you with them. It has gotten to the point that you're beginning to despise the words "what," "why," and "how." "What makes you think you can be successful in that profession?" they ask with a frown. "Why would you want to start a business when you have a good job?" "How are you going to live off of that amount of money?"

Their statements (repeated so many times you have all of them memorized) are even more irksome. "You're living in a dream world if you think it'll be that easy." "It's going to take you forever to rise up in that company," they say. But you dismissed those questions and comments. Well, you had dismissed them until their litany of discouraging words made you start to rethink your plans. After all, your loved ones wouldn't question career and life choices you feel strongly about unless you were really heading in the wrong direction, right?

Wrong. Only your heart can lead you in the right direction. Other people can push you toward the path you need to take, but at the same time, they can also push you backward onto a road going nowhere if you allow them. You begin taking those backward steps the moment you start questioning your goals and dreams because of someone else's fear of change, failure, or success. But instead of letting certain people call you naïve and reckless for setting your sights high, you have to call these people out for what they are. These people are naysayers. And naysayers stand in your way of success—however you choose to define it.

Now You Tell Me?

One of the lessons that I grew up with was to always stay true to yourself and never let what somebody else says distract you from your goals. And so when I hear about negative and false attacks, I really don't invest any energy in them, because I know who I am.
                                                —Michelle Obama

---

Our society is filled with naysayers bent on telling people why they should settle for less than what they desire and deserve. What's worse is that sometimes it's our most cherished family and friends who offer us incredulous looks and discouraging words instead of the smiles and good wishes we hope for.

Yet this is not unusual. Most people who consider themselves successful will tell you that they didn't get all the pats on the back they expected as they strove for that success. They received unconstructive criticism, crazy looks, and a whole heap of whys instead of why nots. And they got this from the people whose opinion mattered the most—their mom, dad, grandparent, sibling, teacher, aunt, uncle, best friend, mentor, and significant other. But they're where they are today because they had the courage to ignore their naysayers instead of ignoring themselves. That is so very hard to do.

When faced with important decisions, we want to have the support of others. We want to be cheered for and bragged on for taking the initiative to better ourselves. But we have to realize that sometimes those cheers and bragging words just aren't going to come. More important, we have to realize that a lack of support doesn't mean we're making the wrong decision. It simply means we're making a decision that someone else would not make. That's okay because we have our own lives to live.

A couple of my family members admonished me for planning to move to New York. I remember one of them asking how a "little ole" thing like me was going to survive in that "horrible place." Nevermind that this person had never set foot on the East Coast. Instead of working in the publishing industry, I was advised to stay in Texas and become a high school teacher. From my family member's standpoint, working as a teacher would guarantee me job security, a steady paycheck, and keep me from moving across the country to a place he was afraid would be riddled with more terrorist attacks. I eventually did go into teaching, but at the time this was not what I wanted. I think the worst kind of teacher is one who teaches out of necessity instead of love. If I had stayed and taught, I would have spent more time daydreaming about the life I could have had in New York than educating students.

Now You Tell Me?

One thing I look at before I consider anyone's words is how the person is doing in his or her own life. Is this person's life the kind of life I want to have for myself? If the answer is no, then I'll discount what the person says. By following his or her words, it can only get me to where he or she is, not where I want to go. —Celestine Chua, personal excellence coach

---

Whether you're venturing into a male-dominated field, quitting a good paying job you despise for a lower paying one you love, or moving across the country to pursue your career, don't let anyone's doubts stand in the way of your ambitions. Of course, you should listen to those you trust and respect. It's wise to take heed of all the warnings you are given. But then you have to ask yourself what *you* want. The question should be what will make *you* content and proud. Envision the future you can have if you do what is necessary to achieve your career goals. And then, despite what the naysayers say, go after what you have envisioned.

POINTERS ON OVERCOMING THE NAYSAYERS

1. Make up your mind: Naysayers cause us so much trouble because we're still waiting for their approval and blessings. We feel like our decision has to be justified by someone else in order for it to be the right one. We wouldn't feel this way if we would just make up our minds about what we're going to do, and then stick to that decision.

2. Don't ask naysayers anything: We usually know how someone is going to respond to something. So why do we request advice from people we know will give us a negative response? Don't ask naysayers how they feel about such and such or what they think and what they would do. You open yourself up to negativity by asking the wrong people for advice.

3. Surround yourself with positive people: Positive people may tell you that they don't agree with your decision, but unless they fear you are at risk of self-harm, they will offer you their support anyway. You should gravitate toward and surround yourself with these people. Negative people, however, will shoot down your decisions and continue to criticize you even after they know you've made up your mind. If you can't remove negative people from your life, then at least avoid them while you're trying to make an important decision.

4. Ask for support: Ask for the support you're seeking from the naysayers you truly need support from, such as your parents. Tell them that you're not seeking their advice or approval; you just want and need their unconditional support.

Now You Tell Me?

I always did something I was a little not ready to do. I think that's how you grow. When there's that moment of "Wow, I'm not really sure I can do this," and you push through those moments, that's when you have a breakthrough.

—Marissa Mayer, CEO of Yahoo, Inc.

Diary of a Careeranista

CARMILLE LIM ON
BEING YOUNG AND IN CHARGE

*I*n college, I had hoped to find a career I'd love and enjoy the success that comes when you work hard to achieve your goals, but I never imagined myself being in the position I am today. If you had told my 20-year-old self that I would one day not only be working in public policy advocacy, but also serving as an executive director in the field before I turned 30, I may have laughed at the idea in disbelief and dismissed the comment.

My career has been nontraditional, in the sense that I took on a number of leadership positions at an early age. After college, I applied and was accepted to grad school, but then changed my mind and made the conscious decision to postpone a graduate degree so that I could gain "real world" experience. Little did I know how much of an investment real world experience would be for propelling my young career. I was appointed by Hawaii's governor to a state commission by age 24, was managing fundraising and advocacy for an organization's three branches by age 25, and was hired as an executive director of a political advocacy nonprofit organization by age 26.

My seemingly swift rise to a leadership position also came with lessons I had to learn equally as fast. I learned early on that being a young woman in an executive position and in the political advocacy industry is tough. Although my official role is to advise legislators, partner organizations, our members, the public, and the media on legislative issues, it often feels like getting others to see past my age, gender, and ethnicity is a job in itself. Sometimes it even feels like the potential barriers that these three factors represent are more difficult to get a grasp on than the technicalities of the policy and lawmaking process issues that I work on. In an industry still heavily dominated by men, my expertise has often been overshadowed by misogynistic and sexist views. It's unfortunate that many people still think women do not belong in politics or advocacy. Also, Filipinas are not widely represented in state or local politics, which further impacts my work and my perceived effectiveness. However, with all of that said, the biggest challenge I have faced as an executive is my age.

I have found that age—specifically, people's feelings on what someone of a certain age is capable of—truly does play a role in how people view you. As a 26-year-old leading a 40-year-old organization that serves as the leading voice in good government reform in our state, it can be awkward working side by side with executive peers who offhandedly comment that they have interns or grandchildren my age. It can be another challenge managing people old enough to be my grandparents.

On one occasion, I met with an advisor at a small business center. I was interested in filing a business license so that I could offer political advocacy consulting; after all, I had been successful in doing this type of advocacy and organizing work for years already. After giving me a quizzical look, the business consultant said, "You're younger than my daughter. What makes you think people here would take you seriously?"

Another time, an executive who was new to his job, and new to the islands, asked to meet with me to discuss possible ways his organization could benefit from or be harmed by a potential policy that would impose a new protection for women. As I came in, the executive looked at me, looked past me at the door, and said, "Is your boss, Carmille, coming?" When I remarked simply that I was her, I received a disappointed and skeptical look, followed by, "Great, I'm going to take advice from a kid." Little did he know that by this time I was 25 and had already done some form of advocacy at the neighborhood, council, state, and federal level.

Both incidences took me aback—did they not trust me because of my age and perceived lack of experience? Or, was their small-mindedness rooted in personal insecurity? I left each incident feeling unsure of myself and frustrated that they and so many other professionals seemed to be more worried about my youthful face than about my resume. So I did what I normally do at a time of uncertainty—I meditated and reflected on my skillsets, strengths, and any areas of improvement I needed to consider. I also consulted with my own personal "board of advisors." Through this process, I rediscovered that I felt confident in my work and experience, and that I knew my material. Also, I took confidence in the fact that I was already being approached for advice by some influential advocates, lawmakers, and business executives, which showed me that not everyone was limited by what and who they saw before them.

After the last experience with the male executive, I vowed not to let further similar experiences discourage me. I also made a point of acting as if my age is a nonissue—as it should be. I now avoid talking about my age at work, and if I am approached with a hostile comment relating to my age, I may respond with a simple: "What were you doing at my age?" or "Does it matter?" or even a "How old do you think I am?" People seem to get the hint: There is a reason I was selected for my position, and it certainly had nothing to do with my birthdate.

But getting past remarks about my age has just been half of the battle. Being young and "in charge" has been a learning experience in itself. In fact, I have accepted that I cannot get by just on my skills and experience alone. As a young executive who has been heavily involved in the community, I have learned industry tricks and best practices from others who have decades of experience, including how to manage up and how important having a polished presentation is to be successful in the workplace. A teacher once told me: "It's important to learn from your mistakes, but even more important to learn from the mistakes of others."

When managing older people, it helps for them to know who I know and hear someone whom they respect—someone their age—vouch for me. Just as important, learning how to interact with the more established individuals also has helped me in developing interpersonal relationships with people much older than myself. I applied this knowledge to the workplace. I learned how to give constructive feedback without sounding like I'm attacking a person, or sounding like I think they are inept. I learned tips like asking, "Can I give you some advice?" or "Can you help me understand why this happened?" when managing up.

Managing relationships and communicating effectively is one thing, but having a polished presentation is another. Having been involved in the performing arts while growing up, I learned early on that being polished is not limited to what you put on; it is also reflected in your body language and how you deliver your message. Because of my theatre and cheerleading experience, I've always been conscious of enunciating my words, monitoring the volume of my voice, and avoiding distracting filler words like "um," "well," and "like," which make young women sound especially indecisive. As a dancer, I'm cognizant of the power of body language—walking with intention, refraining from fidgeting—which could be interpreted as nervousness—and sitting up straight. These may seem like small things, but they have played well into my success. On several occasions, different business and nonprofit executives have told me that they feel comfortable working with me because of how confident I am, or how I present myself. Similarly, older people I have managed have expressed that they feel comfortable working for me because of how sure I appear to be of my decisions.

What took me a little longer to learn was what "dressing professionally" in the workplace truly meant. When it comes to how I dress, I've been known to have a no-fuss, low-maintenance style. But in the past, while I had been dressing in what people would consider professional attire (e.g., slacks, knee-length pencil skirts, cardigans and knit tops, and closed-toe shoes), I had also been known to wear items until they were on their last leg (I attribute this to having been born in a third-world country).

My justification was that if I was going to be successful, it was going to be based on my skill alone, and should not be influenced by what I was wearing. But now I know better: How we dress and style ourselves is the biggest factor in how others perceive us. It plays a key role in whether or not we are hired and promoted, and even affects our overall credibility in the workplace. That's because how we appear is an extension of who we are.

I am glad I discovered this relatively early on in my career. One day, one of my former bosses took me aside and asked why I didn't dress "more professionally." I was shocked and couldn't understand why she was directing this question at me—I had stuck with conventional professional wisdom: neutrals and only modestly showing skin. She explained that that is only surface level; I had to ensure that the items I was wearing were still of decent quality and shape. She then pointed out that my shoes may be closed-toe, but they had scuffs on them; that my tops may have been navy blue or black, but they did not always fit me well and were sometimes pilling; and that although my cardigan was Banana Republic, it had been worn so often that it was now a faded version of the royal purple it used to be. Lastly, she pointed out that my natural beach waves seemed unruly in our conservative office setting. Through her comments, I was able to realize that there is so much more to looking professional—it is truly about looking polished. I believe in "no ask, no get," and, needing more direction, I wasn't ashamed to ask for her guidance in updating my wardrobe, which she gladly provided.

When you are *polished*, you show a sign of respect for other people, your work, and your workplace. Because I live in the United States now, I have also accepted that I can and should spend more effort maintaining an updated wardrobe and tailoring items when I can. Similarly, I make sure I put more effort in lightly styling my hair.

Making these small tweaks greatly improved how I present myself in the workplace. It feels like I'm in a costume and "in character": I'm more assertive than I was previously, and I feel even more confident when meeting people. Now my outside matches my inside. A new state legislator recently told me that he felt that some advocates were simply angry and a little unstable based on their self-presentation. He shared with me that he felt he could welcome me into his office knowing that I had a level head on my shoulders, simply by how I presented myself. He also shared that several of his colleagues feel the same way.

What I have learned so far is what the late R&B singer Aaliyah once sung: Age ain't nothing but a number. If you have the experience, confidence, and polished look needed to lead then you are already positioned for success. And if you have the curiosity to constantly want to learn more about yourself, your industry, and other people, you will go far.

~~~~~~

Carmille Lim is executive director of Common Cause Hawaii. Previously, she worked for a nonprofit focused on women's issues, where she managed the fundraising and advocacy efforts across the organization's three branches. She is a commissioner on the Hawaii State Commission on the Status of Women, and a board member of the National Association of Commissions for Women. She is also past director of the League of Women Voters of Hawaii. In 2012, she was recognized by Pacific Business News as one of Hawaii's Forty Under 40, and as an "Outstanding Young Filipino" by the Filipino Junior Chamber.

31

Battling
Sex Discrimination
and Sexual Harassment

It would be ridiculous to talk of male and female atmospheres,
male and female springs or rains, male and female sunshine . . .
How much more ridiculous is it in relation to mind, to soul,
to thought, where there is as undeniably no such thing as sex.
—Elizabeth Cady Stanton,
leading figure of the early women's rights movement

You know you're as smart, hard-working, and ambitious as any of the
men you work alongside. You have all the makings of a successful
employee, and if given the same opportunities as the men you work with,
there's no limit to what you can achieve for a company and for yourself.

So why do you get the impression that you aren't being given the
same opportunities as Brandon, Byron, and Bill? Why does it seem like
you aren't taken as seriously as your male counterparts? Why do you
get the sickly feeling that you're being treated differently or unfairly
because you lack a certain part of the male anatomy? Perhaps it's
because you are.

Sex discrimination is a common practice in all industries and can
happen at any company. It is also prohibited under Title VII of the

Civil Rights Act of 1964. Sex discrimination appears in many forms. Perhaps the clearest example of sex discrimination lies in the wage gap existing between male and female employees. According to the U.S. Bureau of Labor Statistics' latest research, the typical woman working full time, year round, earns just 80.9% of what her male counterpart earns, and African-American and Hispanic women earn even less. What's more, according to research by the Institute for Women's Policy Research, women earn less than men in nearly all of the 114 most common occupations.

Pay inequity occurs despite the existence of the Equal Pay Act of 1963. This piece of legislation makes it illegal for employers to pay unequal wages to men and women who perform jobs that require substantially equal skill, effort, and responsibility, and that are performed under similar working conditions within the same establishment. And, according to the Equal Employment Opportunity Commission (EEOC), all forms of pay are covered by this law—not just salary—including overtime pay, bonuses, stock options, profit sharing and bonus plans, life insurance, vacation and holiday pay, cleaning or gasoline allowances, hotel accommodations, reimbursement for travel expenses, and benefits. The EEOC received approximately 1,082 Equal Pay Act charges for fiscal year 2012; the majority of these filings were by women. However, as the EEOC has noted, very few people are aware of what their co-workers earn, and therefore most people do not know when they are being paid in a discriminatory manner.

Beyond not receiving pay equal to men's, women may encounter other discriminatory practices, which helps to explain why women filed the majority of the 30,356 sex-based discrimination charges that went through the EEOC in fiscal year 2012. Other ways women may be discriminated against include:

→ Not being hired because of our sex

→ Being made to take tests that aren't required, or having to score higher than men on tests

→ Not being considered for promotions

- Being given easier assignments than men

- Being given menial assignments or jobs traditionally thought to be "women's work," such as answering the phones, filing, and typing—when this is not in our job description

- Being given "behind the scenes" assignments that offer little recognition

- Being excluded from important meetings

- Being ignored when we offer suggestions and solutions

- Being monitored more closely than men

What would possess someone to treat you like this because you were born a woman? Mainly ignorance and insecurity. Despite the contributions women have made in every field men have traditionally occupied, some men and women still hold negative beliefs about women in the workplace. Stereotypes/negative beliefs include:

- Women can't handle pressure like men (tell this to Hillary Clinton, former Secretary of State, as well as America's working single mothers).

- Women can't think as critically as men (tell this to Angela Salinas, major general of the U.S. Marine Corps, and other women serving in America's armed forces whose quick and critical thinking saves lives every day).

- Women can't learn skills as fast as men (tell this to Meg Whitman, CEO of Hewlett-Packard, and other top-performing female executives whose success has depended on not only being fast learners, but being innovative as well).

- Women can't lead others as well as men (tell this to Sheilah Coley, Newark, New Jersey's police chief, and other women serving as leaders in male-dominated environments).

- Women can't solve problems as well as men (tell this to Corinna Lathan, CEO of AnthroTronix, a company making robots that can help children afflicted with diseases learn how to better use their bodies; then state this hypothesis to women who've dedicated their lives to combating poverty, social injustice, and climate change).

→ Women belong at home, not in the workforce (tell this to Sabrina Parsons, CEO of Palo Alto Software and a mom to three boys, all of whom she reportedly took to work with her as newborns so they could nurse).

→ Women should not compete and take jobs away from men because men are the breadwinners for the family (tell this to the majority of American families who depend on a two-person income to support their standard of living).

The good news is that women are refusing to let sex discrimination go unpunished. Companies have a legal responsibility to ensure that women aren't treated unfairly on the job, by anyone. If you believe you've been the victim of sex discrimination, there are steps you can take to remedy the problem.

Now You Tell Me?

Forty-six percent of women said they faced gender discrimination personally, most often in the workplace, according to a poll conducted by the *Wall Street Journal/ NBC News.*

CONFRONTING SEX DISCRIMINATION IN THE WORKPLACE

1. Identify the problem: Determine exactly how you're being discriminated against, and make sure you have the facts to show it while keeping a log of each occurrence. To be clear, facts are what you know, not what you feel or think someone did or said. Making a claim of discrimination against another person is a serious matter that requires fairness and accuracy on your part.

2. Get a second opinion: It is quite possible that your gender is not a factor in the problem you are experiencing. Three men in a row may have been promoted more quickly than you because their work really is better. Your salary may be thousands lower than nearly every man in your position because they negotiated their salary more adeptly than you did. Although your gut instinct is often accurate, it isn't 100 percent reliable. If you can, find someone within your company who you can trust, who has more knowledge about the company and its staff than you, and who can look at the issue objectively. Objectivity is key, which is why your boyfriend or bestie is not likely to give you a neutral opinion; those closest to you may be too focused on your feelings instead of the facts. Also, as a labor specialist once told me, the person shouldn't have a "nickel in your quarter," which means what is happening to you should not have an effect on them in any way.

At the same time, you can get a free consultation from a lawyer with experience in discrimination claims. An EEOC officer is also a good contact. He or she may have public information that could reveal a pattern of discrimination on the part of the party you think is discriminating against you.

3. Confront the offender: If there is clearly a problem, talk to the person at the center of the issue, be it another employee or your supervisor. Calmly state the problems you perceive, lay out your facts, and ask for an explanation for his or her actions. At this point, there is no need to bring up gender as the central issue, unless there is no other way around it (i.e., you were told William was chosen to lead the project because most of the team members are men and will feel more comfortable following a guy's lead). Otherwise, the person's actions should be the central issue.

If the person doesn't change his or her behavior and/or policy, speak to the person's immediate supervisor, and keep going up the chain of command if your concerns are ignored.*

---

* This tactic works best if a co-worker or immediate supervisor is doing the discriminating. When treating women unjustly seems to be a part of the company's culture, filing a claim with HR or the EEOC may be the better course than confronting the offenders(s).

4. File a complaint: If the problem isn't resolved, you should file a formal complaint with HR. Remember: your company has a legal responsibility to end the existing sex discrimination.

5. Report the company: If HR doesn't resolve the problem, the time for talking is over. Ask for a free consultation with a lawyer who specializes in sex-based employment discrimination. Also file a complaint with the EEOC and any state agencies that work to combat sex discrimination.

Now You Tell Me?

The typical woman who works full time, year round, would lose $431,360 in a 40-year period due to the wage gap, according to the National Women's Law Center. This is yet another reason why it's crucial to negotiate your salary and not assume what a company offers is the most it has to give.

BATTLING SEXUAL HARASSMENT

Sexual harassment is just as prevalent as sex discrimination in the workplace. It is also prohibited under Title VII of the Civil Rights Act of 1964. The EEOC received approximately 7,571 charges of sexual harassment for fiscal year 2012; 82.2 percent were filed by women. According to the EEOC, unwelcome sexual advances, requests for sexual favors, and other verbal or physical conduct of a sexual nature constitute sexual harassment when this conduct explicitly or implicitly affects an individual's employment, unreasonably interferes with an individual's work performance, or creates an intimidating, hostile, or uncomfortable work environment.

Even though the law provides a working definition for sexual harassment, it can still be hard to identify. Even women may not be able to agree on what really constitutes sexual harassment because sometimes it boils down to what makes each of us feel uncomfortable. For example, it's obvious that you're being sexually harassed if a co-worker or boss purposefully touches your breasts, demands sex from you, or talks about how much he wants to make love to you. But what if he just talks about how sexy you are and how much he wants to date you? Some women would just find his advances annoying and tolerate them; others might find his actions intolerable and file a complaint.

It's likely that you'll know when someone is behaving in a manner that deserves to be ignored, confronted, or punished through a complaint or lawsuit. If you feel you are being sexually harassed—by men or women—you can follow the same steps outlined in Confronting Sex Discrimination in the Workplace. You don't have to accept being made to feel like a sexual object or toy.

Whether you decide to stay with the company while the sex discrimination or sexual harassment issue is being resolved is a personal decision. Just keep in mind that staying with the company can be quite difficult if you're ignored or treated harshly by your bosses or the men or women angry with you. Also remember that you should work for a company where you feel respected. At companies where sex discrimination seems to be a part of their framework, it's likely that biases against women will remain even if the discrimination does stop due to complaints or lawsuits. So is the case for widespread sexual harassment.

SEXISM OR CHIVALRY?

Some men and women may believe they are doing you a favor by treating you differently because of your gender. These people would never intentionally do anything they thought was sexist. For example, a manager might think he is doing you a favor as a woman by giving you an easier workload or allotting you shorter work hours. That's why it's important to express your dismay and find out the reason you're being treated differently, rather than just assuming it's being done on purpose to halt your growth or demean you.

32

Fighting Racial Discrimination and Stereotypes

I never doubted my ability, but when you hear all
your life that you're inferior, it makes you wonder if the
other group has something you've never seen before.
If they do, I'm still looking for it.
—Hank Aaron, retired African-American baseball player

It's a terrible feeling—to walk into an interview or meeting believing that your ethnicity or culture may play more of a role in how you will be judged than your diverse skill set, great education, and polished appearance. But there is something worse than this feeling—the knowledge that your wariness is justified.

Race discrimination, which often includes cultural discrimination, is still a real and common threat to millions of women across the United States, particularly women of color. Although black, Latina, Asian, and women representing every so-called minority group have continually proven that they can compete on any playing field—be it in the courtroom, the hospital, the classroom, the boardroom, and even in space—too many have found their dreams trampled upon because of their "double minority" status.

Race tends to be a sticky issue, and handling discrimination on the job that is based on your looks or beliefs may be the hardest obstacle you will face in your career. Unfortunately, American employers of all sizes and in all industries have a poor record of providing a work environment free of racial discrimination, as evidenced by the 33,512 race-based charges levied against U.S. employers in 2012 through the EEOC. According to the EEOC, race-based discrimination continues to be its most-filed discrimination claim, followed by sex, disability, and age. The number of EEOC claims helps us see the extent to which race-based discriminations exists, but only so much. There are countless women and men who never file a charge despite having proof they have been discriminated against.

Now You Tell Me?

A survey by Yourblackworld.com revealed that 88.5 percent of all African-American respondents believe they have been victims of workplace racial discrimination at some point in their careers.

Racial discrimination remains a problem despite our increasingly multiethnic society, the marked progress of non-white racial groups, and the fact that Title VII of the Civil Rights Act of 1964 makes it illegal for companies to use race as a factor in hiring, promoting, and firing employees. Individuals in your workplace can discriminate against you in a variety of ways. Some are not very obvious. But knowing some of the signs can better help you recognize and respond to discrimination when it occurs.

SIGNS OF DISCRIMINATION

↪ *Being denied or not considered for promotions you deserved:* Your supervisor will not give you a reason why you were denied or passed over for a promotion, and perhaps promotes someone who is less qualified than you are. You may also notice that others within your racial group are denied well-deserved promotions or are slow to get them.

→ *Being given easier assignments than others:* Your supervisor gives you easy assignments that you are overqualified to handle, and gives less experienced employees within another racial group more challenging tasks.

→ *Being given harder assignments than others:* Your supervisor gives you assignments that you aren't trained for and is unwilling to train you, while training employees within other racial groups and giving them simpler assignments. You may then be punished for your poor performance.

→ Being made to take tests other employees with your position and experience don't have to take.

→ *Being given menial tasks outside your job description:* Being given menial tasks for which you're overqualified or have nothing to do with your job, while employees within other racial groups aren't asked to do these same tasks.

→ *Being given "behind the scenes" assignments:* Your supervisor gives you assignments that offer little recognition or in which you are neither seen nor heard, while other employees of equal standing with you get assignments that bring more recognition.

→ *Being excluded from important meetings:* Your supervisor doesn't invite you to or denies your entrance to meetings that someone in your position should attend.

→ *Being ignored:* Your supervisor ignores your questions, suggestions, and solutions, treating you with less respect than employees within other racial groups.

→ *Being monitored closely:* Your supervisor monitors you more closely than other employees without explaining why.

→ Being discouraged from interacting with clients.

→ Being called derogatory names.

→ Being the subject of racist jokes or comments.

→ Being made to listen to racist jokes or comments.

→ Being asked racist questions.

Now You Tell Me?

Many employment discrimination experts assert that having any type of ethnic-sounding name—such as one often given to African-Americans, Muslims, or Asians—lowers one's chances of being called back for an interview. A study conducted by fellows at the National Bureau of Economic Research found that job applicants with "white-sounding" names needed to send about 10 resumes to get one callback; those with "black-sounding" names needed to send around 15 resumes to get one callback.

It's important to note that although women of color bear the brunt of racial discrimination, white women are certainly not immune to it. The EEOC receives cases yearly in which white women assert that they have been treated differently because of their ethnicity, often when working in predominantly black environments. A close white friend of mine confided in me that she felt as if she was not given the respect she deserved while working for a black-owned company. There was never any overt racism, she explained, but she felt as if she was treated like an outsider by not being invited to attend the high-level meetings someone in her position would have normally attended. Also, she says her boss spoke to her harshly multiple times when she found fault with her work, but never even raised his voice when discussing her black colleagues' performance. Was it because she was white—or for whatever reason, people just didn't like her? She still doesn't know.

Whatever box you check on the census, don't be so naïve as to think your race will never be a factor in how someone acts toward you. And don't expect all acts of racial discrimination to be in your face. It's unlikely someone will ever hurl a racial slur at you in the workplace or tell you outright that you won't get the treatment you deserve. Like my friend, you may come upon situations in which you can't be certain that you're being treated unfairly because of your race, although your gut tells you that is the reason. This is a baffling problem when attempting to confront racial discrimination at work. You don't want to falsely accuse someone of being prejudiced or discriminatory. However, you also don't want to disregard questionable practices or statements just because you're uncertain. Not confronting discrimination can be just as stressful as letting your grievances be known. Regardless of the situation, unlike women of past generations, who often didn't feel empowered enough to combat racial discrimination in the workplace—including because they were not backed by the laws we have now—we are able to more effectively confront and handle bigotry in all forms. You can follow the same steps outlined in the chapter "Battling Sex Discrimination and Sexual Harassment" when you think you are faced with racial discrimination.

HANDLING IGNORANCE

There are countless assumptions people make about others based solely on their racial or cultural background. For the most part, they are all unflattering. Most women of color have grown up either ignoring or battling various stereotypes heard from strangers, classmates, teachers, neighbors, or on the lips of comedians and politicians. Although kids still like to say "sticks and stones may break my bones but names will never hurt me," adults know from experience that this isn't true, especially in the workplace.

It can be exhausting trying to disprove stereotypes, be you fearful of being perceived as just another black woman with no concept of time should you arrive one minute late to a meeting; just another too-meek Chinese woman should you opt to stay silent on an issue; or just another hot-tempered Puerto Rican woman should you choose to disagree with someone. So my advice is to be yourself. It can be equally tiring to feel as if you are expected to speak on behalf of your entire race, as people constantly want your take on the latest controversy and to see how you feel as a ____ American. So my advice is to let people know that you don't represent an entire ethnic group. You are your own person.

As a black woman, I have had to deal with my fair share of foolishness. A female Korean manager once asked me if I knew why black people steal, as if no other group of people steals, and as if I possibly steal, too. A former white male colleague asked me why black men wear gold in their mouths, as if all black men do, and as if I would even know the answer anyway. Equally frustrating but interesting, I have been told countless times throughout the years by non-black co-workers that I don't "act black."

Fortunately, I understand how and why people believe stereotypes, so I rarely find myself getting angry or left with hurt feelings when people say or ask me such asinine things. Instead, because the person felt comfortable enough to show his or her ignorance, I let myself feel comfortable enough to explain why the comment was ignorant and why the stereotype, like so many others, just isn't true. So, for example, I let whoever just said "I don't act black" know that statement comes across as an insult, not as the compliment I guess they intended it to be. I then try my best to explain that there is no such thing as "acting black," or white, Asian, or Hispanic for that matter, and that perhaps they need to develop more real relationships with people outside of their race so they can be more culturally aware.

When you come across seemingly good-intentioned colleagues or managers who say or ask ignorant things, use incidents like mine to educate them—or to at least point out the silliness of their stereotype. It's useless to berate someone who should have known better, but didn't.

Of course, women of color should be mindful that being a member of a minority group doesn't prevent you from being prejudice or putting your heel in your mouth. So watch what you do and say. Everyone should be more understanding and sensitive of cultural differences, and how one's ethnicity shapes the way one thinks about issues, other people, and the world. No one likes assumptions made about them, and even the most playful of co-workers often detests racial jokes and naïve statements.

The ABCs of Succeeding as a Careeranista

In all realms of life it takes courage to stretch your limits,
express your power, and fulfill your potential.
—Suze Orman, financial advisor & author

I hope *Careeranista: The Woman's Guide to Success After College* has been an informational and inspirational tool for you. The "ABCs of Succeeding as a Careeranista" was created to reiterate advice given throughout the book.

Ask For What You Want: A woman who is afraid to ask for what she wants will miss out on countless opportunities. Make your goals and aspirations known to the people who can help you in your endeavors, no matter how big or small.

Be Better Than Your Competition: Know who your competition is and make sure you're five steps ahead of what they know and what they've done, so all eyes will be on you when it's time to get promoted or singled out for a better job with a better company.

Challenge Yourself To Do More Than What's Expected of You: It's the people who go above and beyond what's asked of them who are recognized as leaders in their industries and as the pillars of their communities. Do more than what's merely expected of you, and the rewards you reap will be more than what you expected.

Develop Good Relationships With Your Co-Workers: You don't have to be buddy-buddy with everyone in the office, but you do need to maintain a good working relationship with everyone, from the secretary to the CEO. You never know who you might depend on for something you need in the future.

Expect To Have Some Very Bad Days: Sometimes you might be two seconds away from quitting your job or seriously hurting someone. Realize that bad days on the job are inevitable. Learn how to stay composed and in control when nothing seems to be going right.

Forget What The Naysayers Said: You've made it this far despite all the negative and unsupportive words and gestures of others. Continue to strive for what's in your best interest, and surround yourself with people who want to see you succeed and will help you any way they can.

Get Your Wardrobe Together: "Dress to impress" is not just a catchy cliché. Your appearance is the first thing a person notices and you should dress appropriately for your position.

Highlight Your Achievements: Don't be bashful about tooting your own horn. No one will know of your achievements unless you tell them.

Identify Areas You Need To Improve Upon: There will always be skills you need to sharpen and ones you need to develop to make yourself more marketable. Never become complacent and think you've learned all you need to learn and know everything you need to know.

Join Professional Organizations: The networking opportunities you'll find through professional organizations are extremely valuable. There's truth in the famous phrase, "It's not what you know, but who you know."

Keep Your Private Business Private: It's okay to have a close friend at the office who you can share personal details of your life with during lunch, but everyone shouldn't know about what you do once you leave the office, about your financial woes, or about your cheating ex-boyfriend.

Learn To Negotiate: Whether you realize it or not, you've been negotiating for what you want all of your life. You had to convince someone to give you a later curfew, change your C to a B, let you have the bigger bedroom, and so on. Whether you got what you wanted in the past depended on how well you stated your case. And what you want now and in the future—a raise, better benefits, more responsibility—will also depend on how persuasive you are. Practice negotiating for things you know won't just get handed to you, and buy a book on how to negotiate.

Maintain A Positive Image And Attitude: You never know who is watching you from a distance after five, and what stranger you had an attitude with will be the one smirking as he or she interviews you for a job. Always treat everyone with courtesy and respect, and present yourself as an intelligent, poised, and professional individual whom others would be lucky to know.

Never Compromise Your Values: There will be some decisions others will make that rub you the wrong way, and perhaps you will be asked to do something that you wouldn't if given the choice—that's life and accept it. However, if you're asked to do something that goes against your core values, morals, or religious beliefs, that's life too but you don't have to accept it. You shouldn't do anything that you feel compromises your integrity or something that you wholeheartedly believe is wrong. And you don't need to work for anyone who would ask or tell you to do things that are not in your best interest or are morally unsound or illegal.

Overcome Your Insecurities: You are beautiful, you are smart, you are capable, and you do have something to offer the world. But do you know it? Your insecurities will keep you from succeeding in life. The sooner you get to working on being secure with yourself, the sooner your success will come.

Prioritize Your Goals: List your goals in order of importance and have a reasonable time line that shows when you should have each goal accomplished. Do this so that you won't be trying to get too many things done at once, and then get nothing done at all.

Question What You Don't Understand: Don't go around assuming anything, and don't be afraid to ask people things you think you should know already. Learn to speak up and speak your mind, and you will be a more knowledgeable person for it.

Realize Your Worth And Potential: You have it going on and that's the unconceited truth. Realize that whole worlds of possibilities are yours to explore, and the only thing that can truly limit you is your underestimation of yourself.

Say What You Mean And Mean What You Say: Be straightforward and honest about your feelings. You will gain the respect of others and prevent people from misunderstanding you or not taking what you say seriously.

Trust Your Intuition: Learn to listen to and trust that little voice inside your head that tells you when something isn't quite right or what the best choice will be concerning a decision you have to make.

Use Your Talents: Don't let your talents go to waste. Find a way to use them, whatever they may be, to enrich your life and the lives of others.

Vocalize Your Concerns: If something is seriously bothering you at work, don't be afraid to tactfully talk to the person who can address your concerns. The chances are that others may be frustrated with something going on in your company, too.

Waste No Time In Following Your Dreams: Start actively pursuing your goals and dreams today, even if you can only take small steps in going after what you want right now.

X-amine Your Work: Look critically at your work before others do. Make sure you are measuring up to the standards set by your company and that your work truly exemplifies your talent.

Yearn For Something More: Don't settle for anything; mediocrity is not your friend. Expect the best for yourself and always be on the lookout for ways you can improve yourself and your life.

Zone In On What Matters Most To You: It's what you want for your career and life that should matter most to you—not the desires of your parents, love interest, or employers. You won't get any satisfaction from your achievements if you pursued them to make someone else happy.

Acknowledgments

I could not have completed this book, nor found the courage to pursue my aspirations, if I had not been blessed with an abundance of uplifting family, friends, and former students.

My father, Caryl Foster, should probably be listed as co-author considering the amount of time he spent helping me hone the book's message. He was also the first to point out how the issues discussed in my first book, *Embracing the Real World: The Black Woman's Guide to Life After College,* pertained to women of all ethnicities, and it was his confidence in this book's mission and value that empowered me to write it.

I am particularly grateful to my sister, Cameron Allen-Kyser, who has always doubled as my cheerleader, and I thank her for pushing me to want to be and do my best—as well as for all her great marketing tips. My mother, Charlie Kyser, has a strength of spirit and free-spiritedness that I am still trying to harness, and I thank her for being the type of mother who lets me feel comfortable enough to share my innermost thoughts.

Special thanks to my many friends who provided feedback on various chapters throughout the book: Da'Janai Smith, Teaa Trower, Danielle Skinner, Ramona Crayton, Katesha Washington, Jennifer Dunn, Kira Citron, Kym Strong, Delise Vanvield, Chakie Brown Sterling, Charles Zamstein, and Callie Parker. Special, special thanks to my husband, Keir Pitts, who has supported me in this endeavor and whose loving spirit gives me the confidence to achieve other goals.

Some people I barely knew—at first—showed an inordinate amount of enthusiasm for the book and freely gave their advice and support. Christelle Agboka's detailed comments about my first book assisted me in making this one even more of a must-read, and her knowledge about career-related issues and background in publishing has been invaluable. Kristen Gomez of 100 Pink Pens reviewed the entire draft of *Careeranista* and provided great feedback and edits. Sandra Soto, a seasoned human resources professional, provided much-needed expert advice for various chapters. Valerie C. Harris, a bright, confident young woman attending Southern Illinois University Edwardsville, graciously assisted in my marketing efforts. After learning that I was working on a second book, Carla Jenkins volunteered to read any chapter I needed another set of eyes on—which was all of them—and I appreciate her insight. Also, every few weeks she sent me a short email asking me how I was doing with the book, and those gentle pushes actually helped me finish it faster as I didn't want to disappoint her!

I am grateful to Misty Starks of Misty Blue Media for being a fantastic editor and true friend. She was my go-to person to bounce ideas off of for the book and other projects, and her great work ethic inspired me to work harder to accomplish my goals and to thinking bigger. Elaine Dunn was just the second set of eyes I needed and she graciously proofread my book despite having an already full workload and likely missing a few yoga classes.

And to Dr. Donna Barnes, thank you for your wonderful coaching sessions that served to keep me on track toward releasing this book, and for taking me under your wing when I was an undergrad at Texas State University.

About the Author

Chaz Pitts-Kyser is a writer and speaker with a passion for empowering college students and young professionals to achieve personal and career success. She is also the founder of Careeranista, a company created to inspire, support, and educate young women in their quest to lead more fulfilling lives. Chaz received a master's degree in publishing from Pace University and bachelor's degrees in journalism and sociology from Texas State University. In her career, she has worked as a writer/editor, college journalism instructor, and consultant facilitating writing, self-publishing, and career workshops.

How people manage and become successful in their careers has fascinated Chaz since she first started working at the age of 14 selling popcorn at a $1 movie theater. Of course, in time she moved up at the movie theater (to selling tickets) and then on to bigger and better things with the help of a quality education and a good dose of industriousness and luck.

At the age of 21, she became one of the youngest African-Americans in the nation to serve as the managing editor of a black-owned weekly newspaper. While working in this position and struggling with life after college, the idea for a career guide for black female college graduates came to her. However, she had to wait until she had more career and real life experiences to publish it. Those experiences soon came through more than a dozen jobs, four job losses, a move across the United States and back, an engagement, a broken engagement, feeling secure with lots of money in the bank, negative account balances, dealing with depression from not knowing what she was going to do with her life, and navigating the winding path that led to a career she loves.

After publishing her first book, *Embracing the Real World: The Black*

Woman's Guide to Life After College, and seeing how much it helped young black women, Chaz was inspired to develop a guide for women of all ethnicities that was even more comprehensive and inspiring. *Careeranista* is filled with information that has helped Chaz and countless other young women build a career even more fulfilling than they imagined. She hopes it will help you move more confidently in yours, as well as motivate you to craft the rewarding career and life you deserve.

SUPPORT *CAREERANISTA!*

Loved *Careeranista?* Help get it into the hands of more women and connect yourself to the Careeranista.com community. Start by:

1. Asking the library, career center, and women's center director at your university or alma mater to purchase copies of the book.
2. Posting a review on Amazon.com and on your blog or website.
3. Sending a quick email about the book to six Careeranistas and buying the guide for the friend who needs it the most.
4. "Liking" our website and Facebook page.
5. Connecting with us on Twitter @Careeranista.

ORDER MORE BOOKS

Careeranista: The Woman's Guide to Success After College can be purchased through Careeranista.com or Amazon.com. *Careeranista* is an excellent gift for both college undergraduates and young women striving to get to the next level in their careers. It can also be used as required or supplemental reading material in classes or for book clubs. Discounts are available for individuals and organizations ordering 15 or more books.

The e-book is available through Amazon.com (on Kindle) and BarnesandNoble.com (on Nook).